IN FOR A PENNY

By Peter Hargreaves

A Business Adventure

HARRIMAN HOUSE LTD
3A Penns Road
Petersfield
Hampshire
GU32 2EW
GREAT BRITAIN

Tel: +44 (0)1730 233870
Fax: +44 (0)1730 233880
Email: enquiries@harriman-house.com
Website: www.harriman-house.com

First published in Great Britain in 2009 by Harriman House.

ISBN 978-1-905641-94-9

British Library Cataloguing in Publication Data
A CIP catalogue record for this book can be obtained from the British Library.

Printed in the UK by CPI Antony Rowe

Table of Contents

Author's Note

As a child I never had aspirations to be an author. Indeed if I had shown any early ability in that sphere, the education system certainly missed it! I was informed in 1963 that my school would not pay the entry fee for me to take O Level (now called GCSE) English literature, a decision they only reversed when I offered to pay the fee myself. Their embarrassment was acute when only four boys in my form passed English literature, yours truly being amongst that quartet.

I suppose writing much of the content for the company's newsletters over the years caused me to reappraise my literary skills, during which time I was flatteringly informed that I wasn't a bad storyteller. When I put pen to paper in 2008, my initial plan was simply to write the story of Hargreaves Lansdown, from its modest beginning in my spare room in 1981 to the present day. Stephen Lansdown and I have enjoyed a great business adventure, and my hope was that others might find reading the story as interesting as we have found living it.

Now that the book is finished, there are two other things that I hope readers will take from the book. The parts that I have enjoyed writing the most are the ones that describe the business lessons that we have learnt over the years. I hope that some of these ideas will help others to establish successful businesses, as we have done. I have no wish to be a management guru, but I do know that all the tips you will find here are ones that have worked for us.

It would have been impossible to write a book about Hargreaves Lansdown without also venturing into the minefield of investment. My hope is that readers will gain some insights into the pitfalls that many investors face, and how they can avoid them in future. From very early on in our business, Stephen and I set out our stall by saying our aim was to provide the best information, the best prices and the best service to our clients. That ambition has never changed. Investors need all the help they can get.

This book describes the story of Hargreaves Lansdown and provides readers with information to help them when investing. However the book is not published by Hargreaves Lansdown and Hargreaves Lansdown has no financial interest. The story and the views are solely mine, the author's.

Preface

In For A Penny is both an adventure story and a primer on how to grow a business from scratch. Peter's book will take you step by step from the gleam in his eye when he first heard about unit trusts to the hugely successful business that he and his partner Stephen Lansdown run today.

It is a modestly told story of two men who shared a vision that unit trusts would become a major growth industry. From humble beginnings in 1981 they have built a leading financial services business which now has 240,000 clients and a market capitalisation of £1 billion.

Every chapter is laced with humorous anecdotes and valuable business lessons. Peter tells you how each and every member of his early staff was recruited, how the first word processor was bought and the big day when the office moved from his spare bedroom to its first proper office premises.

I will try not to spoil the story for you, but I cannot resist giving a few of the highlights that impressed me most.

First and foremost Hargreaves Lansdown's three important rules – put the client first, the business second and yourself third.

Second, the way Peter and Stephen have always been prepared to do anything that needed doing, however menial, themselves. Every member of staff is encouraged by example to have the same approach. Coupled with Peter's aversion to meetings, there is never a wasted moment.

Third, Peter's down-to-earth approach of reducing every problem to its basics, and the way in which management and staff have always been encouraged to put forward their own ideas, many of which proved to be real winners with the credit being fully acknowledged.

I particularly like the account of the move to a new office when Peter concealed 1500 square feet of space, boarded it up and decorated over it. He knew that if the space was there, it would be quickly occupied. As the business expanded he made sure that every inch of existing space was used up before the dramatic unveiling.

Another very impressive characteristic of Peter's is his adaptability. This is particularly evident during the so-called PEP wars. The way in which Hargreaves Lansdown's Vantage platform for clients came into being is a model business success story in its own right.

I could go on but it is your turn now. I hope you will enjoy the story and learn how building a market-leading business from scratch is done. Easily said, not so easily done.

Jim Slater
June 2008

Prologue:

The Little Man In Times Square

(Or The Best $100 I Ever Spent)

In the early days of Hargreaves Lansdown, before the arrival of the Financial Services Authority, there were occasions when firms like ours were treated to lavish corporate entertainment by investment providers. One of the most memorable was organised by a small life assurance company known then as Target Life. It was an aggressive business which had some good products, even though the investment performance was due in large measure to its willingness to take greater risks than many conventional life companies dared. John Stone, the managing director, was an extremely able businessman who has since gone on to make a second fortune with an offshore life company called Lombard.

The trip which Target Life organised took a number of brokers and advisers to New York and back on Concorde. Even though my partner Stephen Lansdown and I had only been trading for a short time, we had done enough to be noticed in the industry and earn an invitation. John Stone had identified ours as a business that seemed to be expanding rapidly. The trip was a splendid affair, particularly for Stephen who discovered on the plane that he had won the raffle, the prize for which was an upgrade of his hotel room to a suite on the 44th floor of the Hilton, the hotel in which we were staying. (My initial envy later turned to relief when I visited the suite which had floor-to-ceiling windows. As I suffer from vertigo, I couldn't get within two or three feet of them without my stomach turning over. I could not have slept in that room myself.) The trip included dinner at the top of the World Trade Center and a talk by Art Laffer, the charismatic supply-side economist who advised Margaret Thatcher and Ronald Reagan in the early 1980s.

My personal moment of truth, however, came on our afternoon off. I had wandered up to Times Square and whilst ambling along noticed a man with an upturned cardboard box on which he had dealt three cards, one of them the queen of hearts. He was turning the cards over and switching them around. Three down and outs were gambling on which card was the queen of hearts. Sometimes they got it right, but most of the time they got it wrong. I was bemused by how much money was changing hands and by how much these guys were losing when it was always quite obvious to me where the queen of hearts was. They must have followed this routine three or four times when the dealer looked up after switching the cards around again and said, "You know where she is, don't you?" Having always been wary of any form of gambling, I would never normally dream of playing such a game. Reluctantly I pointed to where the queen was. Gleefully the man turned over the card to show everyone else in the crowd how accurate my choice had been. Turning to his sidekick he said, "Pay the man $100." As this was 1984, in the days when the pound was worth close to $1, $100 would be worth at least £250 in today's money. The sidekick started peeling off dollar bills and, after counting to a hundred, put out his hand towards me. Instinctively, as many people would have done in the circumstances, I reached out to take the money. At that point the dealer said, "You have won the $100, but you can only have it if you can prove you had enough money to make the bet."

Like a sucker I admitted that I had $100 on me. "Show me," said the dealer. I carefully counted out $100, holding it, as you can imagine, very tightly indeed. Again the dealer commanded his sidekick, "Give him the $100 then." As the $100 came my way, he looked up and said, "Now where was she?" I of course pointed to where the queen had been 30 seconds before. The dealer immediately turned the card over to reveal that the queen of hearts was no longer there. Clearly he had repositioned the cards while I was distracted, using sleight of hand (or maybe the queen was no longer there at all – I will never know). Before I knew what was happening, the $100 was out of my hand and the whole gang of four or five, clearly all in league together, were racing off down the street. Discretion being the better part of valour, and not fancying a knife in the ribs in Times Square, I didn't chase after them.

Having fallen hook, line and sinker for a classic manoeuvre, the original three-card trick, I resolved to take away a lesson that has stood me in good stead ever since. The lesson that everyone should learn is: "If anything looks too good to be true, it almost certainly is." I told Stephen about my experience and I have no idea how many times since we have had good cause to say to the other, "Remember the little man in Times Square." I would bet that he has saved us hundreds of thousands of pounds and our clients infinitely more. Back in the UK, the experience was certainly a factor in making us wary of any investments that purported to provide easy and exceptional returns. While some investment schemes of this kind do deliver what they promise, many more, as we will see, are simply variants of the three-card trick, tempting offers that fail to stand up to close scrutiny.

PART ONE

The Making of a Business

Chapter 1

The Bake House and Beyond

A Father's Son

I suspect the story of Hargreaves Lansdown really starts whilst I was at junior school. I had a distinct advantage over most people in that my first home was a flat above my father's bake house. I came home for lunch every day from my junior school and likewise my grammar school was only a three-minute walk away. From an early age, therefore, I regularly served in the shop. My father, although he only went to school at seven and lacked self-confidence as a result, was nevertheless a great businessman. Universally known by his nickname Kendal Hargreaves (though his real name was Tom), he knew what a profit was, he knew how to deal with customers and he knew which customers not to deal with. He never forgave anyone who tried to leg him over but he would service unto death the ones who earned his bread and butter.

One Saturday, I remember my father receiving a telephone call from one of his biggest customers who said that we had under-delivered on dinner rolls. Although I was only 16, he sent me up in the car and asked me to count them. (I hope the police aren't reading this, but I started driving at 15 and I think there was petrol rationing on at the time which made the trip doubly illegal.) The proprietor never found out that I had been to his kitchens and counted the rolls. Every single roll, I quickly discovered, was there. What had happened, as my father suspected, is they had under-ordered. Without saying a word, he baked the extra rolls and delivered them. Why, I asked afterwards, didn't he just confront the customer with the truth? He merely smiled and said, "They will pay for those dinner rolls 20 times over during the next ten years." As they did.

My father could never understand why anyone produced an item at a loss. We didn't have loss leaders in those days. If what he made couldn't be made at a profit, he didn't make it. As he had been away in the war when rations were doled out, he discovered once it was over that he had to pay two shillings a pound (10p) on the black market for sugar. This was at a time when the true price was just 3p. To make a profit, he had to be more efficient than his competitors, some of whom had been there when the rations were drawn up. To get by, he borrowed £400 from his brother-in-law and paid it back within six months. That was the way business was done in those days.

Working in the bake-house was a great grounding for business. Serving people in the shop, I quickly learned to add up. I knew all the prices. In small businesses you see all facets. There was no better training. Every week my father took all the takings and paid all the bills. It was run entirely as a cash business. Anything left over he banked. He used to put a number of half crowns (12½p) away every week for the gas bill and the same amount for the electricity bill. The money was always there when the bills appeared. Other than the £400, he never borrowed a penny and when we bought our first house he did not need a mortgage. Some people might say that he was too cautious. I say he was a great businessman.

In my early days, I often dreamed about going into business. I suspect that when I was at school I must have thought differently to most of the other kids. In order to encourage us in public speaking, the school used to organise an event called "One minute, please". In this, someone's name was drawn out of one hat and then a subject was drawn out of another. The subject was chosen before the next speaker started, so you had exactly a minute to decide what you were going to say. I don't remember this myself but an old school friend is adamant that the subject I was given out of the hat was "change". There were about 400 students in the school and everyone was expecting me to waffle on about changes in the world or something similar. Yet when it came to my turn, it seems that I stood up and talked about change the way I understood it – which was the amount you get back when you hand over a pound note for something that costs 75p (in those days it would have been 15 shillings). As I worked in the shop, that's all that "change" meant to me.

Barry Lancaster, the friend in question, claims that he knew at that moment that I would go on to make money. I wouldn't have disagreed. One of the ideas I had at school was that if I could somehow persuade everybody in the country to give me a penny, I would become very rich. In those days, before decimalisation, there were 240 pennies to the pound (not 100 as there are now) and the UK's population was 50 million. If I could get a penny a year from every one of them, I worked out, that would add up to an income of £208,000 a year. That set me thinking: how could I establish a business where I made a small amount of money from a huge number of people? It was a tradition of students at Clitheroe Royal Grammar School that they wrote their ambitions in the leavers' book when they left. My ambition was simply to "go into finance" and that is exactly what I did.

Learning The Ropes

I started in chartered accountancy. It didn't take me long to realise that I wasn't a chartered accountant and never was going to be one. What did fascinate me were the businesses that I was asked to audit. It also interested me how my accountancy firm conducted its own business. What amazed me most was that audit fees were never calculated on the amount of work involved, let alone on the size of the liability involved in signing the accounts. The fees were calculated solely on the client's ability to pay. That, I have always thought, is a bizarre way to run a business. At the time, which was long before the building societies expanded into the High Street and opened branches to attract retail deposits, one of this audit firm's biggest sources of income was having an agency for a building society. Accountants have always had a much bigger say in where people invest their money than most people appreciate.

I can still remember some of the businesses for which I carried out the audit. There was a family business that sold Vauxhall cars.

The father and his two sons were as keen as mustard. They were involved with every aspect of the business and knew where every penny was going. At the other end of the spectrum, there was a potentially first class engineering business which made machinery for industry. The proprietor was a marvellous engineer and made fantastic machines, but his wife, who thought she was a businesswoman and was full of her own ability and importance, was absolutely clueless. In my experience, someone who thinks they know what they are doing, but in practice hasn't any idea, can be very damaging to your wealth.

The characters whom I came across during my time as an articled clerk, while training to become a chartered accountant, gave me a wonderful grounding in what is good and what is bad in business. One of my audit clients was an egg producer. He would have made money in any industry. If he came into the office to ask about capital allowances and the tax implications for his business, you soon found out that he was only coming in to have confirmed what he had already read and worked out for himself. He didn't need us to sort out his tax, as he had it all planned already in his head. Few clients, however, were quite as savvy. For example, I found a business which made woodware – step ladders, fencing and many other items made of wood. It was a fantastic business with a brilliant factory manager. Unfortunately, the firm had four directors who each took out a huge salary and contributed absolutely nothing. The business was slowly going bust, purely because it was being milked of cash by the salaries of these four incompetents while nothing was being put back into the business. So impressed was I by the factory manager's skills that I almost ended up buying the firm. I raised the finance only to get cold feet at the last moment. I knew that if I could cut out the four directors' salaries and plough the money saved back into the business, it could have been very successful. Having made my decision, I didn't waste time on regrets. That has never been my style. I suspect that I knew one day there would be another venture to take its place.

Having initially qualified with a small provincial practice, Collingwood Burrows and Riley in Blackburn, I realised that I needed next to seek some experience with a larger international firm. So I moved to KPMG (then Peat Marwick Mitchell) in Manchester and found the experience to be illuminating. I soon discovered that large businesses were no different to small businesses, in that there were good and bad at both ends of the spectrum. My experience is that large businesses are more often badly run. Auditing larger firms for the first time brought me into contact with meetings. I simply could not believe how much time large businesses wasted in meetings. Sometimes it was impossible to get hold of anyone who could give an answer to an audit query because they were all in meetings most of the time. It soon became clear to me that working for one of the big practices was not for me.

In the end, two partners called me into an office and explained that it was not Peat's way to sack anyone. They then promptly did just that. Their one concession was to give me three months to find another job. I have thanked them ever since for telling me to go. It merely brought forward a decision that I would have made myself. Fortunately I was already being courted by one of the firm's clients, a business which had a great management team. I joined them and enjoyed my time with them. It was while working there that I really learned about cash flow. Unfortunately, because the business was badly under-capitalised, it was soon having to factor its debts. The managing director was a good man but he also had delusions about how much he should be paid, like the directors of the woodworking firm that I had looked at years before.

I could see the writing on the wall and felt I had to leave, but I did so reluctantly because I loved my time there and it gave me some wonderful business experience. I next worked for what I thought was a marvellous firm – it was called Burroughs Machines then but is now known as Unisys. They sold computers: well, they called them computers but we wouldn't think of them as computers nowadays! Burroughs was completely sales-driven and provided one of my most educational times in business. I soon realised that, whilst salesmen were invaluable in the computer industry, they were extremely costly and nowhere near as productive as they could be.

It was while I was working at Burroughs that I discovered direct mail marketing for the first time. One of the machines which the company sold had the ability to store names and addresses and, even though the machine used a serial printer which printed characters one by one, I found I could use it to write the same letter to lots and lots of prospects. This was back in 1973 and I think the only other firm that was using direct mail as its primary sales channel back then was Reader's Digest. By combining my new-found direct mail marketing skills and my knowledge of accountancy I managed to sell a number of these machines to accountancy practices; and I did so very profitably, too. It was probably my first inkling that somewhere in my future business career direct mail marketing was going to play a prominent part.

In 1974, the market for all types of capital equipment fell apart as Britain's economy reeled towards bankruptcy. Only North Sea oil saved us. I looked around at what was going on and realised that I needed to go somewhere safer for a while. I landed a job at one of the big brewery companies. Strangely enough, the sale of beer went up during the three-day week. Perhaps it wasn't that surprising – when people weren't at work they were down the pub. Even when we had the power blackout, people's televisions went off but the pubs carried on operating with candlelight. They were packed. The brewery was a wonderful place to work. It was a paternalistic company but once again I witnessed the curse of interminable meetings. In those days, there was little incentive to be hugely profitable or even to pay big salaries since most of the profits went in tax. Also at that time people's salaries, above a certain level, were taxed at such ludicrously high rates that perks were more important than pay.

I can remember Charles Woodgate, a colleague of mine at the time, and still a friend, suggesting that, as brewers were one of the two big peddlers of recreational drugs at the time (tobacco being the other), it wouldn't do to make too much profit! Such an attitude summed up the crazy state that the country was in during those days. Enjoyable as it was, I have to admit that the great insight I gained from my stay at the brewery was what not to do in business. For many years afterwards, and certainly during the early years of Hargreaves Lansdown, when thinking about a decision I often stopped to ask myself, "What would the brewery do in these circumstances?" Invariably, my answer was: do the opposite! Unkind, but true.

While I was in accountancy, I audited two firms that used to deal with each other. One was owned by a shrewd plumber who also had a successful launderette business. The other business was, on the face of it, an incredibly successful joinery business. The plumber employed three or four people, whereas the joiner employed 30 or 40 people. Yet I was mystified to discover that the plumber made considerably more profit than the joiner. The reason was that the plumber was a smart businessman while the joiner was not. I remember the joiner telling me a story which I thought was priceless and which perfectly illustrated the difference in business know-how between the two. He had noticed, he told me, that the contra account between the two of them was only ever settled when the plumber owed him money. In other words, the plumber would ring up the joiner and say, "Can we sort out our account?" As the joiner was always desperate for cash, he would invariably agree to give the plumber a discount on the payment, something that didn't happen when the shoe was on the other foot! What amused me was the joiner telling me exactly what the plumber was doing while he himself never tumbled to the deal.

Meeting The Other Half

The funny thing is that Stephen Lansdown and I might never have met, let alone set up in business together, had it not been for a bizarre set of coincidences. This is how it happened. One day, while I was working for the large brewery group mentioned above and living in Lancashire, I saw an advert for a job in Bristol for accountants to work in the investment industry. I rang the guy, who turned out to be Bill Sandham. I spoke to him and he offered me an interview. When I sat down afterwards I thought "I really can't be bothered going all the way to Bristol" and decided against it. By chance however, the following day a friend of mine called Chris Wood rang me and said "What are you doing for holidays this year?" We were both bachelors at the time. I had nothing planned, so he said "We are going to Devon. It will be a good crack. Why don't you come with us?" I said "Fine. When are we going?" And that was that. It was only when I considered the journey that I realised Bristol was on the way to Devon. So I rang Bill again and told him "OK, I will come for an interview after all." I attended the interview and he offered me the job on the spot. On the way back from Devon, I called in to see him again but it didn't seem that exciting a prospect. I pretty much decided that I wasn't going to take the job.

One reason was that the brewery had offered me a job in London that I really fancied. I was ready to take it, but at the last moment they annoyed me by saying the job was going to move to Luton. They wanted me to live in Luton, which didn't please me at all. I suggested I could move to London and later commute to Luton, but they wouldn't play ball. I got very cross and thought "To hell with it, I am going to take that job down in Bristol." So I rang Bill again and said "I have changed my mind. I will take the job", only for him to tell me "I am terribly sorry. I have given the job to somebody else." That person was Stephen. Then a week later Bill rang me again and said "I have been thinking about it for a week. I really want you and I have decided to take both you and Stephen on." The only reason he hadn't given the job to Stephen straight away was because of his age. He was only 25 whilst I was 33, an age which had more gravitas for older clients. I think he was worried that Stephen was too young to talk to clients about their investments.

That was how Stephen and I came to work together for the first time. If I had taken the job when Bill had first offered it, he would never have given Stephen a job and so the two of us would never have even met. If the brewery hadn't annoyed me so much, I wouldn't have taken the job either. I don't believe in fate, but the string of coincidences that brought Stephen and I together makes you think. As it was, once we had started working together, we immediately got on well. I used to go out with him for a drink after work. He was the only one of the staff in the office that I did that with. I think it was clear even then that we were very different and that is the reason why the two of us have always worked so well together. He does all the things that I hate doing and I do all the things that he hates doing. We are like chalk and cheese.

Stephen and I started work together at Sandham Davis on 1st September 1979. It was the beginning of the Thatcher years. I suspect we could not have had a better experience. Our mentor had one good point and a whole host of bad ones. The good one was that he was probably one of the greatest salesmen to have walked this earth. God knows he sold his concept hook, line and sinker to Stephen and myself!

We had an intensive two weeks during which we learned all about unit trusts and especially equity income funds. We learned about the taxation of investment bonds, top slicing, all the intricacies of the business. We learned about some of the proprietary inheritance tax plans, what a whole of life policy was and the difference between unit linked and with profits policies.

What we learned in those first two weeks has proved invaluable in the years since. Bill Sandham's investment plans were simplicity itself. You kept 10% in cash and, depending on how much income the investor wanted, you placed the rest in a combination of fixed interest (gilts) and income unit trusts (equity income funds). When you had generated enough income from that source, you looked at growth funds to give the portfolio a bit of spice. Most of our investment plans today are based on exactly the same principles. The only pity is that Bill didn't stick to those simple investment plans. Perhaps he shouldn't have taken both of us on as he was certainly undercapitalised and winning business from accountants and solicitors, the target market he was chasing, wasn't going to occur overnight. It takes 12 months of calling on an accountant or solicitor before they are likely to give you your first piece of business. You can't blame them. They need to be confident that you know what you are talking about and that you'll be around to follow through.

They were good days. I loved the industry. I had never worked in an industry which enthralled me so much. I enjoyed talking to accountants and solicitors and I found a remarkable thing. Surprisingly, solicitors seemed to be far better businessmen than accountants. Perhaps that's because, amazingly, the one professional training that doesn't include business training is accountancy, or so I assume. The other thing that astonished me was that, if you were ever in an accountant's office and you asked how to get to your next appointment and how long it would take, you could invariably stop and have lunch on the way within the accountant's timescale. You had to be Lewis Hamilton to get there within the solicitor's timescale.

One further thing I discovered was that, when you talked to an accountant or a solicitor, the one that was most aggressive towards you, the one who asked the difficult questions and grilled you, the one that frightened you to death and left you thinking "I failed there" was the guy that was interested and likely to do business with you. The guy who listened and said nothing but at the end said "I'll bear you in mind" was unlikely to ever deal with you.

In my time with Bill, I met some real characters. For example there was an accountant in Cheltenham who, although he claimed to have clients with millions and millions to invest, was nothing but a name dropper. He never did any business. Then there was a firm of solicitors, again in Cheltenham, on whom I made a cold call. I handed in my card and suggested that I had Inheritance Tax plans that might interest the probate partner. The offices of this firm were sumptuous beyond belief. I could hardly see my shoes in the carpet so plush was it and, instead of having room dividers, they had bookcases with law volumes to split up their offices. The receptionist wore a Chanel suit.

Suddenly, out of one of the rooms strode this most confident young man in an Armani suit and Gucci shoes. He took me into an interview room which had similar décor to the rest of the establishment and grilled me. I was pretty naïve. He probably knew 15 times more about Inheritance Tax than I will ever know. Although I got on well with him, and we had a good laugh together, I remember him making a statement which is exactly the opposite of how we have always carried out business. He was arrogant enough to state quite openly, "We are probably not the best lawyers in the country, but we definitely are the dearest." No prizes, therefore, for guessing who paid for the Armani suit, the Chanel suit, the bound law volumes and the Wilton carpet – his clients. I shall never forget him and I am sure he wouldn't even mind me mentioning his name, but I will respect his confidentiality.

During this period, Bill Sandham was paying us generous salaries and providing company cars. Yet despite our efforts the business really wasn't happening. Solicitors and accountants are cautious people, as they should be, and we were not yet turning our relationships into a flow of business. It was clear that Bill was having cash flow problems. As a result, he started introducing weird and wonderful investment schemes which he marketed to his client base. I was nervous that they were outside the normal parameters of investment: in other words they were what I would now call "unauthorised investment schemes". In fact, some of them would be illegal today.

One of these schemes was an arrangement under which the promoters of the plan bought buildings in London that were heavily tenanted. The deal worked on the basis that a tenanted flat is worth only 40% of one with vacant possession. The promoters would luxuriously refurbish the common parts of the building and a few vacant flats, giving them fabulous bathrooms and kitchens, and then put them on the open market. Of course, they sold for high prices. The promoters then offered a choice to the tenants – either buy your apartment for much less than the price of the refurbished flats, or accept a bribe to move out. The schemes were known as flat break-ups. The first two or three made a fortune for the investors, but this turned out to be a sprat to catch a mackerel. There was nothing inherently wrong with the concept, but many of those who promoted these schemes were less than scrupulous. The people who bought the first plans at least paid a sensible price. The rest were all disasters. Later plans were sold through an offshore company and a huge mark-up was added before the poor private investors were involved. Fortunately, as Stephen and I only had a few clients, we had no exposure to these investments. I should have been alerted to the nature of the business when the sales director of the company came to Bristol one Christmas and took the whole office out to lunch. He bought the most expensive wine on the list. I'm always wary of people who are flash with their money.

Unsurprisingly, none of the investors in the later property break-up plans made a profit. Unfortunately, by then, Bill Sandham had been sucked in. I suspect it stemmed from his desperation to balance the books. He also got involved in other "unauthorised investment schemes". Some were quite crazy, such as the limited partnership which set out to create tax losses for clients. It produced the losses all right. Bill had been around long enough to know he shouldn't have got involved, but the commission was just too tempting. The final straw came when he linked up with two gentlemen who had worked for Barlow Clowes long before that infamous business became notorious and who had a scheme to make money out of the gilt market. Although you would think that nothing could be safer than government stock, investors lost serious amounts of money from this scheme, which also brought down a well-known firm of London stockbrokers.

Our time with Bill Sandham turned out to be one of the best experiences that Stephen and I could have had. It took us right to the peak of the learning curve. It taught us never to get involved in the weird and wonderful, the unusual, the get-rich-quick or anything that was an unauthorised investment. When we later set up our own business, the experience helped to keep us out of Barlow Clowes, precipice bonds and many other investments which many of our competitors couldn't resist because of the commission they paid. Bill was to pay a high price for his involvement in unauthorised investments. He ended up going bankrupt and criminally bankrupt at that. Fortunately, Stephen and I could see the danger in these unauthorised schemes and decided to get out at the right time. We were never tarred with the Sandham Davis brush.

Bill's bankruptcy happened many years after we had left and the clients with whom we had been involved there were all in authorised investments, so their money was safe. However, I learned two important positive things from Bill. One was that equity income unit trusts are probably the best investment that anyone can buy. It is the one investment that we have provided to clients both during the Sandham days and subsequently, year in, year out. We still await a complaint. The other lesson I learned, the most important of all, was that "you have to make investment easy for people". I have fought a vendetta ever since that time against lengthy, complicated, difficult-to-complete application forms. In investment, I have always said that for every question you ask on an application form you lose 5% of the potential investors – ask 20 questions and you are not going to do any business.

Shortly after my departure from Sandham Davis, I met a man called Brian Strath, who was operating a small postal advisory service for unit trusts. He invited me to join him and I worked with him without pay for a short time just to learn what his business was about. I couldn't believe what a good concept he had, but I also knew that he was only doing it half-heartedly and that I would not be able to work with him for long. By chance, someone who knew Bill saw me having lunch one day with Strath and reported back. Bill then phoned me at home. At the time, Stephen's wife was seven months pregnant and he was still working for Sandham Davis. Bill said that I would be better off with Stephen. He obviously meant working at his firm, but I decided to read it another way. Was this not the time to persuade Stephen to set up with me on our own? I went straight round to see him. Remarkably, Maggie, his wife, despite being close to producing their first child, backed him to set up with me. And that, in a nutshell, is how Hargreaves Lansdown came into being.

We started in my spare bedroom, leaving a message with the best secretary at Sandham Davis to say that, if she was released from employment because of our departure, we would be delighted to take her on. That is exactly how Valerie Gill, our first employee, came to join us. We borrowed a couple of desks, Stephen's father converted the built-in wardrobe into a stationery cupboard, we bought a filing cabinet and then put in an extra phone line. When one of the borrowed desks expired, we bought a new one. As we couldn't decide who should have it, in the end we gave it to Valerie. Next, we had to decide on a name. We tried every combination you could imagine. They included Lansdown Hargreaves but I managed to persuade Stephen that it sounded better the other way round. Since it was my bedroom and I was older, we eventually settled on a name which we have never regretted choosing. We were so busy that I don't think we noticed what the date was, but Stephen reliably informs me that our records date from 1st July 1981. It was the year that Prince Charles and Diana Spencer got married.

Chapter 2

The Money's in the Post

A Short Journey to Work

I can remember our first day quite clearly. I awoke, went to the kitchen, devoured a bowl of cereals and a cup of coffee and walked back up the short flight of stairs to what would be our first office. We had one phone (my home number), a borrowed typewriter and some new dictating equipment. As the phone was my home number, and I was the first into the office, I got to sit at that desk. At 8.30, Stephen turned up and I presented him with a front door key. We had no income and no clients. Stephen's wife was expecting their first child in a couple of months. It certainly focused our minds.

At least we had done our homework. We knew from the start that we wanted to specialise in unit trusts. Even then we could see that they were the best way for private investors to make the most of their capital. In order to trade profitably in unit trusts, you first had to apply for a "marketing allowance" from the unit trust groups. To do that, you needed two unit trust groups to sponsor you. We had good contacts with Henderson and Save & Prosper so it didn't take long. Peter Pearson-Lund, now with Rathbones, processed our paperwork at Henderson and a man called Peter Sanderson helped us with Save & Prosper. The standard commission on unit trusts was 1.25% but it rose to 3% once you became an accredited broker, eligible for marketing allowance. Our business model was simple. If we could do a million pounds worth of unit trust business, we would earn £30,000. That was £10,000 each and £10,000 to run the business including Valerie's salary, petrol for the cars, telephone, postage, stationery and so on. It seemed a tall order at the time but it's certainly a long way removed from the £2 billion and more per annum that we invest in unit trusts for our clients today.

One of the company's earliest priorities was to sort out a suitable business address. We didn't think that 15a Gloucester Street sounded like an office building in the commercial quarter of the City of Bristol. As window dressing, therefore, we bought a brass plate and after much thought put up the name "Kendal House". On walking past it recently, I noticed that the house still bears the same name. Why Kendal? It's a family name. In fact, it's what the "K" in Peter K. Hargreaves stands for. It was also my father's middle name and the name by which he came to be known. He was always proud that we called our first offices after him and, to this day, our current head office still bears the name "Kendal House".

Valerie arrived at 10 o'clock. She was part-time. Indeed, when we had no work for her, we would sometimes tell her not to come in or send her home early, as long as one of us was there to man the phone. Once all three of us were in, I set off down the road until I came to the nearest bank. It happened to be the National Westminster (now part of RBS). I went in and opened an account. I worked on the principle that all banks were the same so we might as well use the nearest. I haven't changed my mind about banks since. What I have changed my mind about is bank managers, who vary a lot. The way to choose your bank is to find the best bank manager (but beware – if they are any good, they won't be there for very long). Our relationship with the various banks we have used has always been trouble-free, mainly because we have never borrowed a penny in the years since we set up Hargreaves Lansdown. I suspect the banks prefer borrowers. Think of all the arrangement fees, interest, etc!

After opening the bank account, my next job was to persuade British Telecom that we needed a second phone. In those days, that horrible bureaucratic State-run monopoly was just as difficult to deal with as anything the State runs today. I did, however, learn an important early lesson in business, which is that the squeaky wheel gets the oil. The more fuss you make, the more attention you will get. I asked Valerie to write the same letter 17 times and posted all 17 to British Telecom. They were back within four days to fit the phone.

Shortly after we set up, Stephen identified a client with significant sums to invest. This man had fortunately taken a shine to

Stephen. He trusted him and duly invested enough money to earn us our first commission. That kept the business going for the initial two or three months. Whilst the accountants and solicitors with whom we had struck up relationships would bring us a small flow of business, neither of us were of a mind to play a waiting game. Sharing commission with others always seemed a bad deal to me, as we did all the work yet ended up with two masters and only earned a portion of what we would have done had we gone to the client directly. I had, meanwhile, been examining the alternative of selling unit trusts through the post, which I could see was working exceedingly successfully for others. This was the route I wanted to explore whilst, at the same time, keeping our accountant and solicitor contacts warm.

Beginner's Luck?

The next step was to persuade the national press to allow us to advertise. Clearly, a newspaper's reputation is at stake if advertisements creep in for products or services which are not bona fide. Brian Strath, whose sales operation I had seen up the road, was, perhaps unsurprisingly, the main objector. He felt aggrieved that I had looked at his operation and was now planning on copying it. We needed an edge, some way of distinguishing our advertising from his. His advertisement was what is known as a "six-double". That was six centimetres from top to bottom across two columns. Strangely enough, these small advertisements sometimes made a greater impact than large advertisements. The copy in our friend's advertisements was fortunately less than inspiring. It said he would tell you how to invest your money, based on his research. In practice, I knew that his answer was always the same: a unit trust.

As I knew nothing about advertising, it was a case of working everything out for myself. My thinking went like this. Since I was selling unit trusts through the post, I didn't feel it was worth my while talking to anyone who didn't already think they wanted to buy a unit trust. I had a brainstorming session with Valerie and

Stephen and we came up with the simple heading "CHOOSING A UNIT TRUST". It fitted neatly across the top of the two-column advertisement. That was my first edge over the competitor. The second was that I managed to get my advertisement as a five-double. In other words, it was a centimetre smaller and 15% cheaper. The advertising manager at the Telegraph, Hugh Searle, told me he had received a couple of objections to my advertising. ("I wonder where those came from," I said to him but he couldn't see the knowing look and smile on my face at the other end of the telephone.)

I couldn't understand why it was slightly cheaper to advertise in the *Sunday Telegraph* than the *Saturday Telegraph*. Knowing nothing about press advertising, I plumped for the cheaper option. From memory, I think it cost £200. I ran it as soon as I got the thumbs up from Hugh Searle and then had to rush round frantically to find a way of responding to the expected flood of replies. I noticed an advert for a firm, I think called The Secretary Machine, which advertised a word processing service. It was a business to which I could easily relate as it also ran from a spare bedroom in Clifton. (Today, Clifton is still full of little cottage industries.) We must have written and rewritten the initial response letter a hundred times. My advice to anyone in business is to remember that if you are going to send the same letter to a huge number of people, divide the time you spend on the contents by the number of people you intend sending it to. You can't spend too long getting such a letter right.

The only thing I knew about writing marketing literature was something that I had read and committed to memory: never talk about yourself, concentrate on the reader. Don't waste time introducing your service, telling people who you are and what you are doing. People are just not interested. Tell them what you will do for them, how you will do it and how they will benefit. When I give lectures on direct mail marketing, the one thing I tell everyone is this: suppose I took a photograph of you all today and brought it back in six months time. Who would you look for first on the photograph? The answer, of course, is yourself. I then say, "When you are writing to someone, talk about them. They are the important ones, not you. They need to know that what you are telling them is important and something they ought to read."

How many times have you received an unsolicited letter that says "before you bin this..."? In my book, that is a crazy way to start. You have already told the reader that they are going to bin your letter. Invariably, this sort of letter goes on to explain how long the promoter has been in business, what a proud and upright firm they are and how they love treating their clients well and all the rest of it. You sometimes have to read two-thirds of the letter before you find out what they actually do! Most people would have binned it long before they reach that point.

Our advertisement finally appeared in the newspaper. I must have been the first at the newsagents that morning and was delighted with the position that we had been given. It stood out on the page and was right next to a much bigger advertisement by a unit trust provider. My little £200 advertisement was saying subliminally, "Can you see this huge advertisement next to me? Respond to this advertisement and we will tell you whether or not you should be buying the unit trust described in the big advertisement."

We had decided what we were going to recommend to any investors who responded and assembled the pack telling them how our service worked. A huge amount of work had gone into that pack. Even so, for the next three days we sat and waited...and waited. There were no responses at all on the Monday. This was not surprising since in those days, apart from the all-night post office in Trafalgar Square, there were no postal collections on a Sunday. We had a disappointing two or three responses only on Tuesday. We received slightly more on the Wednesday at which time I suspect I had started to write the advert off, thinking that perhaps I had got the whole thing wrong.

By the time Thursday arrived, we didn't really expect anything. Our office was over the garage in the little mews house where I lived. There was a long corridor down the side of the garage with a door into the house at the end. I opened that door on Thursday morning and peered down the end of the corridor. The floor was littered with envelopes! That day was one of the biggest landmarks in the history of Hargreaves Lansdown. I walked down the corridor and sat down elated in the middle of this huge pile of envelopes. I picked up two handfuls and threw them into the air. Every bone in my body told me we had a success on our hands. I can remember quite clearly telling myself: "Now I am going to be a millionaire."

In all, we received 168 responses to our first press advertisement. It was what was known as a coupon response advertisement. Half the advertisement was taken up by a space for people to write their name and address. All they had to do was cut out the advertisement from the newspaper, put their name and address on it and pop it in an envelope to us. Of course, people who have money tend also to be people who are careful with their money. When they cut the advertisement out of a paper on Sunday, they put it in an envelope and (here's the important point) use a second class stamp. They post it on Sunday or Monday and either way it gets in the postal system on the Monday and takes, second class, until Thursday to arrive. Thursday was therefore always the big day of the week in the coupon era. Today, people are reluctant to return coupons at all. Now you have an 0800 number (Freephone) or you direct them to your website but the principles are exactly the same.

We were astounded by the response to the advertisement. It worked out at just over £1 a lead and what wouldn't we do for £1 leads today? We were even more astounded by the kind of people who responded. It showed how desperate people were for independent information. In those days, the only thing we had to do was make our literature and recommendations better than those of the competitors. There were plenty of others promoting investment at the time, not just Brian Strath. We suspected, rightly, that the people who were responding to our advertisements were also responding to everyone else's. Thanks to our training, what we were able to offer was an investment plan for those who responded, which not all our competitors could do. Essentially, we sent out a questionnaire which asked people to detail where their investments were held, how much money they had and so on. Stephen or myself would then prepare a report and, if necessary, go and see them with it.

People started investing but, to be honest, it wasn't quite what I had intended when we started. I thought I would be sending people a unit trust suggestion every five or six weeks and some of them would invest and some of them wouldn't. No, they wanted bespoke plans and that is what we provided. I was, however, still convinced that our best hope of building a sustainable business was to build a large community of investors who wanted unit trust ideas and for us to mail them with funds that we felt were well managed, in the right sector and likely to provide excellent performance. That remains our philosophy today.

The Joys Of Word Processing

Our first attempt at a newsletter would look very amateurish by today's standards. We had not perfected our art and, whilst we were always aiming to improve everything we did, the literature we sent out in those days was by no means the best. We shall never forget the first one we put together because the word-processed letters, the literature and everything else were all finally collated on the morning of the Prince of Wales and Lady Diana Spencer's wedding. My little mews house had a tiny postage stamp of a lawn at the back with a wall no higher than a couple of feet between us and the adjacent garden. I got on well with my neighbours, who were called George and Marcia. (We could never resist privately calling them George and Mildred.) She was really into the royal wedding, something that Stephen and I could have taken or left. We had given Valerie the day off. It was a lovely day, as I am sure everyone will remember. In those days, our mailings were all stuffed by hand. I had an old picnic table which I put on the lawn with a couple of chairs. We took the phone out on a long extension lead and sat there stuffing the envelopes in the afternoon whilst the wedding was in progress. Marcia insisted at every important juncture that we came in to watch the latest wedding highlights, each visit requiring a fresh glass of champagne. I hope we got all the right pieces in the right envelopes but I am not so sure that we did.

Before too long the business started to pick up. Stephen looked after the accounts and had his own clients while I concentrated on the marketing. I remember the telephone ringing one Friday afternoon when I was in the office on my own. It was a gentleman calling from Andorra. It was so long ago that I suspect it wouldn't matter if I used his name but we have never divulged clients' names and it would be a shame to break that rule now. We had suggested a Jardine Fleming Far East fund and he wanted to place a telephone deal for £30,000. For two lads who had just set up in business, that was a big order to accept on the strength of a telephone call from a complete stranger. I must have sat and thought about it for five minutes before I rang Save & Prosper, who carried out dealing on this fund, and placed the deal. I decided that as we had a 3% commission to play with, unless the price collapsed (which I thought unlikely), we were reasonably insulated from the risk of a loss before we saw the client's money. His cheque came about a week later and we all breathed a sigh of relief. As it happened, in the following year, the Far East Fund was among one of the top-performing unit trusts, so I am sure the gentleman in Andorra was even more pleased than we were with the commission we made on his deal.

The Lansdowns' baby finally arrived a few weeks later, so we had to cope with Stephen being in and out for a few weeks. Fortunately, everything went smoothly. We had certainly vaulted the first hurdles. Within weeks the business was making a decent profit. It helped that we were awarded an agency for M&G. The firm didn't automatically provide you with 3% commission when you got on the UTA list (a list of agents who specialise in unit trusts). You had to go for an interview at which you had to commit to sell their life and pension products as well as their unit trusts. Fortunately, a former colleague who had set up on his own down in Devon had tipped us off not to recommend any M&G unit trusts until we had successfully crossed this little hurdle. At that time, M&G were the blue chip unit trust group. One couldn't fault their performance and the saleability of their product. They had a massive presence in the national press, where they ran full page adverts every week in most of the Saturday and Sunday newspapers. Although they were the longest-established unit trust, they weren't quite the biggest. That title belonged to Save & Prosper which had a more successful life company which bought units in their own unit trusts, pushing them to the top of the sales league. Within five years of Hargreaves Lansdown starting out, however, M&G had climbed to the number one slot.

One morning when Stephen came in the office I sat him down and discussed a client to whom I had been talking more or less since we had set up in business. He was a client who had been introduced by one of my supporting firms of accountants. I had been preparing a very comprehensive plan because he was quite a wealthy man (for those times), having sold the family business for a substantial six-figure sum some months prior. I told Stephen that, if this client decided to give us his business, we would earn enough to buy the one thing that I coveted more than anything else – our own word processor. I knew if we could produce our mailings in-house we could make our literature significantly better. It would also save me having to walk across Clifton to the bureau that we had previously used. Having checked with Stephen that he was happy with this arrangement, I was more determined than ever to win this particular piece of business.

What the client who paid for our wonderful life-saving word-processor had never sorted out was how to generate significant income from his capital. The solution I came up with was called a capital and investment bond, provided by a firm called Skandia Life. Interest rates were very high in 1981. At one point, as those who were around at the time may remember, Mrs Thatcher raised them to 17% to combat inflation. This particular product had an option which worked like a gilt. The yield of 10% was guaranteed: however, if interest rates went up the capital would decline and if they came down the capital would appreciate. At the time, it seemed a one-way bet that interest rates would not remain as high as 17% much longer and the client agreed with my hypothesis. I think this was the only time I ever sold this product but it was absolutely perfect for that client and, as interest rates tumbled, he became a happier and happier client as the capital value increased. We eventually switched to another fund when we thought interest rates had declined enough. It was one of those investments that just worked out perfectly and the client has a great part in the history of Hargreaves Lansdown because after he had agreed to proceed, we could afford to buy our very first word processor.

The machine was called a Pet Commodore. I also bought a £500 word processing program called Wordcraft, which was the cheap part of the arrangement, and a printer made by the Nippon Electric Corporation (NEC) in Japan. This turned out to be the Rolls Royce of printers. It was called a NEC Spin Writer and it was the most superb piece of equipment. Indeed, until it became obsolete, it was a part of our office equipment for many years and simply never went wrong. The same could not be said for the mechanical sheet feeder that sat on top of it. This piece of equipment, known as a Rutishauser, caused more trouble than all of the office equipment we have ever had in the history of Hargreaves Lansdown, even though it was supposedly the best cut-sheet feeder on the market. I remember kicking it across the office one day in sheer frustration. Whilst I didn't damage the Rutishauser, I certainly didn't do my foot any good.

Our new equipment cost, unbelievably, £7000. Today, you could buy a PC, with a word processing program thrown in, and a laser printer for under £1,000. Valerie and I sat down and attempted to learn how to operate it. We must at this stage acknowledge someone whom I had met in Bristol through a mutual friend, a man called Spencer Hall. In those early days, we owed a lot to Spencer. It was he who had directed us towards our word processing set-up and, although it cost £7000, we had a much better printer than we would have had if we had bought a dedicated word processor. More importantly, the Pet Commodore was one of the first microcomputers and we could use it for many other functions. Spencer had written a fund management program which he supplied us and this gave us computing power in our early days which even much larger firms didn't possess. I thought we would pay for the new machine within a couple of years. In practice I think we created £7000-worth of extra commission within three months. What an investment it turned out to be!

As we got more used to the word processor and increased the size of our list of potential clients, the business started to enjoy a steady stream of income. In fact, for the first 18 months the business doubled every three months. As we became bigger and bought more supplies, we managed to start negotiating better prices. One thing that anyone going into business should remember is that everything is negotiable. Anyone who pays the asking price for anything, especially in your early years of business, is mad. You should always get a second quote from someone else and, if necessary, play the two off against each other.

The first new piece of equipment we bought after the word processor was a desk. One of the early beaten-up desks expired or perhaps wasn't strong enough to hold the extra equipment that we were buying. We decided at that time that we should buy something good that would last (we still have it). However, when the new desk arrived, we couldn't decide whether Stephen or I should have it so we gave it to Valerie. That was an early example of the culture that we have always tried to create at Hargreaves Lansdown. Everyone has always been equal in the firm. It has never mattered what a person's status is. If somebody is busy, the person who is quiet does the photocopying, stuffs the envelopes and for that matter brews the tea. That still occurs today.

When we started out, we couldn't work out how we could always man the phones. As people were constantly ringing us up to talk about the investments suggested in our mailing, one of us needed to be there all the time. Since we were still soliciting business from accountants and solicitors, we needed some mechanism whereby I knew I could make an appointment without referring to Stephen and vice versa. The solution we came up with was simplicity itself. Stephen and I had an agreement that I could book any day with an even number and Stephen could book any day with an odd number. It worked perfectly and we used the system for at least our first 12 months, after which we didn't need to call so often on accountants and solicitors, although we did have some extremely good contacts and we would regularly have days out to keep those relationships going.

Business Takes Off

By the beginning of December 1981, just five months after we'd started, there was a regular stream of money passing through our hands. Clients would send in cheques for investment which we would bank and then pay on to the various investment product providers. In those days, remarkably, anyone could handle client money. When I think back, it was a frightening situation and it is hardly surprising that there were many scandals. Indeed I wrote to one lady whom I had been to see in Oxford. She was a super lady who, sadly, had lost her husband to a brain tumour. She had two young boys and I don't think the firm for which her husband had worked had been that generous, but she had some tens of thousands of pounds to invest and I put a plan together for her. I suppose we struck up an affinity, not least because we were both from Lancashire originally. I suspect she just trusted me but, when she decided to proceed, I received a cheque for a significant sum of money (in fact almost every penny this lady had) made payable to me personally. I banked it and placed the investments. I also dropped her a letter to say that while her money was safe, there were many unscrupulous people in the world. She should be more careful about whom she made cheques payable to, especially someone that she had only met once.

It was at this time that I first realised that bank managers were not all equal. The bank manager that we had acquired when I opened our first account had absolutely no ambition and was simply working out his last couple of years to retirement. Naturally, being keen to make the most of the money that was passing through our hands, I wanted to set up an arrangement whereby the money that we were holding would earn interest. The manager was completely uncooperative, maybe because he didn't understand what I was trying to do. I knew it could be done because I had seen it done elsewhere. We soldiered on with him for a few more months, but eventually he lost our account.

In October 1981, we decided to produce our first newsletter which we called "The Unit Investor". Although the business was starting to blossom, we were still very keen to keep costs down. I had looked through a catalogue for the different typefaces you could buy for our NEC spin writer. There was a 15-pitch typeface without serif which I thought looked like something you might see on a printed newsletter. We bought this print wheel and we printed out various articles for the newsletter in narrow columns and then literally gave them to the printer to paste up and print from. This saved us the cost of typesetting but also it saved us a huge amount of time. We only had to check our own copy: we didn't have to re-read it again after it came back from the printer. For those days, it looked fine. It may not have been the smartest newsletter in the industry but we are still proud of the content to this day and it certainly cost the least to produce.

One day, while I was in the office, I received a call from a man who represented a small unit trust group based in Henley-on-Thames and who wanted to come and see me. He duly arrived one morning and produced some facts and figures about a unit trust that had provided its investors phenomenal growth. The name of the fund was the Perpetual Growth Fund. Although I had still not met the little man in Times Square at the time, I have always tended to be sceptical about performance that seems too good to be true. I talked to Stephen about it when he came in the office later that day and he was just as sceptical. He said, "Why don't you go to Henley and see them, have a look at them and get a feel for the place?" It was an obvious solution. Clearly, if that performance could be continued, it would be a fantastic investment for our clients. I can't remember everyone I met at Perpetual, but I do remember seeing their dealing book (unit trust business in those days hadn't long passed the quill pen days). I couldn't believe the famous London stockbroking names that were buying the fund. Martyn Arbib, who ran the fund, was a chartered accountant with a reputation for being a successful backer of racehorses. He had always been interested in the stock market and thought he could make a better job at investing than most institutions. As it happened, having survived the stock market collapse in 1974, his business was brilliantly placed to prosper in the great bull market of the 1980s and 1990s.

When I visited them, the Perpetual Growth Fund still had no more than £5 million in assets. The newer Income Fund was only £2 million in size. After discussing Perpetual with Stephen and saying that I was comfortable with the firm, we did a mailing for them. It was one of the most successful mailings we have done. In fact, although Martyn will never admit to this, I suspect that we helped put his fund in the limelight. We have subsequently had a lot of dealing with Perpetual, not all of it amicable, but they have been a significant factor in Hargreaves Lansdown's growth and I think vice versa. Many years ago, I had a bet with Martyn that one day Hargreaves Lansdown would be capitalised at a higher value than Perpetual. He was sceptical at the time but, over the years, I've regularly reminded him of this and I think now he is getting worried that I might just be right! The most recent bet I had with him was at Royal Ascot, where we had a side bet on which of our horses would win a race. He won that one and, when I saw him shortly afterwards at Henley, I duly paid up. The only thing that worries me is that we never specified how much money is on the bet about the capitalisation of Hargreaves Lansdown!

During the early days, we became more convinced that we had a potential success on our hands. Whilst it was probably bravado at the time, I remember saying to Stuart Pirelli, the Fidelity Sales Manager, "We intend being the largest unit trust advisory service in the UK." I remember Stephen adding, "And I want us to be the best unit trust advisory service in the UK." I think that really set out the two prime missions of the business. They were decided during our first six months. Stephen wanted to be the best and I wanted to be the biggest. I suspect it was many years later that I realised the only way we could become the biggest was if we were also the best. At the time we certainly weren't anywhere near the best, as we could tell when we compared our literature to that of our competitors. They say strong competition is good for business and I am sure that is the case. Having great competition sharpens both of you. There was little doubt that there were some firms whose literature was better than ours. At the time, we thought we were good at making recommendations but we realised, even in that area, we needed more scientific research. What we needed was both qualitative analysis (talking to fund managers) and quantitative verification. It was many years before we developed what we now believe is the best unit trust research team in the country. One of our golden rules of business is never to give up attempting to improve everything we do, whether that is marketing, research, administration, client calls, staff training and quality.

In January 1982, there was a constant stream of literature going to those who responded to our advertising and we were handling all of this in-house, which kept us busy and working long hours. For instance, I regularly set up the word processor at 10 o'clock at night with a letter to be merged with all the names and addresses of our clients. I would fill the hopper with letter-headings, start the thing going and wander down to the pub at the end of the street for a last pint. Normally, when I came back, I would find the batch processed properly but there were times when the cut-sheet feeder screwed up one letter very early in the run. Then I would have to start again at quarter to 11 at night or get up early the following morning to get the mailing out. There really wasn't time during the day, so busy were we becoming. We were no longer sending Valerie home when we were quiet and it was clear that we needed another employee. It was also clear we needed to do what Stephen had always wanted from the start, which was to move into an office.

By chance, a small office suite that we had looked at briefly when we were still debating whether to start in an office or from my house came back on the market. The business that had intended to move in never did so, despite having paid six months rent. The office was above the estate agent from whom I had bought my house and I still knew the estate agent well. He phoned me and told me that the offices were available. What is more, because the other business had an extended lease, they were prepared to pay us to go in there. In other words, we had the chance of moving into offices which would cost us very little. That, however, was the only good thing about them. They were called Heaps Chambers and that pretty well described them. Stephen was right, however, that if you are in business you really should be in business, and that means you should incur the overhead of offices expenditure. So we took the plunge and signed on the dotted line for our first "proper" offices.

Chapter 3

Enter the Rochdale Cowboy

A Tough Choice

Whatever anyone says, luck, fate or whatever you call it can make a big difference in business. It has certainly played a huge part in the history of Hargreaves Lansdown. I doubt, for example, whether we would have considered the offices that were suddenly available seven months before. Nor would I have so impetuously agreed to move into the investment business had not the company I worked for before coming to Bristol caused me so much grief. Equally, if I had not dithered initially about making that move, I would not have met Stephen, as he would not have been employed there when I arrived. Now, when we had found the offices and knew we could occupy them on such advantageous terms, we were at last able to start recruiting.

There are two lessons that anyone who starts out in business needs to learn. One is only to recruit when the existing staff are so overworked that they will accept anyone new. There is no better way of settling in a new employee than if the existing people are desperate for their help. The second lesson is that you should only move offices when you are already heaving at the seams. People don't care where they go or what the new offices are like, so long as they have more space. Although people hate change, they will be much more ready to accept it when they are desperate. Valerie was a fantastic employee but she was part-time and had a young family. So, although we pushed her hours out as far as they would go, we knew we needed assistance.

I have always been a believer in advertising job vacancies. Using agencies to find new employees is a sign of laziness on the part of the employer. The staff you recruit from agencies are often of the same ilk. People who desperately want to work for a decent firm look at every available source of new jobs. It is a shame that very few employers today advertise and very few potential employees do other than go to agencies. We welcome, and have always welcomed, people who scan the situation vacant columns of newspapers. In fact, we normally give them preference. Why? Because it shows that they are making an extra effort. Many employment agencies are no more than post boxes. We have never found an employee from an agency who has been properly vetted and interviewed before being sent to us. What usually happens is that you pay the agencies a fee and end up doing the job of interviewing and vetting them.

When we advertised for our first full-time employee, we didn't know exactly what we wanted. We simply said that we were a small dynamic business that was growing rapidly and we needed someone who was happy to carry out whatever we threw at them – which could be secretarial work, administrative work, whatever. In those days, you could state the sex and even the age of the prospective employee. A young woman was what we wanted. To my surprise, I also had a phone call from someone whom you definitely couldn't describe as a young woman, namely George Budd, a man who reappears later in this story. At the time, he was the branch manager for Target Life. "Peter, a little lass that worked for me would be absolutely perfect for you," he said over the telephone one day. "She is willing, bright and not afraid of work."

Of course, we interviewed her and George was right. She was exactly what we wanted. I almost regretted paying for the advertisement but as we had several applications for the job, we also interviewed two other young women. The first of them escapes my memory. The second came for her interview to my little mews house in Clifton Village on a Saturday morning. I remember she turned up in a green dress looking a little windswept. I immediately got on with her. She was very bright, had a degree in politics from Bristol University, couldn't find a job and had done a graduate secretarial course.

At first, I thought she might be one of life's perpetual students but that is not how she came across. I thought she was great but that she was probably far too good for us. I didn't know how we could give someone with her credentials enough to do. Nevertheless, she seemed keen to join. Stephen and I agonised over which young woman to choose. In the end we offered the job to the girl that George had recommended, only for Fate to take a hand when she turned us down. I think over the years I must have knelt and thanked God a thousand times that she did turn us down. It meant that the Bristol graduate who had gone through secretarial college was our only option. Her name was Theresa Barry and I can categorically state that Theresa has been no less important than Stephen or myself in the development of Hargreaves Lansdown.

Unfortunately, we didn't learn the obvious lesson that day, which is that you should always try to recruit people who are too good for the job. Theresa herself naturally reminds us regularly of what was nearly our biggest mistake in business. The reason I make this point is that young, uneducated, low achievers rarely persist through what they see as boredom in business to eventual success. Brighter, more intelligent employees don't mind doing a boring job for six months because, provided their company has a culture where talent and commitment is rewarded, they know they will be given a better opportunity one day. Maybe those who can see no further than the mundane job they are doing today complain of boredom because they know they are consigned to a life of it. The really bright people can see that one day there will be an opportunity to do something more rewarding and interesting.

So came the Ides of March. It was on the 15th March that we moved into 16 Merchants Road, the name which we preferred to use for our offices in preference to Heaps Chambers. Mrs Heap, the character who lived in the flat above us, was proud of the name because apparently a relation had offices in Sydney, Australia, which were also called Heaps Chambers. But "heap" was still the word that best described the premises. The building had been rewired about 16 times without the old wires being taken out. The offices were also highly inconvenient. The room that Stephen and I worked in, for example, was not connected to the remainder of the offices. You had to cross a hallway to reach them. The stairs were narrow, dark and dingy. Heaps Chambers was 600 square feet of disaster yet we loved every minute we were there. Theresa and Valerie never seemed to mind the inconvenience. In fact, none of us had time to think about where we were working.

Below us was a little estate agency called Harrop & Co. Graham, who owned it, had sold me the house in Clifton from where we started the business. He was a sound businessman, never spent a penny where a ha'penny would do and had worked out that if you employed temporary staff it saved you National Insurance because temporary staff never earned enough to incur more than minimum National Insurance contributions. Like all estate agents, he had a photocopier. (Estate agents were the first people to employ photocopiers because it made more sense to copy their blurb when it was required rather than print a large number, many of which might then be wasted.)

Graham had what, for those days, was a state-of-the-art photocopier and had worked out that it made sense to offer a photocopying service to others. In fact, he once told me that it was such a good source of income that it paid for one of his temporary staff. His copier was also ideal for us. We didn't need to buy our own because it was only a flight of stairs to get something photocopied. Graham ran a little account for us and we settled up from petty cash whenever he needed a few quid. There was always a bit of fun with the girls down in the estate agency. We never stood on ceremony. If you wanted something photocopied you took it down yourself. We never asked anyone else to do it. If you gave it to somebody else, what would you do while you waited for the copy to come back? Answer: nothing. You might as well do it yourself and not stop somebody else working. This is a principle that we have always applied in Hargreaves Lansdown and still apply today.

A year or so after we moved into Merchants Road, it became clear that, given the time we were spending on photocopying, especially the time spent socialising on the ground floor, it would make sense to have our own photocopier. So we duly acquired one. Before this, we had probably paid for 30 or 40 copies a day downstairs. How many copies a day did we make when we had our own machine? The answer is at least 250 a day. When we were paying for copies, and had to go downstairs to make them, people were much more frugal with their time and our money. I suspect that if we didn't have photocopiers today, we would probably end up making do with fewer than 1% of the copies we currently generate. The moral of the story is that simple cost projections can be hopelessly wrong, however obvious they might appear at the time.

A Brief Digression; And Learning From Our Mistakes

The history of photocopying, incidentally, is one of the more amazing stories in business. In the early 1960s, there was a small photographic processing firm in Rochester, New York, that hung on the shirt tails of Kodak, its far more famous local employer. One day one of the boffins at this small firm went along to the managing director and said, "I have been playing around with a photographic process that doesn't take photographs, but instead burns images into a piece of paper. What it means is that you don't have to wait for a film developer in order to make a copy of something." At that time anyone who wanted a copy of something had to use a photographic process. The photocopiers of the 1960s were very poor things that needed special photographic paper. The process which the boffin showed his boss was quick and easy. It used ordinary paper and it produced a document which you could easily send straightaway to a client. His boss was wildly excited. In fact, his enthusiasm surpassed that of the boffin himself (boffins are not normally known for overt enthusiasm!).

The board of this little company sat down and wondered what they had got. One bright spark said, "Why don't we mail all the companies in the S&P 500 (America's top 500 companies) to find out what use they would have for our invention?" Everyone thought it was a great idea. So they mailed all 500 companies. How many of those S&P 500 companies replied saying they might have a use for this wonderful new invention? The answer is: just two. Undeterred, in one of the biggest business gambles of all time, the board of this little company decided that the S&P 500 companies were wrong and spent the equivalent of three-years' profits developing the process. The company was called Xerox. Xerography, the process they developed, is not only the basis on which all photocopiers work but also how laser printers work. The gamble certainly paid off. Soon after the launch of its first photocopier, Xerox had produced no fewer than 130 millionaires.

I am not surprised by that. I have always been astounded about the way that photocopiers get used (and misused) in business. When I worked for large companies in the 1970s, they used to have special "photocopier operators" where you went and said, "Could I have a copy of this?" My experience was that however many copies I asked for, I never got what I needed. I always received at least twice as many. Today I suspect that most laser printers and photocopiers still produce many more copies than are really required. Yet it keeps the manufacturers of the machines and the suppliers of the paper and the toner (the material which photocopiers depend on) clapping their hands with delight on a daily basis.

Despite the less than palatial surroundings, our days in Merchants Road were happy ones. Although we were running the same old "Choosing a Unit Trust" advertisements, one advertising agency had noticed our presence in the newspapers and decided to revamp the shape of the advertisement. Instead of a five-double, which was five centimetres deep and spread across two columns, they re-designed it as a ten-single. I had discounted this shape earlier because with a five-double you had an extra couple of millimetres between columns for free, something you didn't get in a single column. There are times, however, when what looks to be the best value isn't. The advertising agency which had drawn up our ten- single had a point. The first time we ran the advertisement in this shape it had a lot more impact. I remember Martyn Arbib, the hands-on managing director of Perpetual, ringing me up and moaning almost to the point of tears that he had paid several thousand pounds for his advertisement and yet my little ten-single had more impact on the page. That was a great endorsement and proof that the innovation was worth the effort.

Not only did the advertisement in its new shape have more impact, it also meant that the reply coupon need only take up a third of the advertisement space instead of half. This gave us an opportunity to sneak in a couple of questions about what the investor wanted. Did they want income or growth? How much did they want to invest? And so on. With this extra information, we set about trying to tailor plans for clients more carefully. We worked out how to send those who replied to the advertisements a complete bespoke response. If they said they had £30,000 to invest and wanted income, we would give them a list of income unit trusts and suggest a couple of fixed interest unit trusts as well, while leaving £5000 in the building society. Our response would also show how much income they would get and how the whole plan linked together. In the case of clients who opted for growth, we would list a number of UK growth funds and then, depending on how much they had to invest, perhaps two or three overseas growth funds as well.

Naturally, we thought that what we had produced was absolutely brilliant – but we were totally wrong and it taught us an invaluable lesson. The problem was that our investors varied so much, from the ultra-naïve to the ultra-sophisticated. While we probably hit the right note with the sophisticated investors, there were far too few of them. Investors today are far more knowledgeable but, in those days, most investors thought that "growth" was what happened when you allowed income from a building society account to roll up. In the event, most investors ticked the growth box – but the way we responded to that was wrong. What we should have done was send virtually the same plan to everyone. That plan should have been based around income funds. For those who wanted income, we should have suggested they took the income from the income fund. For those who wanted growth, we should have suggested that they simply rolled up the income from the same income funds.

The insight into the power of income funds that we have gained from over a quarter of a century has been invaluable in helping us give investors what they want. As an adviser, you have to interpret what the client is requesting. The response to our advertisements provided us with invaluable intelligence. The response to those early coupon advertisements allowed us to continue honing our literature, our products and our advice – something that we have never ceased doing and still endeavour to do today.

Playing The PR Game

Very early on in the evolution of Hargreaves Lansdown, we noticed that journalists in the personal finance columns of the newspapers were looking to quote so-called "experts". All the papers wanted comments on new products, comments on the market and comments on financial planning. At the same time, there seemed to be a groundswell of opinion that unit trusts were a good way to invest. Investors love past performance figures and huge numbers of investors choose investments on nothing else. As the stock market had bottomed in 1974, by 1984 any investment from that time had great ten-year figures to boast about. Two of the funds that launched in 1974 were ones with which we became heavily involved. One was Martyn Arbib's Perpetual Growth Fund and the other was an income unit trust that unusually had been launched by the offshoot of an insurance company; namely Provincial Life. They called their investment arm Prolific. Prolific High Income became one of the best loved and best-known income unit trusts in the UK, in part because of our own efforts at promoting it.

In fact, by 1982, unit trusts were becoming so popular that the Money Programme selected a panel of experts to choose which unit trusts they thought would perform best during a calendar year. It ran the competition in conjunction with *The Times* newspaper. The general public was also asked to compete. I noticed in *The Times* that there was a section for professional advisers and after some thought I entered a fund. I didn't expect the readers who chose poor funds would get pilloried but I did suspect that the four experts who were sticking their necks out on television had a real chance of being pilloried, which was exactly what happened. The panelist that did the worst was ejected from the panel, meaning that a new expert had to be found. I felt at the time that it should have been ourselves, but someone else who had just come into the unit trust industry and played the PR game extremely well was chosen instead. Kean Seager, the guy in question, based his whole business on PR. I sometimes thought he must have spent more time in Fleet Street than in his own business (yes, Fleet Street was at that time still home to a few newspapers). In the competition, I was the leading professional adviser at the halfway mark with my choice of Britannia Hong Kong. My picture was in *The Times* and I found myself commenting on investment after only being in business 18 months.

We were also in a competition in a magazine called *Planned Savings* and the portfolio that Stephen had selected was doing well and getting mentioned in the national press. It was clear that PR was going to be an important tool in building the business. So it became an obsession of mine to work out how we could become proactive rather than reactive at PR. Since the journalists didn't know who we were, let alone our address or telephone number, I didn't imagine that they would phone us up out of the blue and nor did they. One night I was in my local where I used to meet a couple of chaps from Lancashire who like myself were in exile in Bristol! One of them was in PR and I asked him how it was done. "It's simple," he said, "you need to give journalists ideas. They have a column to write and a blank sheet of paper, so they welcome all ideas with open arms."

"I don't need a PR agency then?" I asked. "Well," he said, "PRs can introduce you to the journalists and help you with your plans, but essentially no."

The other important thing he told me was that I shouldn't give all the journalists the same story. No journalist likes writing a story and finding it being carried by three other national newspapers the same day. Now, at least, we thought we knew what we were trying to do. Stephen and I sat down and came up with seven different stories. I got on the phone and booked half hour appointments with seven journalists from seven different newspapers in one day. I didn't know then that wasn't the way that a PR firm would do it. Its solution would be to take the journalist and myself out to lunch, then charge me for all three meals and repeat the operation for seven days running! I travelled up to Paddington station, joined the taxi queue and told the first taxi driver who came along that I wanted to go the *Daily Mail's* offices, which in those days were close to Fleet Street. I got on well with the taxi driver so when I got to the *Daily Mail's* office I said to him, "I will be half an hour. Keep the meter running. I'll be back." From there it was on to the *Financial Times*, the *Telegraph*, the *Sunday Times*, the *Guardian* and the *Observer*. I had a different story for each journalist. I remember seeing Joanna Slaughter at the *Guardian* and Chris Hill at the *Sunday Telegraph*. The only one that I failed to see was Louise Botting, who presented Money Box on the BBC. She expressed doubts that someone that had been in the industry for such a short time would have anything particularly authoritative to say. I hope she was surprised when she saw the newspapers that week!

After that, I never looked back. We struck up some great relationships with the journalists and today I still talk to some who were around then. Lorna Bourke still writes a column. Roger Carroll, who was also at the *Telegraph*, contacted me when we announced our flotation because he went to work for a PR firm and wondered whether his firm could do our flotation. In fact, we chose someone else but the flotation was one of the few times that we have appointed a PR firm. It was such a different field that it was wise not to risk getting it wrong. The only other time we have employed a PR firm was for our stockbroking side where Richard Hunter, who is regularly quoted on stock market matters, was ably assisted by an excellent PR firm for a while. The advantage of having a PR firm is that they know the ropes, know the people and know what stories journalists will like. Journalists have confidence that the better PR firms won't waste their time. I was impressed with the PR firm that we appointed for our float. The day we announced our decision they had pre-booked times for every national newspaper, all the news services and various specialist publications. Stephen and I sat in a room as the calls were put through. The following day we had comment in every single national newspaper. Over the years, of course, we had become known by the financial press even though these journalists were on the City pages rather than the personal financial pages. Many of them had cut their teeth in the industry's trade publications and some had gone to the City pages via the personal financial columns. It was easy talking to them because we knew them, we knew what we were doing, we were relaxed and I have to say they were exceedingly kind in their comments the following day.

Unwanted Visitors And An Interesting Lunch

One incident at Merchant Road sticks in my mind. The layout of the offices, as I have described, forced Stephen and I to walk across the top of a landing if we wanted to get to the rest of our office space. It was very inconvenient. One day we were both away from our room, doing something in the other office. When I returned, I suddenly came face to face with two shady characters coming out of our office. I held out my arms as if to capture them. Stephen went into our room and shouted, "My wallet's gone." At that point, the two lads shot past me and down the stairs. I followed in hot pursuit.

I caught up with the second one and, having squarely planted my foot in the middle of his back, kicked him down the last flight of stairs. (You can be very brave when the circumstances demand it.) With the help of a young man who was working in the estate agent down below, I managed to make a citizen's arrest. You don't have a lot of fight left in you when you have been kicked down a flight of stairs. Sadly, that was the last I heard of it. Although there was eventually a court case, and both offenders were caught, we never received the money back, nor a word of thanks from the police. In court, the lad whom I had kicked down the stairs asked for four other offences to be taken into consideration. Two of them were for grievous bodily harm so perhaps I had rather a lucky escape. In those days we could not be accused of lacking passion.

Another thing that became very evident to me with our early mailings was that the amount of business we did was directly proportional not just to the quality and desirability of the products we were recommending but also to the size of our list. Our early list probably had no more than 1000 names. Stephen and I often discussed how much business we would do if we had a list of 10,000 names instead and, in time, we got to find out. We have always had a good feeling for what clients wanted but it soon became apparent that response rates did not fall off when we expanded the numbers we mailed. This was mainly because our lists all came from the same sources and those who didn't invest were removed from the list, so we were, in effect, concentrating our list all the time. After we had established this, the game became one of growing the list as fast as we could. For the first 15 years of our existence, you could say that the most valuable commodity we had wasn't Stephen, Theresa or myself but the list. All I can say for the three of us is that we knew how important the list was and did everything we can to make the most of the strength it gave us.

As the business continued to develop, we realised that we couldn't just confine ourselves to unit trusts. We needed to look at other options. Despite 25 years of criticism, life companies still have some valuable products. People do need life assurance and when people retire they do need to buy annuities to secure a lifetime income from their accumulated pension funds. We have never been wildly impressed by the talents of most of the life company people who have called on us. We always wondered whether they were just innately low calibre people or whether the environment in which they worked cultivated mediocrity. However there was one young lady who impressed us immensely. She worked for Commercial Union and, after a short period of time, we started to give her business, not least because the service she gave us was second to none. One day she came to me and said, "My branch manager has been asking me ever since I opened your account whether he could come and see you." She smiled winsomely and said, "I have put him off so many times that I can't put him off any more. He is a complete jerk and it will be agony, but would you do it for me?" I thought it could be a bit of fun to bait the old rascal so I agreed.

We met in a restaurant close to the office. (We are lucky that Clifton Village has always been a place where people go out to wine and dine.) We sat down and Hilary's appraisal of her boss proved to be entirely accurate. He had risen through the ranks more by longevity and luck than ability or intelligence. "Peter," he told me earnestly halfway through our lunch, "I have got to tell you about something we have just acquired in our office. We're a big company and so we can afford it but I wouldn't be surprised if you have one, too, within a few years. It is a word processor. The amount of work it will save and the things we can do with it are just amazing." I answered him by asking him, "How many staff have you got in the Bristol office?" "I suspect around 90," he said. "Really," I said, "we have three office staff and they have a word processor each." Hilary's face was a picture. It was one of the best business lunches I can remember, if only because I have laughed and dined out on it for years. Needless to say, we employed Hilary the following week. She just couldn't bear to stay where she was any longer. When she joined us, it enabled us to set up our own pensions business.

The Rochdale Cowboy

One evening during our tenure in Heaps Chambers I received a telephone call from the unit trust rep for Target Unit Trusts, a man called John Simmonds. As we were both bachelors living in Clifton, we used to bump into each other in the local hostelries and struck up a friendship, perhaps because we were both Lancastrians. I used to call him affectionately "The Rochdale Cowboy". He has since had an illustrious career, most recently at AXA, the large French insurance group. When it was rumoured that we were about to float Hargreaves Lansdown, he was despatched by his bosses at AXA to meet me. I half suspected what the meeting would be about and I was right. His message was that AXA would be willing to buy Hargreaves Lansdown before the float and pay a very substantial sum. It was suggested they might pay more than the company would be initially capitalised on the stock market. I had to explain to him that I was almost certainly unemployable and that, reassuring though his words were, a life company would have ruined the business. I asked him what would happen if the chief executive of AXA telephoned me one evening and said I needed to be in London for a meeting the following day and my reaction was simply no. How would AXA deal with that? I think at that point he realised that the deal would not have worked out well.

I was able to remind John that back in 1982 one particular call had played a large part in the development of our business at Hargreaves Lansdown. At the time his call had a certain frantic edge to it. "I have got John Stone down tonight and the broker in Bristol who was supposed to be having dinner with him has cried off." Knowing that I was a bachelor and probably doing nothing, he asked if I could take the broker's place. The deal was dinner at Harvey's, arguably Bristol's best restaurant at the time. John Stone was the head of Target Life and had previously been head of Vanbrugh, the Prudential's unit-linked business. It was an opportunity that I could not miss. I had never met John Stone before although, whilst working for Bill Sandham, I had attended a presentation at a seminar in a country club on the outskirts of Bristol. It was one of the most remarkable seminars I have attended. During it, he cleverly wound up all the investment and pensions brokers from the Bristol area by telling them about a new concept in personal pensions which was brilliant in its simplicity. It was the way he toyed with the audience that was so impressive. He was a very charismatic presenter and none of that charisma has left him over the years.

The new product that John Stone was presenting to his audience was called Loan Back. It worked on the basis that few successful businessmen could afford to make pension contributions in their formative years, mainly because their businesses when embryonic consume so much capital. Pension contributions in those days were even more tax advantaged than they are today. At the time, the highest rate of income tax you could pay was 60% but on top of that there was the so-called investment income surcharge, which meant that unearned income paid an extra 15% tax, making a top marginal rate of 75%. Pensions, however, were exempt from the income tax surcharge. A pension contribution of £100 in effect cost you just £40 if you were a higher rate taxpayer and potentially saved you another 15% as well.

The deal Vanbrugh was introducing was so simple that it was remarkable that nobody had thought of it before. It involved making a contribution to a pension plan and then immediately borrowing back the amount of the net premium. This is how it worked. If a 60% rate taxpayer paid in £10,000 to a pension plan, it effectively cost him only £4000 because he got 60% tax relief on his contribution. If he immediately borrowed back the £4000 from his pension plan, it meant that he had actually paid nothing, albeit that he owed his pension plan £4000. The net effect was that he ended up with £10,000 in his pension without having to part with any cash. Of course, he had to wait to reclaim the tax, so there was a cash flow problem. This is where Vanbrugh proposed to come in with its ingenious new Loan Back scheme.

The company's plan was to make short-term loans until the person who had made the pension contribution was able to reclaim the tax on his pension contributions. As John Stone was explaining his new scheme, I noticed that the room suddenly started to empty. I couldn't at first understand why. The content was spellbinding. The reason for their exodus turned out to be quite simple. Most of the brokers in the room had clients who should have been putting more money into pensions but didn't have any spare cash. As soon as they had grasped what they were being offered, the brokers were jumping into their cars and driving off to see those clients before someone else got to them with Vanbrugh's new scheme! I have never seen anything like that before or since. John Stone certainly left a lasting impression on me.

The chance to meet such a charismatic figure was not one to be missed therefore. I turned up at Harvey's bright and early. John Stone and John Simmonds were already there and I was duly introduced. We had the most enjoyable dinner. We all seemed to hit it off together extremely well, so well indeed that our table became the noisiest in the restaurant and the last to be vacated. I suspect there was more than the odd bottle of wine drunk. I was fascinated by John and his stories and he seemed interested in my business. Although Hargreaves Lansdown was only embryonic in those days, he could see we had a goal and we seemed to know how we were going to achieve that goal. I suspect it was quite late in the evening when he suddenly looked at me and said, "So Peter, how are you doing this direct mail?"

It seemed a rather silly question but I answered it all the same. "Well, John, it's coupon response. We send the respondents a few mailings and if they haven't invested after six months, we drop them off the list." I don't know why I told him we dropped them off the list. I just happened to say it. He looked at me over the top of his spectacles, perched on his above-average sized nose, and he uttered three words, two of which were expletives. I will say no more than the first word was "you" but the rest of the statement indicated that I was making a very serious mistake!

I have found that if somebody makes an impassioned statement like that, you are usually going to hear something important. I still didn't realise what I was doing wrong but John was quick to explain. "After six months is just when they are going to invest." Nothing more needed to be said. The following morning, I went back to the office, told Theresa the story and we resurrected all the names we had abandoned and mailed them again. It turned out that John Stone was very right indeed. It was one of the best pieces of advice I have ever had in business and I hadn't even paid for the dinner.

An Early Bombshell

We had only been in Merchants Road – I still can't bring myself to call it Heaps Chambers – for about 15 months when Theresa informed me that she intended to leave. I was stunned and desperate to know why. "It's not because of the business," she said, "because I love it." The reason was that she had a boyfriend who years before had followed her to Bristol University. It was he, I found out later, who had brought her to her first job interview on the back of his motorbike, which is why she had appeared somewhat flustered on the day. Paul had obtained a job in Kent to which he was commuting on a weekly basis, leaving at the crack of dawn on a Monday morning and coming back on Friday evening. It was not so much that Theresa missed him but that the 150 miles or so journey between Bristol and Kent twice a week in all weathers was causing her concern for his safety. The day of her announcement was one of the worst days we had experienced since starting the firm. We knew already how important Theresa was to the operation. She had shown a real aptitude for marketing, finding out what clients wanted and helping us give it to them. She was learning the business, learning the trade and soaked up information like a sponge.

When I asked Theresa what she was going to do, she felt that she might try to find a job in the City as that was within easy commuting distance of where she needed to live in Kent. We wrote a few letters, as we have done for many employees who have needed to move for personal reasons. One of the letters must have struck a chord because Theresa found a job working for the unit trust division of Abbey Life, who in those days had an excellent investment business. Her boss, a man called Jack Bourne, was someone for whom we have always had a soft spot at Hargreaves Lansdown. Jack had earlier been part of the marketing team at a successful unit trust business called Schlesingers, famous for having the best marketing in the industry.

Her intended move was going to leave a huge gap. When it came to replacing Theresa, we decided that we needed someone to look after unit trust dealing full-time. It had been a job that Theresa had done before as part of her many duties. By strange coincidence, the young lady who applied for the job had worked for the same firm that had originally given me the idea of selling unit trusts through the post. She knew the job and was a bright, intelligent girl who, while she would never be a Theresa, was just right for what we wanted. Theresa agreed to stay on and train her. The young lady told us how much she required as a salary and we agreed it. Within days of starting, she was astounded to discover how big our volumes were in comparison to her previous employer. At the end of her first week, therefore, she came into the office that Stephen and I shared to say, "I don't think the salary you are paying me is enough." I replied, "But I agreed to pay you exactly what you wanted." She gazed back and said, "Yes, but I didn't realise how much business you were doing." I thought it was completely immaterial how much business we were doing. She was being paid to work from nine until five, with an hour for lunch, and that was the end of it. Nevertheless, I said I would consider her request.

Then I went to the pub with Stephen, as I often did in those days. We generally found that a snack and a beer in the pub was the perfect environment for discussing things and for holding management meetings! Stephen had sat there in silence while the girl had been talking in the office and continued to say nothing. "Should we give her what she wants?" I asked. "Perhaps we should meet her halfway." I must have agonised aloud for about ten minutes. Stephen never said a word. In the end, I said, "Oh hell, lets sack her. She will always be a problem. Whatever we offer her now she will want more in the future. I can't do with someone who wants to change her contract within a week." Stephen looked at me and smiled. "I thought that an hour ago," he said, "but I thought you would come to the same conclusion if I left you to blow off steam."

The young lady went that afternoon, despite telling us that she really didn't want the rise and would have carried on working for the same money. The problem was that we could never have trusted her after that. To replace her, we contacted the college where Theresa had done her secretarial course. We were confident that we could teach their students the job. In the end, we found two young women who were absolutely great and took them both on. Theresa trained them and finally left us to head for her new life. My last words to her were, "If you ever come back this way, make sure your first letter is to me."

The two young women we recruited were both efficient although very different in character. Rosemary Young was perfect for us because she liked being in a small firm and didn't mind the shabby surroundings. She was a real character and I still have some contact with her today. Penny Foren was more formal and eventually moved into marketing when she left. I shall never forget how one day, having been asked by a journalist on a national paper to write something, I asked Penny to have a look at it and write it. I knew she could do it but she had less confidence in herself than I had in her. After I had walked out of the office, Penny turned to Rosemary and said, "Peter has asked me to do this but I haven't got a clue what it's about, I don't know what I am doing and I don't know what to do." Rosemary looked at her and laughed. "Well, it has never stopped Peter in the past." It was one of the saner comments made about Hargreaves Lansdown. Penny wrote the article and the journalist never knew.

Chapter 4

Where are the Customers' Yachts?

Unit Trusts Or Investment Bonds?

As we became more successful and achieved a higher profile, many people questioned what we were doing and why we were doing it. One of those was George Budd, who had found us our ideal employee (the one who even more fortunately turned us down). George was a great character and one of the old school in the investment business. "Why are you guys selling unit trusts?" he demanded to know one day when he came into the office. "Don't you know that you can get 6% commission from investment bonds? And it is 7% for volume sales! What is more, if the clients are basic rate taxpayers, they need never pay any more tax and can take 5% per annum tax-free out of the bond forever. If they are a higher rate taxpayer, they can take the same amount for at least 20 years without paying tax." It was a good question and one that many of our competitors could not understand either. However, we never did subscribe to his views about investment bonds. Nor at the time did we tell him why.

The reason was partly to do with tax. In those days, only a few investors had generated sufficient capital gains to be at risk of paying capital gains tax. The advantage of unit trusts was that the funds did not pay capital gains tax. Investors in the funds only paid capital gains tax when they sold their units. You could therefore choose exactly when and how much you sold and could time those disposals to take full advantage of the annual capital gains tax exemptions. Investment bonds by contrast resided in a life company's funds, which suffered capital gains tax.

There were however other good reasons not to use investment bonds. The problem with an investment bond was that you were locked in to the investment expertise of just one company's funds.

In practice, very few investment funds managed by life companies performed anything like as well as those offered by pure investment houses which lived and died by their investment performance. (Target was one exception to this rule, as were M&G, Prolific and Equity and Law.) Life companies sold so many other things that investment performance was never such an important part of the equation. Before April 5th 2008 there was a genuine case to be made for investment bonds, though it depended on investors' personal circumstances. Today investment bonds are less attractive. In the past there was a case for using investment bonds, especially for someone who was incurring capital gains tax; you can no longer make that case. The new 18% rate of capital gains tax means that the maximum tax that any taxpayer can pay on a gain is 18%. Within the bond any gain is taxed internally at approximately 20% (there is a composite rate which can be slightly less or slightly more than this) and then a higher rate taxpayer when encashing would pay a further 20% on any gain that his bond has made, i.e. a total of circa 40% whereas externally only 18%. In the case of basic rate taxpayers they will also be paying 20% on any gains on the investments within the bond and it is highly unlikely that many basic rate taxpayers would incur capital gains tax on their investments by using their annual exemptions. I am sure that this much less favourable regime for investment bonds will not stop brokers selling them because they still have one very desirable feature – they can pay up to 7% commission to the broker.

There was another reason for not favouring investment bonds which we have kept secret since we started but which I shall share with you here. The problem with investment bonds is that they are produced by life companies and all life companies employ incompetent twerps whose job is to produce lengthy, unusable, incomprehensible application forms. The forms they produce are the biggest deterrent to business imaginable. A single premium investment bond is on the face of it about as simple an investment as you can find. All the life company needs from the investor is a name, an address and a cheque. Yet the twerp who designs the application forms for life companies invariably manages to turn this simple requirement into a six page version of *War and Peace*. Their application forms include a myriad of questions which are completely irrelevant, such as age, sex and two whole pages of health questions, a multiple choice application form for 19 different investment choices and more questions about the level of income.

The one lesson that anyone in the investment business needs to learn is that for every extra question you ask you will lose 5% of your investors. If you ask 20 questions, therefore, you risk getting wiped out. No one ever told the designers of application forms for life companies this and, even though I have told them so regularly for many years, they remain blind, deaf and daft. The average life company form contains about 40 questions and for some pension contracts the form runs to 17 pages. By contrast, to sell a unit trust you only need a person's cheque or sometimes just a telephone instruction. Even today you don't need a signature to carry out an investment in a unit trust (or stocks and shares for that matter).

While the commission on investment bonds is more than twice the commission on unit trusts, I have always found I could sell ten times as many unit trusts as bonds, so turning down the high initial commissions was not as difficult as others seem to have found it. I did not even have to rely on the unit trust groups' own application forms which, although brilliant in comparison to those of the life companies, were also horrific. I could and did design my own forms which consisted of surname, Christian name, address, postcode and whether the customer wanted income distributed or rolled up. If the forms are going to people who are already clients, we sometimes now send them application forms that have already been partially completed: all they need to do is attach their cheque. As a businessman, I would rather have 3% commission on £100,000 than 6% commission on £10,000 any day. More importantly, when you encash an investment bond, there is a horrific tax calculation (top slicing in the industry's jargon) that only a few people in the country can do correctly. Many people's accountants still don't carry it out accurately.

This is not to say that investment bonds have no place at all in the investor's armoury. There are situations where they can be useful for tax planning purposes, and we have used them in that way. For instance, someone who is using their annual capital gains tax exemptions, or a higher rate taxpayer who will one day revert to being a basic rate taxpayer, could find an investment bond a useful interim tax shelter. Investment bonds have also sometimes enabled investors to access investments that are not available through other types of collective investment product. For instance, for many years the only sensible way to gain exposure to commercial property was through an investment bond. The same went for exposure to life company "with profit" funds. The way we have often sought to overcome the problem of high upfront commissions has been to ask the life companies to add back a significant portion of the commission due to us for the client's benefit. As is now our normal practice, we negotiate instead a renewal commission that comes out of the annual management charges in the bond and therefore does not cost the client anything more.

Talking about the complexities of financial planning reminds me of a story involving one of the industry's colourful characters. Many years ago, I had a very wealthy client who was selling two businesses and had a complex flow of income during the next three to four years. He wanted an investment that would create taxable income and/or capital gains at specific times. There was a considerable amount of money involved. A guaranteed income bond seemed a sensible solution. They were structured through a life policy and each bond could be structured differently. Some bonds produced taxable income, some had chargeable events every year, some had chargeable events every other year and others had a chargeable event only at the end. I therefore furiously started ringing round all the providers of guaranteed income bonds to find one that would fit the bill.

In those days Schroders had a life company and employed a character called Nick Welsh. His real name wasn't Nick, it was Roger, but having been a Russian translator for the RAF in Berlin, he found his colleagues drew the line at saying "Roger, Roger". After the RAF he worked at GCHQ and had also been a tax inspector. "Nick," I said when I was put through to him on the phone, "your guaranteed income bond – how is it structured?" He asked "What do you mean?", to which I replied "Well, I want to know when the chargeable events are, what sort of taxable income it throws off and so on." He then started laboriously describing the bond in minute detail, explaining what a chargeable event was and everything else. "Nick, for Christ's sake," I said after a while, "I just want to know when the chargeable events are." He just ploughed on with his list of minutiae. "Nick, for Christ's sake, I'm a chartered accountant. Please cut to the point!" "Oh sorry, Peter," he said. "I didn't know you were a chartered accountant. I'll speak a little slower." I have laughed about that for the last 25 years. At the time and since I have pretended to be offended. Only now will he find out how I saw the funny side.

Royal York Crescent

The 600 square feet in Merchants Road didn't take many people and so it wasn't long before we again needed more space. By the summer of 1983 we were once more straining at the seams. One of our biggest problems was not accommodating people but finding room for clients' files. Filing cabinets, in my experience, are just about the worst way of storing paper ever invented by man. My advice to anyone starting in business is simple. Don't buy one. There are lateral filing systems which are much easier to use and far more economical on space. Nor do they have drawers which come off the runners and jam closed. Initially, we kept the clients' files alphabetically but alphabetical filing soon becomes very unwieldy when you have over 1000 clients. So we decided to change to numbers and use our small computer as a search engine. What you did was type in the name of the client and the computer told you their number, allowing you to trace their file that way.

So, after only 18 months we were on the move again. It turned out not to be difficult getting rid of Merchants Road even though we had taken out a lease that had still not expired. Spencer Hall, the computer expert I mentioned earlier, had by now set up a new business called Accounting Software and he needed offices. That produced a neat solution. He moved into Heaps Chambers and we moved out. I had heard that there was space available in a building at most a hundred yards from Merchants Road. A firm of consulting engineers had been in there but they had outgrown the premises. Because there was little demand for office space at the time, the engineers were prepared to offer us a bribe to move in. We have been lucky in all our office moves as we have never had to offer a rent-free period to new tenants when we left but we have in our new abode frequently benefited from such an arrangement ourselves.

I had more or less agreed the deal when I was told by the agent that the people on the top floor of the building had also expressed an interest. This was a government quango which purported to train social workers. They not only wanted to take the space but said they would pay a premium to do so. Clearly, they knew nothing about the office market but then it wasn't their money they were spending – an early experience for me of how wasteful government can be. My solution was simple. I went to see the manager, whom I doubt could have managed herself out of a paper bag. I mentioned that, if she proceeded with the deal, I would certainly make sure her ineptitude with taxpayers' money was given maximum publicity. Surprise, surprise, I heard that afternoon from the agent that the people on the top floor had decided they didn't need the space after all.

The new offices were fantastic and for the first time in our history we learned about the wonders of partitioning. We sent for one of those firms that come in and divide an open plan space up exactly as you want it. Ironically, over the years we have come to the conclusion that as little partitioning as possible is best but at the time we didn't know that. Stephen and I had separate offices. We also had a filing room, two interview rooms and more new desks. It all seemed fantastic. There was one parking space and, because the offices were only a short walk from where I lived, I gave the space to Stephen. Even that wasn't strictly necessary because there was a huge disused school playing field right outside the offices. Someone had helpfully put tarmac all over it. Although there was a sign up saying it was private land, no one seemed to take any notice. It proved to be a most useful free car park. As it was laid out as a netball pitch, we also held a few inter-staff netball matches there in the early years.

When the day came to move, Stephen had a little hatchback car which just took a filing cabinet (one of those things that no one should ever buy) and we did the move ourselves. We had one person on the phones at the office we were leaving and arranged to switch the phones over at 5 o'clock that night. (BT were being co-operative for a change.) In the midst of the move, the local representative of Henderson Unit Trusts arrived at the new offices with a case of champagne, which he had even had the presence of mind to chill for us. I was astounded as I had only seen him about twice before and that was only because I had complained to the sales director at Henderson that he had never called on us. He was a lovely guy, but how he managed to get through life remains a mystery to me. I don't think he once did a full day's work. Many years later he was working for another company when he heard that his boss was looking for him. He rang his boss to explain that he was not feeling very well and had decided to have the day off. Just at that moment in the background through a loudspeaker system came the immortal words, "They're under starter's orders – and they're off." He must have been close to 60 at the time. I imagine that was his last job.

His champagne was at least a nice gesture. Without the assistance of Steve Garrahy, the Schroder branch manager who had turned up to help us move, I doubt we would have opened more than three or four bottles. Steve opened the lot. It was as well we had got most of the move done by then. A few of the bottles were shared with our neighbours in the building, although we didn't risk giving our wonderful public workers on the top floor a further excuse not to do their jobs properly. We thought that would not be terribly public spirited.

By the time the move was completed, business was really starting to boom. Unit trusts had become a vogue investment and by 1984, ten years after the low point of the great 1970s bear market, their historic ten-year performance figures were looking superb. The truth was that any unit trust that had been around in 1974 and had survived to tell the story was bound to look good. Their past performance figures, on which investors always unfortunately rely when picking investments, were nothing less then phenomenal. We had a team of four people who did nothing but place unit trust deals. I remember saying many times to Stephen that we ought to go and find out how our competitors did this part of the job, because the process seemed incredibly inefficient and cumbersome. In fact, unit trust dealing has been archaic since the formation of the industry in the early 1930s. It is only recently that a new unit trust dealing system called EMX has brought unit trust dealing into the 20th century. They haven't quite moved into the 21st century yet.

In retrospect, however, it is probably a good thing that we never went to look at how our competitors were doing it. Whilst the unit trust groups were hardly models of efficiency, they looked like the kings of industry in comparison to the systems used by brokers. During our time at Royal York Crescent, the government started to make noises about regulating the industry for the first time. There was little doubt in my mind that something needed to be done. To set up as an investment adviser in those days, all you had to do was put a brass plate on your door and persuade a few life assurance companies or unit trust groups to give you an agency. There was no vetting whatsoever. You could handle client money from day one, something that astounded me. We never encouraged clients to make cheques out to us, suggesting instead that the clients made their cheques payable to the eventual investment provider. Many other brokers were not so scrupulous.

Remembering The Little Man In Times Square – Again!

Around this time, one investment was being advertised on a massive scale in the newspapers. Sometimes you would see the same advertisement for the product in three different places in the same paper. It was certainly an eye-catching scheme. The idea was to use gilts, the safest government securities, to create a 10%

income. Many pundits at the time said that they would never invest in this scheme as it was impossible to get a yield of 10% out of the gilt market. That was true but it was not the only reason why brokers should have been more circumspect about using this scheme.

I remember the day that the firm, which was called Barlow Clowes, came to see us. They had heard that we were contracting significant amounts of unit trust business and offered us highly advantageous terms to sell their gilt plan. It was easy to be wary, given the far-from-subtle hints that "supporting brokers" would get an invitation to Peter Clowes' yacht on the Mediterranean or perhaps to his ski lodge in Switzerland. If you were really good you might even be flown there in the private Lear jet!!

Fortunately, the accountant in me was unconvinced. So I investigated not just how they were creating the 10% income but also the security of the underlying investments. The story they gave us was that a clearing bank was custodian for all the investments and therefore we had nothing to worry about. I then asked a question which I suspect no one had asked before, which was "who issued the certificates?" I was told that Barlow Clowes' head office issued all the certificates. In that case, I pointed out, all the clearing bank was offering was a safe deposit box. The Barlow Clowes salesmen didn't understand what I was saying so I had to spell it out. Unless a clearing bank is issuing the contract notes and certificates, how can it know how much of the investment has been issued? In a unit trust, there is always a designated trustee, which is often a clearing bank. The trustee holds all the investments and issues all the certificates. They are always in a position therefore to add up the amount of investments they are holding and make sure that it matches the amount of certificates they have issued.

Barlow Clowes, it turned out, was not doing this. It could easily have issued certificates for £150 million and only deposited £50 million-worth of certificates with the bank. The bank itself would be unable to monitor both the issues and the deposits and check for discrepancies. I was amazed that the clearing bank had lent its name to such an arrangement. However the events of the sub prime debacle have taught us not to be surprised at anything banks might do. But, of course, when you read the small print it was quite clear that the bank was not a normal custodian or trustee. It purely provided a safety deposit box arrangement. There was no real security in having its name associated with the product.

What I feared might happen was exactly what did then happen. Peter Clowes, the founder of the firm, was living a champagne lifestyle without either making a profit of any kind, never mind creating the 10% income he had promised investors. I imagine that even the principals of Barlow Clowes themselves couldn't reconcile what they had. It was only when this became public knowledge that everyone began to realise why they were running so many advertisements. They had to attract new money to bolster the difference between what they were paying out to their investors as 10% income and what they were actually receiving in dividends from the gilts they held. As long as they could go on bringing in new money, it didn't matter to them that the investments were yielding less than 10%.

When you also took into account the cost of their many salesmen, the jollies they provided for brokers in the Mediterranean and on Mr Clowes' private jet, they must have known that at some stage the volume of redemptions would outgrow the new money that was coming in. That is what duly happened. Mr Clowes went to prison, which was scant compensation for the clients who had lost many millions of pounds. While we thought we had sheltered our clients from the debacle, we were surprised to learn later that many of them had bought into the bogus gilts fund under their own steam. In some cases, they did this even after they had taken the trouble to ask us about it and we had advised them not to get involved. 10% income is a very powerful draw and one which most investors find difficult to resist. But, of course, these investors haven't had the benefit of meeting my little man in Times Square.

There was one amusing sequel to the Barlow Clowes affair. The heavy losses incurred by British investors ensured that there was a debate in the House of Commons in 1989. A certain young backbencher on the Labour side of the house put his hand up to demand that investors should be compensated in full. Would the Government admit, he demanded, "that, while the need for compensation is agreed, the reason for the payment of this public money--our public money-- is not the fecklessness, gullibility or incompetence of the small investors, but the fecklessness, gullibility and incompetence of the Government who, for months and years, ignored all the warnings about Barlow Clowes that were available to them?" The Conservative Government acquiesced and agreed to pay compensation to investors who claimed for their losses. It is interesting to note that the same backbencher today is proving far more reticent to pay compensation to investors who lost money as a result of poor regulation, despite another damning report from the Ombudsman. The backbencher in question was of course Gordon Brown, the current Prime Minister. The investors to whom he has so far refused to offer compensation are those who were duped into investing money with Equitable Life. Admittedly Government finances today are much less robust than they were at the time of Barlow Clowes, but whose fault is that? After ten years as Chancellor of the Exchequer, Mr Brown can hardly duck his share of responsibility.

Moving into insurance

We loved every minute of our time in Royal York Crescent. It had fabulous views to the south west of the city. In the winter we could see the traffic streaming into Bristol down the A370 and in summer we enjoyed the delights of seeing the balloons at the balloon festival. Indeed one evening I was talking to a solicitor who did business with us while we were waiting for the Friday evening ascent of the balloons. I didn't realise that there was another event scheduled beforehand. I was discussing a client when suddenly there was a deafening roar just outside the window. "What the hell is that?" we both exclaimed. It turned out to be the Red Arrows, who had come in low straight over the top of our building. I could damn near see the pilots in their cockpits.

A year or so after we moved to Royal York Crescent, I had a game of squash at a local club with a man called Chris Ladkin. As squash is a sociable game, my games invariably ended with a couple of beers. Chris told me that he worked for a national insurance broker. And he asked me what I did and how we got our clients. I said, "Well, predominantly from newspaper advertising, but we also have very good accountant and solicitor contacts." Nothing more was said at the time. Then a couple of months later he telephoned me to ask if he could come and see me on a business matter.

His proposition was short and to the point. He explained that one of his colleagues was doing very well with providing professional indemnity (PI) insurance specifically for accountants. There had been one or two scandals in the accountancy profession at that time. As a result, premiums were very high and commission payments on the premiums were very lucrative. He wondered whether, in return for a share of the commission, we would be interested in mailing 10 to 20 of our accountants every month to offer them a second opinion on their PI cover. I had to admit that while it had some appeal, I have always believed in businesses sticking to their knitting. I didn't know Chris that well and I thought, "Why would I risk losing a relationship with an accountant who was giving me investment business if they botched his PI cover?" So I declined. We did however arrange to have another game of squash a week later. In the bar this time he confided that he and two colleagues were not happy with their current employer and were thinking of setting up on their own. Could I help? Now that really did interest me a lot more than his earlier proposition.

Many external observers think that people in the investment industry, especially those who sell life assurance products, are very similar to general insurance brokers. In reality, they are chalk and cheese – or at least they were in those days. Brokers in general insurance liked to think they were far superior. They sported qualifications like ACII and FCII and, to be honest, were much more professional. The other good thing about insurance broking is that you earn a commission every time the client renews a policy. With most life assurance products, by contrast, you only earn commission once, when you sell the product to the client. The quality of earnings in insurance broking is therefore much higher. Regular repeat commissions are more valuable than having to go out and constantly find new customers. I therefore quickly arranged to meet Chris and his two colleagues. I liked them. They knew what they were talking about.

Gary Horswell, the colleague who was most knowledgeable about professional indemnity insurance, impressed me immediately. The one thing I was fairly sure about however was that it was unlikely these three guys would have set up in business on their own. They might know how to sell insurance and how to place risk. But the step from doing that to recruiting staff, finding an office, raising the capital and so on was not then in their make-up. This is no criticism of them. It is the main deterrent for most people going into business. Marital commitment was also a factor. While Chris Ladkin was a bachelor, the other two were married and one of them had children.

There and then I put to them a proposition. I would find them everything their new business needed – office space, cars, a small salary and all their accounting and secretarial requirements – in return for a controlling stake in the business. They said they would think about it and needed time to decide. This delay allowed me time to think further, too, and when they eventually came back and said yes, I had slightly modified my offer. I explained that they would probably need around £30,000 to get the ball rolling and provide adequate working capital until they started bringing in business. The disadvantage of insurance broking is that you can only do the business when a client's insurance policies come up for annual renewal. That meant they could have to wait for up to a year to bring in business, even from their best clients.

My plan was simple. Stephen and I would form a new company and issue 100 shares at £1 each. We would then lend them £10,000 each and allow them to use it to buy 10% of the shares in the business. We also committed to funding any additional working capital that would be needed over and above the initial £30,000. We would end up owning 70% of the business to their 30%. Whilst we had provided the working capital, they owed us the money. I drew up the loan agreement on a single sheet of paper which we all signed. When it was tested many years later, even though a solicitor had never seen it, it was deemed completely enforceable. There is a moral there. Too many people in business reach unnecessarily for their lawyers. The loan agreement was my security that the three guys wouldn't just walk away. Nor, if the business was successful, could they steal it away from us (I knew that I certainly wouldn't have been able to run an insurance brokerage).

When the final details of our new insurance business had been agreed, I realised that one thing I hadn't taken into account was where to sit them. There was one office in which we used to keep the noisy printers that ran off letters for clients. To say it was small was an understatement. I knew we couldn't get three desks in there but we did manage to fit in two tables down the side of the office. There was just about room for three chairs. The three lads were brilliant. They didn't really care about the space, because they knew it was still a lot better than if they had tried to start out on their own. One of them brought in some white sticky tape and marked off a third of each of the two tables. The three guys of course were sure that all their clients from their previous employment would move their business over to the agencies that we were acquiring.

It was then that reality set in, reinforcing my suspicion that they would have struggled had they set up on their own. They received a solicitor's letter from their previous employer threatening all sorts of action if they dared talk to any of their previous clients. I couldn't persuade them for some time that they should just burn the letters and ignore them. I urged them to write to all their previous clients to say that they had left their previous employer, to thank the clients for their support and mention that they would be delighted to renew their relationship, should the clients wish to call. There is very little that a previous employer can do in those circumstances. You are not soliciting for business: you are merely extending a hand of friendship.

The three lads, however, were naturally alarmed by the solicitor's letter. It took me a week to convince them. What they didn't expect was that virtually none of their previous clients indicated they would jump ship. If you are in business and have a significant amount of insurance with a long established national firm, why would you suddenly change to an upstart business which might or might not succeed? One of the lads specialised in marine insurance.

He had a client who thought the world of him, but whilst the people who dealt directly with him wanted to move the business, the board of the company wouldn't let them. Had they been on their own, I suspect the business would have failed right then.

The boys were clearly concerned. Only Chris Ladkin, the one who had started the ball rolling, remained reasonably philosophical. Of course, he was a bachelor and probably felt he had to put on a brave face. I was also concerned because, whilst I had the loan agreements for £30,000, had the business failed I would have had to write it off to experience. It was only when I was back in the bar at the squash club with someone else that the answer came to me in a blinding flash. I remembered the conversation that Chris had had with me about chartered accountants' professional indemnity insurance. I had laughed about it with Stephen at the time, partly because one of the reasons I hadn't gone for it then was that I couldn't believe that he only wanted me to mail 15 or 20 leads a month. With a mailshot of 20 names, you would have been lucky to get one response.

Accordingly I called the lads in the following day and suggested that we went for professional indemnity insurance in a big way. Gary said he knew how to place the business and Chris Ladkin and the other Chris, Chris Green, felt that with their sales experience they could go and knock the business down. We made a few phone calls to the biggest writer of PI at the time, namely Sun Alliance, which was excited about the thought of someone focusing on accountants' professional indemnity insurance. If the lads thought I was going to write to 15 or 20 firms of chartered accountants, they were quickly disabused. That morning I got my team of typists keying the entire list of accountants in the country into our database. We even took on a few temps to finish the job. I underlined a partner's name at each firm, not knowing which partner might be responsible for PI but reckoning that any partner who got a letter with his name on it telling him that we were the best thing to happen to them since qualifying was likely to pay some attention. Within a week I had mailed every chartered accountancy practice in the country with a letter including a reply coupon at the bottom allowing them to write in the name of the partner responsible for PI and the date when their PI was renewable.

I hardly saw the three of them again for the next two years. They had never worked so hard in their lives, but at the end of two years they had put together what was probably one of the biggest professional indemnity insurance practices in the country. They were sure that the success was down to them and, indeed, there is no question that they did the work. Without that first mailing, however, I am sure that the business would have been stillborn. Whilst the guys were involved in their tour of Britain, they would on occasions come back into the office with beaming smiles on their faces to present "letters of appointment" from firms of chartered accountants. These pieces of paper supposedly indicated that when the chartered accountant's professional indemnity insurance came up for renewal, they would do the business through us. My view was that these promises were based on nothing more than "a wing and a prayer". On the rare occasions I saw the three of them in the office, I enjoyed telling them I would believe they had the business only when I saw THE CHEQUE. To be honest, I rather think that I added an adjective to the word cheque which I would prefer not to reproduce in print!

On the whole, though, I was extremely pleased at the success of the PI business, not least because of its favourable earnings characteristics. At the time, most provincial accountancy practices contracted their PI through a local insurance broker, who in many cases might also be one of their clients. Fortunately, because of the size of our book, the insurance companies were prepared to give us favourable terms to help us hold on to the cover that we had placed. Once we had made the initial sale therefore, we were able to achieve some excellent renewal rates. It meant that I finally had the business I had long wanted in the Hargreaves Lansdown group, one that was going to chuck in a profit every year no matter what happened to the stock market. The insurance brokers business was to become very important to us in 1988, as you will hear later.

Chapter 5

The Crash of '87 and Other Headaches

Broadening the Income Base

Not very long after we moved to Royal York Crescent, we were once again straining at the seams. The partitioning firm was working round us as we desperately tried to engineer more space for our growing numbers. This was good news, of course, because it meant we were busy. But even better news was also on the way. Towards the end of our tenure in Royal York Crescent, I received a letter from a lady in Kent. It was a very brief note. It merely said, "Peter, Paul has got a job back in Chippenham. We are thinking of moving back to Bristol. You always said if we ever came back to the area to drop you a line. Theresa Barry. PS I enjoyed my stay at Abbey."

The day before, by chance I had received a mailing from the firm that I thought in those days was the best direct mail marketing firm in the investment field. I say the best marketers deliberately, because I was always less impressed by the quality of their recommendations. I suspect that the level of initial commission they earned was more relevant to them than whether the investment would be good for the client. (I won't mention their name, although a few owners later they did go spectacularly bankrupt.) I had brought the mailing in that morning. It was as always brilliant and I loved the opening gambit in the letter. "We make no apologies for once again recommending this investment to you." It was brilliant stuff. My letter to Theresa was therefore easy to write. "Theresa, tell me when you are back, tell me when you want to start and this is your job. Have a look at the enclosed mailing pack. I want us to be better than them. Yours sincerely, Peter."

We finally had to change our computer systems. The little Pet Commodore was no longer up to the job and no one was writing software for it any more. By then, IBM had committed what looked like one of the biggest commercial errors of all time by producing what everybody now knows as a PC (personal computer). IBM had decided to make the PC using "open architecture": in other words, anyone could build them. Even more amazingly, it had allowed a third party to produce the software for the operating system. It meant that any manufacturer in Taiwan, Korea or even back home in IBM's native America could produce a PC and know that all the software that had been written would be compatible with the machine.

We had already bought our first PC and Spencer Hall was helping us write software for dealing in unit trusts. It was a system that we called Dealing Book. The simple fact was – Hargreaves Lansdown was reaching the size where running the business off small computers was no longer viable. All the big computer manufacturers were trying to make us buy what in those days were called mainframe computers. I knew about them, of course, as I had worked in the computer industry ten years before. All I remembered about them was that they were costly and unreliable, needed specialist staff and were not compatible with each other, even for peripherals. In other words, a Burroughs line-printer wouldn't work on an IBM computer and a Honeywell terminal couldn't be connected to a Sperry Univac computer.

Computer manufacturers and suppliers were often naughty too. I remember one line-printer that was marketed in the early 1970s which was available in three models: 60 lines per minute, 120 lines per minute or 180 lines per minute. They were also priced accordingly, with the fastest costing twice as much as the slowest. Contrary to what you would expect, the slow model cost more to make than the faster ones. That was because all three printers were identical. They all ran at 180 lines per minute but the two slower ones had a logic card in them which deliberately slowed them down. The whole industry was rife with such con tricks. Today, when everything more or less plugs into everything else, no manufacturer could get away with such ruses.

One day Spencer Hall told me that the future of computers would be intelligent terminals connected to a huge central data storage system known as a file server. This was then the leading edge technology. Whether through naivety or bravery I was persuaded to go down the route of buying a file server and attaching numerous IBM PCs to it to form what is called a local area network. No major user in the UK had yet made the same move and, because our business was growing so rapidly, at one stage Spencer reckoned that we probably operated the largest such system in the South West of England. These systems now are commonplace throughout industry.

At the same time, the original word processing program that we had bought known as Wordcraft sadly became obsolete. I was particularly upset because, while I could use Wordcraft, I never learned how to use IBM's equivalent word processing program. We then went out and bought an off-the-shelf database for the ridiculously low cost of £200. It was called Cardbox and lasted for something like 10 years. The author and owner, a Mr Kohanski, was a real gentleman. I negotiated a deal with him early on so that one license fee would cover any number of terminals. Theresa learned to use this database very skilfully. It enhanced our ability to contact clients. And it improved our filing and client information records. When we finally had to replace Cardbox with a fully relational database (of which you will hear more later), the Kohanskis told us that our system had the most records and the most users of any Cardbox system in the world.

Meanwhile, Stephen had been searching the market for suitable office premises. It turned out that a building that we had looked at briefly before we found Royal York Crescent had almost a full floor available. At 6000 square feet, the space was roughly four times the size of Royal York Crescent. Stephen took me down. We were met by the agent and we opened a door into an open space which looked bigger than a five-a-side football pitch. We both stood there open mouthed. "Pete," said Steve, "have we really grown this big?" I suspect at the time we only had about 17 or 18 staff. It was a huge commitment but then Fate took a hand again. They always say it is better to be born lucky than good looking and that certainly applies to me.

A local investment firm called Tyndalls which also managed unit trusts (albeit not very well) had a life company which was failing. They had another floor in the same building and were desperate to dispose of their lease. Their floor was identical in size though a little bit tatty as it had already been occupied for some time. The availability of two such similar offices at the same time enabled us to stage a Dutch auction. Tyndalls would come back with the offer of a rent-free period and then the landlord would come back with an even better offer. It was clearly in the landlord's interests to let the space to us because it meant that if we moved in the building would be fully occupied. Although Tyndalls had moved out, they were still paying the rent. I think the landlord had a potential buyer for the building if it had full occupancy. I think he gave us an allowance for partitioning and two years rent free. Stephen couldn't believe the deal he finally arranged.

As 17 employees would have looked pretty silly in an area the size of a five-a-side football field, I did something which to this day still surprises people. I partitioned off the end quarter of our floor. We just built a partition right across the office. There wasn't so much as a door. Only Stephen and I even knew that the other part of the office existed. The staff assumed we were operating in 4500 square feet, which was two and a half times bigger than our previous office. No questions were asked. I didn't want people to spread into 6000 square feet and then find ourselves running out of space again and have to rein them in. This meant that people bought smaller desks and were more careful with the space they occupied. A few years later, when the insurance broking business had grown and we had a telephone help desk for clients and we had formed our own investment department, we were once again straining at the seams. With a great flourish, I got our favourite partitioning firm in to open up the back. There were a few cobwebs, lots of spiders and the windows needed cleaning but after the carpets were vacuumed we suddenly had another 1500 square feet to play with.

Even that soon wasn't enough. It wasn't very long after we had opened up the back of our original space that the remainder of our floor became available. This had been occupied by a small life company run by an Indian gentleman. I can't remember his name but I think in some way he was connected to the Bank of Credit and Commerce, which went spectacularly bust, but I am not sure whether this company went bust or just disappeared. It was from this gentleman in any event that I learned "the art of the deal". Indians have the reputation of being great businessmen and we have evidence of that with people such as Lakshmi Mittal, who has created one of the world's most successful businesses in steel, an industry which everyone thought was dead 15 years ago. This guy certainly knew how to do a deal. He taught me a lot. For example, he refused to speak to me directly and insisted that I negotiate with someone I came to call his henchman.

It was a crazy situation because we both knew he wanted to get rid of the office space and we both knew that I wanted it. It became a war of attrition, one which I am not afraid to say that he won. His henchman would always put a deal to me on a Friday. He knew it was one I could never possibly accept but he insisted on leaving me the weekend to think about it. In desperation I tried inventing a fictional piece of space elsewhere in order to try and frighten them that I might move the whole business out. I did everything I had learned to try and regain the advantage, but each time the henchman simply informed me that he would be lynched if he agreed to my deal. It became a war of nerves. Initially I had expected him to assign the lease and maybe make a small payment plus legal costs. In the end I found myself paying the legal costs.

However, although it cost me money, I have no regrets about being bested on this deal, as I have used the henchman idea many times successfully since. The chance to use a business ruse of this kind comes up all the time, more often than you might think. It is particularly helpful in purchasing. No matter what we are looking to buy – whether it is letterheads, envelopes, advertising space or office equipment – I always make sure that someone else in the office starts the negotiations. That only happens after I have been briefed and introduced to the supplier. My job at that first meeting is to breathe fire at the poor unsuspecting salesman. When it comes to agreeing a price later, my employee then begs them to offer a better deal – on the basis that I will kill them if they have to come back to me with the lousy price that they first suggested. This stratagem must have saved us thousands of pounds over the years. I think I learned almost as much from the inscrutable Indian boss as I learnt from the little man in Times Square.

The Mid-1980s

Although I would never take away from the success we enjoyed in Embassy House, I would have to say that our offices in Royal York Crescent were a happier place in which to work. The Embassy House offices were probably the least enjoyable of the places in which we have worked. It was one of those buildings that fostered illness. Maybe it was the fumes from the traffic. One of Bristol's busiest thoroughfares ran past the building. We also had the problem of an ambitious landlord. It was a great argument for reading your lease carefully. The amount of work the owners did to the building at our expense was beyond belief, quite apart from the disruption. Having scaffolding outside was like issuing an open invitation to the criminal fraternity to come in and do their worst. We were lucky that they did not take the chance.

Business was prospering, however, so it was easy to put up with the disruption. 1985 and 1986 turned out to be the golden years of the unit trust industry. Investors clamoured for new funds with exciting names. We focused on growing our list and improving the ways in which we presented the various propositions to our clients. New unit trust groups sprung up. Richard Thornton had parted company with GT, the unit trust group he had started with Tom Griffin, and had formed his own unit trust group. There he recruited Jim Mellon who has since gone on to create his own investment empire and a considerable personal fortune. It was the time of the weird and wonderful and investors couldn't get enough of it. The riskier and more esoteric the launches, the more the investors piled in. Everything went up and the country had a phenomenal confidence as Margaret Thatcher's policies came to fruition.

It was the time of the yuppie and the whiz kids. Many of the people who had lost their jobs when economic policies had laid much of our industrial heritage to waste had risen from the ashes and created new businesses rather than the horrible union-ridden government-supported industries that existed before. Those should never have survived. The only reason why they had survived was because the pound had been regularly devalued and the government, in many cases, had poured in aid. Some people look back affectionately at the 1970s. In my view, they were our nation's years of shame. Britain didn't just become the sick man of Europe. Britain was the sickest economy in the world. A job needed doing and we have to thank Margaret Thatcher for doing it. By the time she was ousted (outrageously in my opinion), she left Britain with one of the best economies in the world. In the mid-1980s, we were still firmly on the recovery path and the markets definitely got a little too confident and exuberant.

In 1987, the Chancellor of the Exchequer, Nigel Lawson, launched the PEP, the first of the tax-free "wrappers", with the stated aim of encouraging people to save and invest more. In retrospect, the first PEP was a poor product. It allowed you to invest £2400 (a miserably small sum of money, even then) in a tax-free shelter. Only a quarter of that could be in funds. The rest had to be in quoted shares. I think Nigel Lawson must have seen all the whiz kids in the City in their red braces at the time and thought that was what an investor looked like. It showed that he had no feel for what the general public was like or wanted. The problem was that the man in the street, even if he knew what a share was, had no idea which shares to buy.

It was no surprise therefore that in its early years the PEP was not a success. Once Margaret Thatcher had been re-elected for her third term in 1987, however, the stock market celebrated with such exuberance that there wasn't a bear in sight. Every journalist, stock market pundit and private investor was convinced that the only direction for the market was upwards, indefinitely. Symptomatic of the time was the exorbitant price that Britannia Unit Trusts paid for the unit trust group owned by the NatWest Bank. In the same category was the extravagant launch of a new range of unit trusts by Royal Insurance, one of Britain's best-known insurance companies, based in a large iconic building in Liverpool.

"The Royal event", as it came to be known in the industry, was one of the most lavish unit trust launches of all time. The company desperately wanted to get into the investment market and spared no expense in the effort. It produced the most brilliant marketing I have seen from an insurance company which, on reflection, may not be saying that much. Their best innovation was to make their unit trust application forms look as similar as possible to a prospectus for the privatisation issues that had been so successful in the early 1980s. In every privatisation issue, from British Airways, British Steel and British Telecom to the power and water companies, the City had persuaded the Treasury to spend a fortune on underwriting the offers for sale, despite the fact that the companies were already being sold at a bargain price. It was a gravy train for the City and easy money for those investors who took part. By making the Royal event look as much like a privatisation as possible, the company encouraged investors to pile in with the same expectation of success.

What made the Royal event remarkable in the industry was that almost any Tom, Dick or Harry with any sort of agency arrangement with Royal Insurance could participate. Even if their agency was just for endowment policies to back mortgages, they were allowed to take part in the Royal event. In fact I remember receiving a mailing about the Royal event from a firm of estate agents in Bristol. I telephoned them to ask why they had sent it to me and from where they had got my name. Their answer was that I had enquired about a property that was on their books when I had moved to Bristol in 1979. That made me smile when it came back to me. This firm had been the first to show me round when I had arrived in Bristol. They had showed me a part of Bristol which has the posh and exotic-sounding name of Montpelier though it is anything but posh or exotic. Quite frankly, it was (and still is) a dump. The agent told me that it was "coming up" as an area. After looking at two properties, I was able to tell him that if it was coming up, it certainly wasn't going to happen in my lifetime. The story goes that many estate agents in that part of Bristol were always trying to sell properties, some even owned by themselves, in the area to suckers who are moving to Bristol from out of town. I wasn't sucked in.

No one knows how much Royal Insurance spent on the Royal event, but everyone remembered how many prospectuses they received. My personal tally was 14. It showed how, if everyone sings from the same hymn sheet and if every single broker in the land sends out particulars of the same investment, it increases the amount of business that eventually gets done. Whatever you think about the wisdom of Royal's policy, it was an example of what blanket marketing can do. They not only produced all the marketing literature for any agent who wanted to take part. They also produced complete mailing packs, together with a suggested accompanying letter. We knew the man at the Royal who was in charge of the broker side of the event. When I contacted him and said that we would like to use our own letter in the Royal event, he was delighted. As we wished to direct our clients to just two of the three funds on offer, we simply sent him the letter that we wanted to see go out under our name.

In practice, Royal Insurance did virtually everything for anyone who agreed to take part. They even paid the postage for the mailings. All we did was send them a small parcel containing labels with all our clients' name and addresses. We did nothing else. The applications went back to the Royal, rather than to us, and they did all the processing. All the applications were coded and a few weeks later the Royal sent us a cheque. Perhaps we should have done what some other people did, which was buy any old lists – dentists, doctors, chiropodists, opticians, you name it – and send the labels off to the Royal. We were a little more concerned about the ethics of such indiscriminate mailings. We also wanted to give investors some guidance. Of the three funds that were being launched, we thought one was unlikely to perform particularly well. We therefore guided our clients towards the other two, which duly turned out to be a better home for their money.

Before we could be vindicated, the industry had to endure the storm that erupted in the financial markets in October 1987. Many people are surprised when they see me socially in the evening and ask me what the market has done that day. It is normally quite rare that I know. Unless you are a trader, the daily movements of the market should be immaterial. The only time I look closely at what is happening is during periods of extreme volatility. October 1987 was one such occasion. The Wall Street collapse started with the US market falling on Thursday 15th October. In those days I used to go out for a run with a couple of pals. We used to run six or seven miles. We had a circuit that went past each of our houses in turn. We then showered at our respective homes and met down at one of the local hostelries in order to have a couple of beers. When I got to the pub, one of the guys had had time to switch on the television where it was being reported that Wall Street had collapsed. The US market's fall had started in the afternoon, UK time, but was not severe enough to have a big impact on the UK stock market before it closed.

By chance the famous storm which poor old Michael Fish, the TV weatherman, has for some reason taken the blame for started later that night or early the following morning and blew all day on the 16th, prompting the joke that Sevenoaks had now become Fouroaks. London was so disrupted that many people in the City failed to get to work and British news services, being naturally more interested in the storm, failed to report the events on Wall Street where the market again fell more than a hundred points on the Friday the 16th. Such was the devastation of the storm that the troubles on Wall Street remained virtually unreported over the weekend. It was only on Monday when the City of London got back to work that the financial markets were finally able to appraise the situation. The UK stock market fell by 10% and even that wasn't the end of it. When Wall Street opened on the 19th there was a further sell off and whilst much of the fall was after trading hours in the UK, Wall Street ended up down by a mighty 22%, the biggest one day fall of all time. The UK fell a further 11% on the Tuesday.

My worries about how bad things might get were initially proved wrong. Every pundit that the media could find was trying hard to convince people that there was no need to panic – instead it was a great buying opportunity. To my surprise, the first few weeks after the crash produced brisk business for us, as bargain hunters entered the market. This boost to business was short-lived however. The problem was that between May and the beginning of October 1987 huge numbers of investors who had never bought an equity based investment in their life before had come into the market, attracted by the big gains being made. I had a letter from one new client who had lost huge amounts of money in 1974 when the market had previously crashed. He told me how he had vowed at the time never to invest again but had succumbed to temptation just five weeks before the crash of 1987. I suspect he never ventured back into the markets again.

The ironic thing was that anyone who had invested some money in shares on January 1st 1987 would still have been showing a profit on December 31st. Although the market hadn't fallen below its level at the beginning of the year, the scale and speed of the October fall shocked investors to the core. The crash also coincided with the privatisation of BP. Because of our position, we had been offered a small amount of underwriting on some earlier privatisations. Underwriting means you are paid a small commission by the seller of the shares, in this case the British Government, on the understanding that if there is insufficient demand for shares in a flotation, you will pick up any shares that fail to be sold at the offer price. In most previous privatisations, underwriting had proved to be an unnecessary luxury and a boon for the investment banks that were bringing the various companies to the market. Whereas they had initially doled out the underwriting to a wide circle of brokers and others, later on they started to restrict this so as to keep more of the proceeds for themselves and their cronies. In this particular privatisation, which involved selling shares in a well-known company that had been quoted on the stock market for many years already, they kept it a very closed shop indeed. The market was soaring when the BP privatisation was announced and we weren't offered even the tiniest amount of underwriting. It turned out to be a blessing in disguise.

In the event, the timing of the BP float could not have been worse. The prospectus was out and the issue open for subscription when the stock market staged its collapse. Amazingly, some private investors still went ahead and put their money in the new shares at the offer price, even though this was above the price you could have bought the existing shares for in the market. Nothing could be much dumber than that. Despite the fact that a few stupid investors still trotted up with their cheques, the bulk of the issue was left with the underwriters who promptly went cap in hand to the government to plead to be let off their commitments. They got short shrift, thank goodness. The Government pointed out that if they had done the underwriting job properly and not kept the bulk of the issue to themselves, they wouldn't be in this trouble. Their greed cost them many millions of pounds and it took several years for them to sell out their stock.

After the short-lived euphoria, as investors thought they were buying bargains in the hope that the market would immediately bounce back, our business volumes more or less collapsed. We learned a hard lesson, which is that investment it is not like any other industry. When there is a recession in the car industry, car manufacturers sell seven cars instead of ten. In the case of the investment industry, investors don't buy anything. They don't need to do so as they can always leave their money on deposit. In 1987, the government, knowing that almost every stock market crash had heralded a recession, slashed interest rates to try to keep the economy going. In the short term, they were reasonably successful but this did not prevent these being dreadful times for us. Low interest rates caused the rest of the economy to boom. The housing market was soaring and many companies were being bought and sold because of the availability of cheap finance.

In a commercial city such as Bristol, we could not fail to notice that the accountants were doing well, the solicitors were doing well, and our two main industries, aerospace and the life assurance industry, were also doing well. We were competing in the same job market for staff. In 1987, unlike today, sales of life assurance products were not particularly sensitive to falls in the stock market either. Most of the money channelled through life companies still went into so-called with profit funds that were designed to be unaffected by any sudden falls in the market. As the market ended higher at the end of the year than at the beginning, most life companies increased their with profit bonuses the following January.

By contrast, even as the rest of the world was booming, we suddenly found ourselves wrestling with a savage downturn in business that showed no sign of ending any time soon. The problem is that when you are quiet you are always at risk of losing your best staff. The phones didn't ring and because interest rates had collapsed neither were there any high-yielding investments that we could suggest to our clients. Misguidedly we continued to inform our clients of investment opportunities in unit trusts. Some clients appreciated the fact that we continued to contact them but really we shouldn't have wasted our money. One thing did stand us in good stead for the future. Several of our clients unfortunately welched on deals that they had placed just before the crash. We were not alone in this. Most brokers in the land faced a similar situation. The difference was that even though we didn't get paid, we settled the deals and took on the investments ourselves, even though they were worth considerably less by the time we acquired them. I think the fund management groups in the unit trust industry appreciated our action. We believed that honouring the deals was our responsibility. Some brokers claimed otherwise but we were "del credere" agents. (A del credere agent is one who stands the financial risk of a deal not being completed. In other words, if his customers don't pay, the agent pays). It still irks me that one broker who welched on his deals still trades and on occasions gets quoted in the press.

For the first time in our history, the business shrank. Our financial year end was (and still is) June 30th. In our accounts for the year to June 1988, we were able to show a profit, based on the phenomenal business we had contracted in the first 3½ months of that year, leading up to the October crash. The following year was a different matter. Investors had disappeared and the only game in town as far as we were concerned was our insurance broking subsidiary. In the year ending June 1989, the insurance broking subsidiary made a quarter of a million pounds profit while the rest of the group recorded a quarter of a million pound loss. This made the three principals in the insurance broking subsidiary difficult and demanding to deal with. A few months before the crash, we had consolidated all the businesses in the Hargreaves Lansdown group. The share exchange left the insurance-broking directors with a small stake of about 2.5% each in the top company. I thought we were badly advised to carry out the consolidation but by then it was too late. It meant we were left with a situation where three people with a very small stake in the business were making all the group profit. We had to acquiesce to some of their demands just to keep the business together but it left a sour taste in the mouth.

It was not as if they were growing the business very fast any longer. Eventually Gary Horswell, the one with the most business acumen, decided to leave. He was philosophical about it. He shook my hand and told me that he had enjoyed the experience but had decided to go out on his own and try to prove himself as a businessman. I remember him saying that he would never forget everything that he had learnt at Hargreaves Lansdown. It wasn't a total disaster for us. Perhaps the other two directors felt aggrieved that they hadn't been invited to join the new venture; in any event they seemed to be galvanised by Gary's departure. A few years later, having proved that he had the courage to set up on his own, he was made an offer he couldn't refuse by a specialist insurance brokerage. We will never know whether staying with us would have been a more profitable route than the one he took. Having bumped into him again the other day, we shared an enjoyable trip to London together, reminiscing about our venture. He informed me he had once again started up a new business. I was able to wish him well in his latest business venture, which I am sure will be a success.

The Lean Years

As we went into 1988, we were experiencing a period of trading which was completely alien to us. Our first seven years had been ones of continual growth without a hiccup. We were just not used to such a downturn. We were concerned both about our ability to generate business and keep our staff occupied. Some had been trained for three, four or even five years in skills that you can't just get off the shelf. Some of the best ones left out of boredom. We had always been frugal in our expenses. Our only overhead other than staff costs was the rent we paid for the office space we occupied. All our computers and desks were paid for. This conservatism now came into its own. It would have been very easy to borrow money, lease equipment and pay ourselves huge salaries for a champagne lifestyle during the good times but we never did that. I can safely say that a good part of our success has been because we have always had money available when there was an opportunity to grow and always had reserves in the lean times.

From the beginning, we had been told that our industry was one of feast and famine. We were finally sampling the famine. Many commentators were convinced that the famine would be short-lived. Compared to 1974, when the country was nearly bankrupt and would probably have defaulted on its debt had we not mortgaged North Sea oil, times were different, they suggested. The economy wasn't in bad shape. I was dubious about these arguments. I believe in economic and market cycles. I could remember that it had taken six years for investors to venture back to the stock market after 1974. My view was that if we worked on the principle that it might take us as long again to restore business to its boom time levels, we wouldn't be disappointed. However, the issue remained: as a business that was focused on promoting unit trusts, what should we do? Our main competitor at the time was a company that by chance had set up within a month or so of us in 1981. This was a company called Chase de Vere. It was an excellent business in those days, ably run by Michael Chadwick and Michael Edge. We didn't come across them a great deal as they initially set up in London. Later, they moved down to Bath, just a dozen or so miles away from us.

Chase de Vere had a successful direct marketing business and had always focused less on equities and more on guaranteed income bonds and fixed interest. That was certainly the right place to be in 1988. I don't think they suffered as badly as we did during the downturn. The product they excelled in was guaranteed income bonds and in those days they had a significant market share, second only to the clearing banks which were shovelling millions into the product. The market for guaranteed income bonds was tighter than for unit trusts, as most issues had a finite sum and were backed by a specific gilt or other fixed interest instrument. Chase de Vere had a lot of experience in this area and had a great feel for how much they could sell of each issue. The life companies were happy, therefore, to keep them well supplied with tranches of new issues. With our shorter track record, it took us a couple of years to become a credible player in this market. We have always felt that competition was good for our business and seeing their success naturally made us try harder to keep looking for new opportunities.

One event that proved something of a bonanza for us, although to this day we don't know why it happened, was the Government's decision to end the tax-free income that you could draw from life assurance savings plans. Until then the rules were that, if you funded a life assurance policy for a minimum of ten years, the amount of money held in that policy at the end of that period could be used to generate a tax-free income, no matter what rate of tax you paid. This had never been a big deal for investors, largely because life company funds had to pay income tax and capital gains tax on investments held within the funds, so the tax benefits were marginal. By chance, shortly before the announcement was made, I was talking to an extremely able direct marketing manager at Scottish Widows about promoting one of their regular savings plans. We had got as far as putting together a mailing pack. The product was not particularly exciting but it could have been useful for some clients.

The change in legislation was announced at the beginning of 1988 just a day before I was scheduled to go on holiday. My main concern that day was to clear my desk and make sure that everyone had something to do while I was away. I didn't, therefore, give the news much thought. The next day, we set off on holiday. Unusually, we took the train to Gatwick rather than drive. On the journey between Bristol and Reading, where we were due to change, I saw a comment in the newspaper about the change in legislation. The fact that I had been thinking of promoting a plan with the ability to take tax-free income on maturity in any event made me think. If we were going to do it before, then we should certainly do it now before the tax privileges were about to be withdrawn. Much to my wife's dismay, I borrowed a sheet of paper from someone in the train and wrote a few brief notes to Theresa (there were no mobile phones then). I gave her the name of my Scottish Widows contact in Edinburgh and all the reasons why we should have a go. I put this letter in an envelope and posted it when we got to Gatwick. Then I disappeared on holiday and never gave it another thought.

Theresa received my letter the following day and talked to everybody in the office who was involved in life assurance savings plans. She couldn't get any enthusiasm at all. Perhaps it was just as well that she couldn't contact me. She took out what I believe is the marketing manager's most important tool, namely a calculator. She keyed in a few figures to work out how many of these plans we needed to sell in order to recover the cost of mailing 20,000 people. This was something that I would never have done but it looked an achievable target. She rang up my contact in Edinburgh. They did the deal and when I came back I was impressed to discover how bold and brave she had been. The product turned out to be an amazing success, as well as a huge feather in her cap. Whilst our mailing was in production, the loss of tax-free income on life company savings products became a major story. Nobody else was anywhere near ready to get out a mailing, so ours landed in a blaze of helpful news coverage. The success of this venture gave us significant confidence that the lean years need not be devoid of success. Although unit trusts were dead, investors still wanted ideas for their savings.

Something else that lifted the business's spirits after the Scottish Widows savings plan was an event that we had announced just three days before the stock market crash the previous October. As our staff had worked all hours that God sent handling the phenomenal business of the summer of 1987, we thought we should do something to reward and encourage them. I had come up with the idea of an office trip to Majorca. I had called this trip "The Spanish Connection". That was partly because when I was at Burroughs Machines they had organised a trip called The Italian Job, after the film of that name. Ours was intended to be a parody of another film, the cult movie *The French Connection*. When our business fell out of bed, Stephen and I agonised whether to go ahead or not. In the circumstances, I doubt if any member of staff would have felt aggrieved had we cancelled it. In the end, however, we went ahead and never regretted it for one minute. It was money well spent and a great morale-booster. At a management course I had been on years before, I remembered somebody saying that you should put the most effort into lifting staff when they don't have much to do: when everything is going well, they are too busy getting their jobs done to become down-hearted. "The Spanish Connection" certainly got the firm going again. The years between the 1987 and the early 1990s were the years when we learned how durable our business was.

Changing Our Business Model

As the full effects of the stock market crash of 1987 took effect, we quickly came to realise that we had an inappropriate business model because our main product, the conventional unit trust, was virtually unsaleable in the new market conditions. Chase de Vere, the competitor that we had always watched closely, as they were of a similar age and size, seemed to be in much better shape. They had a sales force and their business model encompassed a far wider range of products. The difference between their model and ours was that if a salesman doesn't make a sale, he doesn't eat. Businesses that are sales-driven rather than marketing-driven therefore find it a lot easier to switch over to other products such as savings plans, inheritance tax planning, school fees, pensions and term assurance. These were areas where we had limited capability and where many products in the market place, we felt, were mediocre, despite offering juicy commissions. Our challenge was to hold firm to our policy of giving our clients only the best. It was tempting to succumb to the lure of high commission products with dubious benefits. While we knew that we were building a long-term business and that taking the pain was an essential rite of passage towards that goal, we still had to find new ways of generating income without compromising our principles.

The years that followed forced us into learning more about the full range of what people who came to be known as independent financial advisers (IFAs) did. We had a few people who could offer personal advice but they had come into it through necessity, not by choice. Whilst many of our clients were very happy to make their own investment decisions from the literature we supplied, we were being asked more and more frequently to supply individual advice. We did it but I don't think our hearts were in it. At least we took comfort in the fact that we had an ethical team of people. They could afford to be ethical because it was the client who was asking for advice in our case. We weren't the salesman with his foot in the door, offering advice whether the client wanted it or not, as happened (and still happens) elsewhere.

One of the problems with investment advice as a business is that there is a lot of abortive work. Most IFAs spend a large amount of their time producing reports and information for potential clients, only to find that the client either opts to go elsewhere or decides not to proceed. It has often been said that people who act on advice end up having to pay for the time that the financial adviser has spent with the people who don't do anything. The advantage of an operation such as ours is that we don't actively promote our advice business. Instead we prefer to wait for clients to come to us and ask for advice. That way we have far less abortive work and it means that our advisers, whom we call Financial Practitioners, not Financial Advisers, don't have to spend a large part of their time prospecting for new business. We can therefore afford to work with lower margins and provide what we genuinely believe is the best advice, rather than having to spend time hunting down the products with the highest commissions. The only other way to make advice work as a business is to achieve sufficient scale that you can spread the costs of prospecting for new business and abortive research across a much broader client base. Some firms have gone down that route but it is not the way we have chosen to do it. As a result, we have been able to avoid much of the stigma that (rightly or wrongly) sticks to anyone who takes commission yet dares to call themselves an Independent Financial Adviser.

One thing we learned quickly was that in bear markets investors never shun the market completely (a bear market is one where most people believe the market will go down rather than up). The one thing you are always certain about after a stock market crash is that you are not buying shares at the top of the market! In the back of most investors' minds, therefore, a niggling voice is suggesting that if only markets were to return to their previous levels, there would be a big rise in the value of their capital. One way that investors try to put themselves back in the game is to place a small amount of money in something very speculative. Often they will want to buy emerging markets or geared investments. We frequently offered these types of products in conjunction with some low risk "banker" alongside them. We might, for example, buy a guaranteed growth bond and a geared share in an investment trust, combine the two and offer it as a product which would give the investor their money back at worst but also offer a lot of upside if markets improved. The result is a no-lose situation with some upside, and because markets did in fact climb from the lows set after the October 1987 crash, investors did very well from small geared plays of this kind.

One smart thing we did in the lean times was to start computerising what we were doing. Although our efforts would look crude by today's standards, we made the effort to record on our computers all the different investments that our clients had bought. Many readers may be surprised to hear that most brokers in the 1980s had no records at all of what their clients had put their money into. As long as our clients retained their funds, having records gave us a crucial advantage; it meant we were in a position to value their portfolios. In turn that meant we could show a comparison between how well they had done and the performance of our in-house managed portfolios. The disparity in returns helped to attract reasonable volumes of business for us. Instinctively many people prefer to let someone else make decisions for them, and having the evidence that our portfolios were in many cases producing better results helped to convince them to change. Many years later, during the market downturn of 2002-03, we were able to draw on our experience in the lean years of the 1980s to even greater advantage. Whereas in the first period, we had maybe one or two people dealing with individual enquiries on a case by case basis, now we have a much more sophisticated process whereby clients can ask us to carry out a comprehensive review of their holdings, something we call a portfolio healthcheck. The lesson we took from the tough times in the 1980s was that having detailed information on clients' holdings, when coupled with a fully manned help desk and a regular programme of mailouts, makes for a very powerful business model.

We also launched a regular investing scheme, on the basis that regular investment has historically been one of the best ways to invest. If you have £100,000 to invest, putting all that money into the market in one go will prove to be either very wrong or very right, depending on whether the market's level turns out to be high or low (something you don't normally find out about until later). We therefore formulated a product which allowed the client to allocate a certain amount of money to the markets and inform us over what period they would like us to drip it into the market. We called it a phased investment plan. We were flattered ten years later when many other firms produced a similar product after the technology debacle and even gave it the same name. Our phased investment plan was a new departure in another way as well, based on our discovery that people like receiving small gifts through the post. I had come across a man who had bought large numbers of the share certificates of "busted bonds", as they were called. These were share certificates of companies which at one time or another had gone bust. Some dated back to the 19th century. Many more dated back to the period shortly after the Wall Street crash.

Share certificates in those days were very ornate and colourful and when framed made excellent pictures to hang on the walls of an office. Accordingly, we arranged that anyone who bought a phased investment plan from us was sent one of these beautiful and ornately engraved share certificates. Some of them even have value as collectors' items. I remember that when Fidelity launched its famous Special Situations unit trust in 1980, the manager Anthony Bolton received significant publicity because one of the investments he had made was in what were known as "Boxer Bonds". These were bonds issued by the Chinese before the days of Chairman Mao. During the subsequent communist regime, the Chinese had (to nobody's great surprise) defaulted. The idea had come from Fidelity's head office in Boston, where they had heard that President Reagan intended to visit China. The idea emerged that the détente between America and China might result in the Chinese making some token payment towards these bonds in case they ever needed to raise capital in the international capital markets. The Boxer Bonds were never redeemed, as far as I am aware, but Anthony Bolton made a tidy profit on them when other people forced up the price in the wake of the improvement in relations between China and the United States.

There was one ugly consequence of the British government's decision to slash interest rates in the wake of the stock market crash. Inflation, which everyone thought had been conquered, suddenly started to rise again. The Government had no option but to raise interest rates which meant that for a while we saw products in the market place which delivered once again the magical income return of 10%. As will be explained later, the two things that are normally true about products with double digit yields are (1) that they are irresistible to investors and (2) that they sometimes fall into the too-good-to-be-true category that the little man in Times Square had taught me all about. On this occasion, for a brief period at least, we were able to launch a genuinely innovative product that delivered real value to the income-hungry investor.

What we did was buy a small portfolio of income unit trusts which at the time (believe it or not) yielded in the region of 7% or 8% per annum. Then we would buy what is known as a temporary five year annuity which delivered a very high rate of income in a tax-efficient manner. This was because the greater part of the "income" was deemed to be a return of capital and so did not attract income tax. Because interest rates were high, annuities were cheap. The only risk the client faced was that the income fund could not earn back the cost of the annuity through capital appreciation. Over a five year time horizon, the investors were in practice taking very little risk. The result was that these plans allowed clients to enjoy an income of 11% while producing a capital sum after five years that was significantly greater than the amount they had originally invested.

Our business soldiered on with the help of short-term fixes such as these. We had however lost the excitement, enthusiasm and buzz that there used to be about the business. So low did things get that we even looked at a merger with a company that had what we lacked, which was a highly incentivised sales force. We got as far as agreeing a price for the deal, only for it to be aborted during the due diligence phase when the accountants (quite incorrectly, as it happened) suggested that we would make a significant loss, not the modest profit that we had been forecasting. By then, fortunately, it was probably immaterial. After meeting the two major shareholders of the company with which we were going to merge, Stephen and I had a lift back to Bristol with the chief executive. This turned out to be a lucky break. As we questioned him about his business, it soon became clear that it wasn't doing particularly well either. We walked away from the deal before it even reached the stage of negotiating the lower price that the chief executive said he wanted. With hindsight, doing that deal would have been a very serious mistake.

Slowly, we started putting the business together again. Necessity proved to be the mother of invention. There were many things that we managed to achieve during those lean years. We were for instance the first brokerage to negotiate a 10% discount on BUPA medical insurance for our clients. We also revisited "roll up" funds which, although their capital gains tax advantages had been legislated against, were still excellent vehicles for deferring tax. A roll up fund is typically based in the Channel Islands and turns income into guaranteed capital gains. The funds were categorised as no longer having distributor status, but they were (and still are today) useful for deferring tax. That is because any annual gains you make are accumulated gross of any tax, and the gains on the gains are also accumulated gross. In effect therefore you have more of your capital working for you for longer. Many investors use them whilst they are working and are paying tax at 40%, knowing that they can sell them when they retire, at which time they will often have reverted to paying basic rate tax. Wealthier investors who plan to live abroad when they retire also use them by waiting until they can be declared "not ordinarily resident for tax purposes". At that point they can sell the roll-up funds and pay no tax at all.

One thing we came to realise during this period was quite how much money investors were putting into so-called single premium investment bonds. These are products which allow investors to make a single one-off payment which is then invested in one or more of the provider's funds, using the investment bond as a wrapper. They have always been popular with many advisers, since they pay 6% or 7% in initial commission rather than the 3% available on unit trusts. Needless to say, when the markets fell, these bonds too went down in value, just as unit trusts did. Many of our clients were keen for us to appraise their investment bonds for them. Our response was we didn't generally recommend investment bonds because in our view the life companies which offered them often knowingly and willingly allowed investors and their advisers to abuse them. Good deals were rare. Many brokers who sold these bonds to their clients would also offer the clients a bond-switching service. The idea was that the client would give the broker the power to switch the money that had been invested in the bond from one of the life company's investment funds to another. In other words, the money might be taken out of, say, the life company's Japanese fund and invested in its US fund instead, while remaining within the overall investment bond wrapper.

Some of the big life companies offered the most crazy terms to brokers for switches that they carried out on clients' behalf. Not surprisingly this inevitably led to cases of abuse. In some cases the life companies would allow a broker to backdate any switches they made for clients by as much as two days. In other words if, as a broker, you saw that the American market had gone up, you could switch cash into the life company's American fund and still capture the gain two days after the event! I could never understand why the life companies allowed this practice. If you allow new money coming into a fund to benefit from a gain that has already happened, it effectively penalises all the investors who were previously in the fund. It was hardly surprising in the circumstances that many bond funds, and especially those where bond switching was actively being pursued, performed badly. The practice has now thankfully died out. One reason was that the brokers who were playing the switching game had for the first time to obtain qualifications to manage clients' money, something that was sadly beyond the grasp of many of them in those days.

Taking stock of our move into new lines of business, we could see that the pension business that we had first set up with Hilary Carden was starting to produce profits for the group. We had an unhappy foray, however, into providing school fee plans. We quickly discovered that they didn't fit our approach to business. We recruited someone who had worked for a leading school fee advice firm. I don't think he can have listened during his interview when we said that we would only want to get involved in school fee planning if we could do so in an ethical way, by which we meant putting the interests of the client first. In the case of most school fee plans in those days, the prime beneficiary was the broker who sold them. In many cases the plans were based on endowments that offered very high commission rates – a nice little earner for the broker but not always such good news for the client. Most of these policies were cashed in long before maturity, not that this worried the brokers unduly. Even when policies were cashed in early, the brokers were still allowed to keep the commission as if the policy had been held for its whole life, which could be as much as 20 years. Sad to relate, for many investors, leaving the money in the building society would have cost them nothing and produced a better result. Unfortunately, the person whom we recruited could not adapt to our way of doing business and our parting with him was accompanied by much acrimony.

The one thing that we did keep going through all those lean years was our newsletter. In fact, I still have a full set, which has been invaluable in carrying out the research for this book. We found out that clients appreciated it enormously if we stayed in contact with them even when they weren't willing to invest. By keeping in contact during the lean times, we have invariably found that we increase our market share. Doing so has only a minimal effect on our bottom line, as the cost of staying in contact is small in relative terms. We always put a cover price on the newsletter even when it was free, as we thought it made the clients value it more. The two most useful things we learned by staying in contact with clients were (a) what type of investments they wanted and (b) when they were ready to start reinvesting. We did, however, take to sending out our literature in the same envelope as contract notes in order to save on postage, which has always been one of our biggest costs.

For a while, we experimented with charging a subscription for the newsletter and had a modicum of success. The offering with which we had most success however was something we called the Savers Organisation, a package of different items which guaranteed clients all our newsletters, all our bulletins and a number of other services including significant discounts on package holidays. At its peak, I think we had as many as 10,000 paying members. One of the very popular perks of belonging to the Savers Organisation was the massive discounts on package holidays through a company named Magic Breaks. Keith Thompson, who ran this service for us, did so well that eventually he made it his main business and extended it into other areas. It was one of a number of businesses in which we took a stake and offered to help along the way. Having participated in some of the capital growth that Keith's business achieved, it was later sold just before the package holiday market collapsed.

Chapter 6

Fighting the PEP Wars

The Investment Trust Bonanza

As business was slowly picking up, we started to take a keen interest in investment trusts. These were (and are) a fascinating product which enjoyed something of a bonanza in the early 1990s. This was in large part, I like to think, because of our involvement, as we took a prominent lead in helping to market what for many years had been a moribund and forgotten sector. Later on, some of the good work that we did in making investment trusts more popular with the general investing public was to be undone by a scandal. The split capital scandal that unfolded in the period 2001-2002 was as good an example as you can hope to find of Gresham's Law, which says that bad money will always tend to drive out the good. Or, as a layman might put it, you can always have too much of a good thing. In a competitive market like financial services, there will always be someone who ends up killing the golden goose through taking a good idea and taking it to excess.

In the 1990s all that lay in the future. Investment trusts date back to the 19th century, and on the face of it do much the same job as unit trusts. That is to say, they invest in a broadly diversified portfolio of stocks and shares. Unlike unit trusts, however, which simply issue new units when new investors come along, investment trusts are known as closed-end funds. That means that they cannot grow by expanding their investor base in response to any new investor demand. The number of shares they have in issue is fixed, so the only way that an investment trust can normally get bigger is through its investments increasing in value. If new buyers for the trust come along, there is no way to accommodate them unless they can find another shareholder from whom to buy their shares.

One consequence of this ebb and flow of supply and demand is that the share price of an investment trust does not always move in line with the value of its underlying assets. Whereas the price of a unit trust is designed to reflect the daily value of its assets, the same is not the case with an investment trust. If a trust is out of favour, the share price can easily fall to a level where it stands at a significant discount to the net asset value. At other times, the shares may trade at a premium. All this makes the share price of an investment trust more volatile than that of a unit trust. This can work both for and against the interest of the investor. In the best case, the investor benefits in two ways. First, the underlying investments appreciate in value and, secondly, the discount at which the shares are trading narrows. This produces a "double whammy" effect and a bigger positive return. In the worst case, the double whammy works in reverse. The investments that the trust has made do badly – and the share price falls even further as a result of the discount widening. Investment trusts therefore require more effort and care to understand properly.

The interest in investment trusts that developed in the 1990s was remarkable by the standards of the past. Far from trading at a discount, as they had done historically, many trusts became for a while so popular that they started to trade at a premium. Whilst investment trusts had gone down during the stock market crash of 1987, just as unit trusts had done, they had one great advantage as far as we were concerned. This was that because so few investors had owned them before, few of our clients had experienced losses with them. As a result they had no legacy of bad feelings about them. Until we came along, nobody had made much of an effort to market investment trusts professionally. The boards of many investment trusts were dozy and complacent, reflecting the fact that the money their shareholders had invested was essentially captive money. In other words, although investors could sell their shares to someone else if they did not like what a trust was doing, they could not ask for their money back directly from the trust itself. This is something you can always do with a unit trust. As a result the boards of investment trusts tended not to see themselves as being at risk. They had little incentive to do a good job.

Admittedly, that had started to change with a landmark event in the history of the investment trust business, when the National Coal Board Pension Fund made a takeover bid for one of the largest investment trusts of the day. The Globe Investment Trust, as it was called, was a particularly sleepy fund that in my opinion had no right to be in existence. Aside from its stock exchange investments, it owned a number of other businesses including Tyndall Unit Trusts, which was based less than a mile from our offices in Bristol. None of these other holdings were great businesses. Unsurprisingly, therefore, the shares in Globe Investment Trust stood at a huge discount to the underlying assets. The performance of the fund had been so pedestrian that no one wanted the shares. The National Coal Board pension fund found that almost everyone who owned shares in Globe was happy to sell. Their takeover of the trust turned out to be a peach of a deal. Once they had taken control of the company, the new owners of Globe were able to sack the board, realise all the assets and make a profit equivalent to the difference between the low market value of the shares and the trust's net asset value – a figure that ran into many millions of pounds. The takeover of Globe had the further beneficial effect of putting the whole investment trust industry on notice that poor performance would no longer be tolerated.

One consequence was that the surviving investment trust companies rallied round to form a trade association and appoint an official to promote the investment trust concept. By good fortune the person whom they chose as the first Director of the Association of Investment Trust Companies, Philip Chappell, was one of the smartest people in the industry. He was ably assisted by a young lady, Lesley Renvoize, who had marketing and sales skills and (I thought) more drive than most of the rest of the investment trust industry put together. Between them, Philip and Lesley set about trying to persuade the investment community that investment trusts were the way that private clients should obtain their equity market exposure. They were able to point to lots of good reasons, including the fact that investment trusts generally had lower charges than unit trusts, and had independent boards who looked after investors' interests (in practice this advantage was a bit of a joke) and could borrow to increase returns.

We had meanwhile taken on a former fund manager from Tyndall, the unit trust business which had been owned by Globe before its takeover. He was an enthusiast for investment trusts and together we set about producing an investment trust management service, providing portfolios for clients who wanted to invest in these shares. This business did well partly because our fund manager picked some good investment trusts but also because the growing interest in investment trusts had the effect of closing the discounts between the share price and net asset value. The sector was going though one of those positive periods when investors were able to enjoy the double whammy effect of rising asset values and narrowing discounts. Our growing involvement in the business brought us into contact with the AITC. Although we were chalk and cheese in terms of our backgrounds, I got on well with Philip Chappell from the word go. He might have been what my father would have described as "old money", but he was both a gentleman and exceedingly able. When I criticised the investment trust industry for its sleepy boards, amateurish fund management and superior attitude. Philip showed an interest in my comments and took them on board.

Michael Scott, our investment director at the time, wanted us to develop a bigger investment trust business. Events in 1990 were to prove how right he was. When Touche Remnant launched a new European trust in September 1990, he persuaded me that we should send details to all the people on our list who had expressed an interest in investment trusts. This was something we had never done before. Our list numbered just 1092 people. Although we were preaching to the converted, the response to our investment trust mailing was overwhelming. In a moment of madness, I worked out how much business we would have done in that one investment trust had we been able to obtain the same conversion rate across our entire mailing list, rather than the 1092 who did receive it. The answer was that it would have been the most successful investment promotion we had ever carried out.

When I rang Philip to let him know how well the launch had gone, he was sufficiently impressed to invite me to address AITC members at their annual conference which was being held in the

Selfridge Hotel in London. My presentation generated a lot of laughter, not all of it intentional. One reason was that the lectern for the speakers was on a dais with a very small amount of space on which to stand. When I make a presentation I like to pace up and down, and I must have stepped off the back of the dais and disappeared at least three times during my presentation, much to the amusement of the audience. My talk was devoted to explaining how investment trusts could be brought to the attention of the general public and how well they would be received if only they were marketed in a more professional way. My message was received with little enthusiasm. Mike Scott, our investment director, was incognito in the audience and reported back how he had heard one delegate after another reacting with horror to the idea of having to go out and market their beloved product. The evening culminated in my suggesting that investment trusts would never become a mainstream investment sector unless AITC members changed their antiquated attitudes.

Never having shirked from ruffling a few feathers wherever possible I like to do something dramatic in my presentations. On this occasion I showed them the figures for the response to our promotion of the TR European fund and explained how much more business I might have done if only we had been able to send out a prospectus. I then took out the prospectus from a recent investment trust launch, which must have weighed about 4lbs, and dropped it from a height right onto the desk of one of the luminaries sitting at the front – anything to grab the audience's attention! With a flourish I said, "To mail that would cost me thousands of pounds – yet you guys wouldn't even pay the cost of printing them." One of the fuddy-duddies in the audience played straight into my hands by piping up to say, "It's the law that stops us." It was exactly the reaction I wanted. I was able to take out a two page spread from the *Financial Times* and slowly unfold a prospectus for an investment trust complete with application form. This had been issued by one of the investment trust companies that were represented that evening. I argued that if an investment trust could legally stick a shortened prospectus like that in a newspaper for anyone to read, it must surely be legal for us to send something similar to clients who had already expressed an interest in owning an investment trust.

I thought I had won my argument but it seemed that nobody, with the possible exception of Keith Crowley, the then marketing director at Britannia, had grasped the implications of what I had said. Mike Scott and I departed depressed because we thought that the investment trust industry was too dozy and cosy to understand that we were offering them the greatest opportunity in their history. A couple of months later, however, I had a tip off that M&G, the company that had invented the unit trust in the 1930s, was thinking of launching an investment trust. I immediately rang Paddy Linaker, M&G's chief executive, and got through to him in his car. I explained my ideas and said, "Before you go any further, may I please see the team that are launching this investment trust?" My enthusiasm must have struck a chord because two people from M&G were in my office at 9 am the following morning.

M&G produced for me exactly what I had unfurled in the Selfridges Hotel a few months earlier. It was a reprint of the prospectus that they were placing in a national newspaper folded down to A4 size. We folded it once more then added our covering notes and a PEP application form, because we felt that many people who bought investment trust shares would want to put them in a PEP. Until that point, investment trusts had only ever been sold to the general public by stockbrokers. They rarely bought unit trusts for their clients because unit trusts were not something that could be bought and sold on a stock exchange. Investment trusts, however, traded exactly like shares so there had never been anything to stop them. The M&G deal was a great success and marked the moment, in my view, when the investment trust industry finally woke up to the bonanza which it was to enjoy in the next few years with our help. The spate of new investment trust launches that followed was instrumental in bringing the private client back to investment after the setback caused by the crash of 1987.

However this was not quite the end of the story. Just as any gravy train is boarded by everyone, you can guarantee that with every bonanza someone will get carried away and cause a crash. After the

M&G launch, it seemed that every single unit trust group had decided to launch an investment trust. I personally persuaded Martyn Arbib at Perpetual to launch one, despite protests from both his marketing director and finance director. It proved to be a huge success for Perpetual. By 1996 the amount of money that was being taken by investment trusts made everyone sit up and take notice. It was not all plain sailing, however, as we discovered when the wave of new investment trusts hitting the market started to become more and more complex. One of the advantages that investment trusts enjoy over unit trusts is that they can offer investors several different classes of share, each with different risk-return characteristics. One class of share, for example, may be structured so that it goes up more quickly than the market in which the trust is invested. By the same token, this class of share will go down more quickly when the market is falling.

It quickly became fashionable in the City to combine several different classes of share in any new investment trust launch. Roger Adams at Warburgs was an expert at making his investment trusts horribly complicated. One of the funds he created for M&G had income shares, capital shares and a zero-dividend preference share, a nightmare combination for those of us trying to sell the deal to clients. We managed to cut through some of the complication by packaging the income shares and the capital shares together to create a geared income share and selling the zero separately. As the zeros were the most popular share class, we decided to offer a discount on the geared income share. The actuary who was working for us at the time, a character called Bimal Balassingham, did all the calculations and smugly expressed satisfaction with his work. We sent out our mailing, only to discover that the discount he had calculated was so great that it was impossible for us to make a profit on the geared package! The news got out and I remember Diana Wright from the *Sunday Times* writing an article with the heading "Oops". It worked out not too badly in the end because we sold so many geared income shares that we also had the lion's share of the market for zeros. However Roger wasn't content and went on to create an even more complicated trust called ISIS while Schroders created an offering so complicated that I would rather not go into it for fear of boring you.

The Privatisation Gravy Train

During the 1990s the other big gravy train for investors was the privatisation phenomenon. So it was no surprise that before long the investment group Mercury Asset Management (now owned by BlackRock) came up with a plan to create an investment trust that invested solely in privatisation issues. The story was that the bureaucratic governments of Continental Europe were planning to emulate the Thatcher Government's successful sale of public industries with a massive series of privatisations of their own. It turned out, remarkably, that just as Mercury were launching MEPIT, as the Mercury European Privatisations Investment Trust was known, their rivals Kleinwort Benson were also working on another product which had exactly the same objective. This created an awkward but comical dilemma for us. Having been made an insider on both deals, we were legally bound not to spill the beans to either side of what the other was doing.

Kleinwort's investment trust, known as KEPIT, involved partly-paid shares and a second call some months after the first, an idea that had also been used in some of the UK privatisations. This gave the fund manager the chance to invest the first tranche of money quickly with the promise of more money to invest later when the second call was made. The Kleinwort fund's drawback was that because of this partly-paid structure the trust could not be invested in a PEP. The PEP rules prevented partly paid share issues qualifying for tax relief. Nevertheless Kleinwort got their trust to the starting block first and had a huge success, much to the discomfort of Mercury, which dillied and dallied over whether or not to proceed with their own issue. I remember a conference call in which I urged them in no uncertain terms not to cancel the issue. They took some convincing but in the end they went ahead.

Their trust took in around £500 million and I shudder to think quite how much income it produced for Mercury. The way in which Kleinwort handled their launch, which was massively over-subscribed, left us deeply aggrieved. We put a huge amount of work into it and spent a considerable amount on marketing, more in fact than anyone else. Yet in typical City grandee style, when it came to allocating shares, Kleinwort gave their private client stockbroker mates in London preference over provincial brokers such as us. We had to send hundreds of cheques back, incurring both the extra cost of returning the money and the wrath of investors who had been unsuccessful with their applications.

As so often, however, this turned out not to be such a disaster in the end. After these two big issues, which dwarfed in size the average investment trust share issue, many stockbrokers dumped the stock after it went to a premium and before long the Kleinwort trust was trading at a significant discount to net asset value. Investors also started to dump stock in the Mercury fund and that, too, went to a big discount. The subsequent investment performance of both trusts was poor. The Kleinwort trust was eventually wound up while the Mercury trust went through several transformations until, in 2004, a third of investors moved to a new trust and the remainder cashed in their investment.

Moving Into Stockbroking

In the early 1990s, we started to offer a stockbroking service through an arrangement with a small local stockbroker who cleared our bargains for us. We didn't make any money out of this but our clients appreciated the additional service and it improved our image. It was only when we became heavily involved in the investment trust market that we realised quite how much business we were creating for stockbrokers. If we wanted to buy shares in an investment trust that had already been launched, we had to use a local stockbroker to buy shares in the open market. When our clients wanted to sell an investment trust, we again had to give the business to someone else. We therefore put out some feelers to discover how we might become members of the Stock Exchange and do the business ourselves. Eventually we were introduced to a retired stockbroker named David Lambert. He had discovered that he couldn't play golf every day and was becoming bored with his new life of idleness. We liked David immediately. So we recruited him and he brought with him someone else in a similar situation who also didn't want to retire.

Having got our ducks in a row, we applied to The Stock Exchange for membership. There were two ways to join. One would make us eligible to deal in shares while the other would make us full members. There was a difference of about a thousand pounds in the price of the two deals. Without consulting me, for which I am eternally grateful, Stephen chose the more expensive option. As members of the Stock Exchange, we added another leg to our business and, just as importantly, learned a huge amount from observing the way in which stockbrokers went about their business. For example, while we had always tried to be efficient, we had never thought it was the be-all and end-all to get contract notes out on a daily basis. In contrast, David Lambert was adamant that every contract note had to go out the same day, even if people had to work until 8 o'clock to get the job done (and when we got busy that sometimes did happen). David and his colleague also insisted on calling all their clients "Sir" and "Madam", something which our stock-broking dealing desk does to this day. I strongly believe that in business you should never call anyone by their first name, especially if they are your client, until you are invited to do so. Many clients write to me and use my Christian name, which I am quite happy about but when I write back I always use their surname. Whilst all my staff call me Peter, I hate it if someone rings me up to try to sell me something and feels they can call me Peter. I do not believe it is professional. My staff are all instructed to call everybody "Mr", "Mrs", "Miss" and if they don't know their marital status "Sir" or "Madam". I believe our clients appreciate the courtesy we extend them in this way. Over the years, our stockbroking business has never stopped growing and we are now the eighth biggest execution-only stockbroker in the country.

There are always great humorous stories in any company's history and the poor performance of commodities led to a story that has made me laugh for many years. In the early 1980s Save & Prosper launched a fund known as their Exploration Fund. This was a fund that invested in companies which prospected for minerals, oil etc. Because it was a time when there was not a massive demand for many of these products, the fund was doomed. Things are very different today. Indeed I suspect the fund would have been extremely successful had it still existed during the 2004-2008 period as China and India scrambled for raw materials. From the moment it launched, however it went down and it continued to go down from then on. I had completely forgotten about it until one day when I happened for some reason to value it for a client and noticed the price was 50p. In those days, many funds launched at 50p and I excitedly said to Stephen, "Look, Steve, the Exploration Fund is back to 50p." He looked at me and said, "Pete, it launched at a pound!"

A few years later, Save & Prosper launched a pension product which they called their Retirement Account. It was for its time an innovative product in that whilst it had a managed option it also allowed investors to invest in any of their funds. I went to a grand presentation in Bristol and sat in the front row with a character called Stephen White. Save & Prosper's top man, John Manser, who eventually went on to be a Fleming main board director, was there. John had launched the Retirement Account for Save & Prosper. He ended his presentation by saying, "And you can link it to any Save & Prosper unit trust." Stephen White next to me chirped up and said, "You can't link it to the Exploration Fund." This caused huge consternation on the platform. They had discussions between each other wondering if Stephen knew something that they didn't. After much discussion, one of the Save & Prosper team spoke up and said they were pretty sure it could be linked, but that they would look into it. They again asked Stephen if he was sure of his ground. Stephen White with a big grin on his face said, "You can't if someone actually wants a pension at the end of the day." It brought the house down, although Mr Manser was not amused.

The Thorn In My Side

For almost 15 years, I was responsible for the PR in Hargreaves Lansdown but I was also running the business and I suspect I didn't court the journalists enough. One trick I missed was not thinking that the trade publications were important. We never sent press releases to the trade magazines. In fact, I was probably guilty of giving trade journalists short shrift when they phoned me, something which I later found out was counter-productive.

During those 15 years, there was one constant thorn in my side. This guy, Mark Dampier, who worked for Whitechurch Securities, another Bristol firm, had done absolutely nothing as far as I could tell in respect of ideas for the press but was still being quoted in the same article as me! On some occasions, it even looked as though the ideas were his rather than mine. The last straw came when we worked on an M&G investment trust and spent a huge amount of money promoting it. Unbeknownst to me, Mark managed to persuade a journalist in the *Daily Telegraph* to write an article about the trust, mentioning that his firm, Whitechurch Securities, was offering a discount. As a result, they took an enormous amount of the business that I thought should have been ours.

My investment team often went to the same seminars as Mark and were friendly with him. Alan Durrant, who was our investment director at the time, was a keen fisherman, as was Mark, and they became good friends. Alan once pulled on an England shirt for fishing when he was younger and the two of them can claim to have persuaded the investment groups to invent the idea of a corporate fishing day. The groups were delighted to back the idea as, with Alan's position at Hargreaves Lansdown and Mark's constant presence in the press, they were a great source of influence in the unit trust arena. Mark had left Whitechurch and set up in business with someone else. It was a period when times were difficult in the investment world and the business was probably not capable of supporting both Mark and his partner. It's the same in any business – if everything is going well, the relationship between the proprietors is always excellent, but when times are bad they can quickly deteriorate. Things had got to a low level with Mark and his business partner and Alan indicated that Mark might be interested in joining us. (Stephen and I have always been lucky in that things have never got so bad that it has threatened our relationship. We have always had an understanding that we would never do anything if one of us didn't want to do it. It's a great formula for success.)

Hiring Mark looked like it could be a good move for us. We had always felt that the press had question marks about our firm, partly because they knew we were a lot more successful than most others in the industry. Journalists are naturally suspicious and some may have wondered whether we really were as good or as strong as we made ourselves out to be. But journalists really trusted Mark. He had courted them more than I had and impressed them as being knowledgeable, honest and straightforward. Although he worked locally, I had never met Mark, partly because I had stopped going to all the seminars and jollies that the investment companies organised, believing that my place was in the office. Mark came in for an interview and we got on immediately. There is an old expression "once bitten, twice shy", and Mark had been bitten twice. He felt that he should have had an equity stake in Whitechurch and left when it became clear that he was never going to be given one. In his second business, he was the minority shareholder and worried that he could be outvoted. Negotiations were a little tortuous because it was a big decision for him but eventually we came to an agreement and he joined us.

By chance, the desk near mine that Theresa had used until then had just become vacant. She had decided to move nearer the help desk where she could hear directly what was going on with clients (surely it cannot have been anything to do with moving further away from me!). At the time, we had two investment directors and I suggested that they toss a coin for Theresa's desk. They decided that, as Mark was older than either of them (or so they said), he should have the space. That meant Mark was within shouting distance of me from day one and, in fact, ever since he joined he has always sat within a few yards of me. He is one of the few senior people in the firm whose internal extension number I still don't know. I have never needed it. I am sure he will agree that my reputation in the industry is considerably different from the reputation I have with employees and clients. People outside the firm regard me as some sort of wild man, as I am outspoken and often fighting battles with the life companies and other providers. In the office, I can assure you that I am a pussycat.

Within two days, it was as if Mark had always worked for us. I don't think anyone has come into Hargreaves Lansdown at such a senior position and settled in so quickly. Mark enjoys the banter in the office and the leg pulling (his is pulled more than most). I think the journalists were startled to see Mark Dampier, the man whom they trusted and admired, joining a company that had the reputation of being aggressive and outspoken street fighters. For a while the only thing they wanted to know was; "What are Peter Hargreaves and his firm really like?" It wasn't long before, thanks to Mark's efforts, it was Hargreaves Lansdown that was being quoted all over the newspapers. I think I can safely say that we have rarely had a bad piece of press since he summoned up his courage and opted to join us.

Since Mark arrived, we have recruited or promoted from within a complete PR team of our own. Some weeks Tom McPhail is quoted more on pensions than Mark is on investment. The rivalry between the two of them is not only good for the business but great fun too. In addition, we have some young investment researchers coming through who one day may be household names as far as investment is concerned. Ben Yearsley has already found a niche with Venture Capital Trusts and also acted as our liaison person for the flotation of the business. We were also extremely lucky in finding Richard Hunter who is frequently quoted in the newspapers and regularly appears on television. As he works in London, it is easier for him to appear in the live media arena.

There is no secret about why Mark is so good at his job. He loves the whole investment arena and eats, sleeps and breathes investment. He loves talking to fund managers. When he is not in the office, he is reading every bit of investment literature that he can find. His second love is PR itself. He loves going to London to meet and talk to journalists (a job which some people would dread). Even after 25 years in the industry, he still can't wait to pick up the newspapers and see himself quoted here, there and everywhere. Mark is always available for a comment whether in the office or down the gym. He has even been known to be quoted from a ski lift in the Alps. The only time he tends not to get reported is when he is fishing, and that is only because some of the places where he fishes don't have mobile service. If it was physically possible, I am quite sure he would happily talk to a journalist while reeling in a 6lb trout.

Apart from his family, the other two loves in Mark's life are skiing and fishing, both of which are a mystery to me. I have never had the patience for fishing and suspect the only fishing I'd enjoy would be with a harpoon gun. As for skiing, I can't understand why people who live in Northern Europe want to go to an even colder place in the winter and wear boots that are uncomfortable and stagger around with planks on their feet. The fact that we are so different is probably why Mark and I get on so well. We go down to the gym together two or three lunchtimes a week. There, we can discuss investment ideas and the business whilst feeling we are doing some good for ourselves rather than sitting across a lunch table, eating and drinking too much.

The PEP Wars

We had been one of the first brokers to embrace PEPs when they were launched in January 1987. PEPs are another idea for which I have to thank Stephen. He persevered and showed the initial enthusiasm. Initially, Fidelity had acted as our plan manager and subsequently, when Fidelity withdrew that service, we became PEP plan manager ourselves. However, the early years of PEPs were not a huge success. It was only when the rules were changed to allow investors to invest the whole of the annual PEP allowance in unit trusts that the idea took off. Until that point, three-quarters of any investments in a PEP had to be individual stocks and shares. The change in rules was a great opportunity for everyone in our business and I am sorry to say that one of our biggest competitors,

Chase de Vere, quietly stole a march on us. The PEP Guide that they introduced in the early 1990s was a fantastic publication that listed the performance of all the available PEPs. You name it, their Guide had the information. The national press lapped it up and journalists regularly recommended the guide in their columns. The PEP Guide helped to make Chase de Vere the biggest PEP broker in the land and secured them huge numbers of new clients, much to our annoyance and frustration.

Meanwhile, I remember having lunch with someone from Schroders, which was regarded at that time as number one for performance and sales, and asking him which of his competitors were doing well. I was surprised to hear that it was Perpetual. Despite having been one of Perpetual's earliest supporters, and always enjoying a great relationship with them, we had fallen out with them over one particular matter. One of their funds had been an extremely poor performer and when Perpetual did nothing to change the fund manager, we eventually advised our clients to switch to another group's fund which was performing much better. Whilst we felt we were right it did strain relations.

Although we later patched things up, the fact was that Perpetual were selling huge numbers of PEPs each year and, because we had lost contact with them, we had not realised how quickly they were growing. We therefore found ourselves in a difficult situation where we had lost our market share in PEPs, had allowed Chase de Vere to steal a march on us and were having problems in our relationship with one of the UK's leading PEP providers. Perhaps we were distracted by our new stockbroking business. Perhaps the popularity of investment trusts had caused us to take our eye off the ball. Either way, we were suddenly paying the price for neglecting our core business which was and always has been unit trusts. PEPs in their new form were clearly the future of the business and it was clear that we would have to redouble our efforts if we were to restore our position in the market place.

There was another development that contributed to the start of the period of intense competition that turned into the PEP Wars. A firm in London called Chelsea Financial Services started to advertise in the paper that they would discount the initial commission on both PEPs and unit trusts. In those days, the standard rate of commission was 3% but Chelsea announced that they were happy to take just 2%. Chelsea Financial Services ran a slick operation. Nobody could blame them for spotting a gap in the market. Although they thought otherwise, I never felt any personal animosity towards Chelsea – but I didn't like what they were doing and lost no time in saying so. My point was that they were doing nothing to grow the market. All they were doing by discounting was changing where and how existing business was transacted. When Barings tried to take away their agency, Chelsea won their case without even going to court. That opened the floodgates for a sudden and dramatic proliferation of discount brokers in the PEP and unit trust industry. Eventually the 1% discounts became 2%.

Overnight, business became very tough. It did not take me long to decide that eventually we would have no choice but to join the discounters ourselves. Convincing the board was another matter. We knew for a fact that some of the discount firms were telling their clients to put themselves on our mailing list in order to get our information and ideas and then do their deals through the discount brokerages rather than through us. Eventually, a firm in Nottingham called The PEP Shop went the whole hog and discounted the full 3% commission. They could do this because there was now another way in which to get paid for recommending PEPs. A few years earlier Fidelity had begun to offer what was called renewal commission on PEPs, although we think it is more accurately described as a share of the annual management charge. Their deal was that every PEP an adviser sold would qualify to earn renewal commission of 0.5% every year, to be taken from the provider's 1.5% annual management charge. Haydn Green, who ran The PEP Shop, had worked out that a regular income from renewal commission of 0.5% a year was potentially far more valuable than the standard 3% initial commission the industry had lived off for so many years. Because it repeated every year, renewal commission made his business worth something in a way that one-off sales commissions could never do. Above a half-page advertisement in the Sunday newspaper for a Perpetual, Schroders, Morgan Grenfell or M&G fund, you could soon see Haydn's little adverts promising a 3% discount to anyone who saw the advert and dealt through him.

There was a way in which the industry could have responded to the new breed of discounters. Sadly nobody would act on my suggestions for dealing with the problem. Whilst it would clearly have been restraint of trade to take agencies away from the discounting firms, I felt that the industry could have opted to reward agents on the basis of effort rather than sales. If the discount brokers didn't need the initial commission to do business, why – I argued – should they be allowed to use it as a marketing tool? None of the unit trust groups were brave enough to try my suggestion of removing initial commission from the discounters which is why I came to the conclusion that if we could not beat the discount brokers, we would have to join them. It also aligned our future even more closely with our clients. For 12 months, I argued to the board that we should take the plunge and switch our business model to one based on renewal commission. To get anywhere in business, however, you have to take people with you. Initially, only Theresa Barry was on my side. Admittedly, it was a very big decision to give up the 3% commission on which we had always relied to fund our business. A change would mean a serious hit to our annual profit.

I was becoming more and more concerned, however, that investors were using our marketing for ideas, only to place their deals with the discount brokers instead. The feedback from our focus groups showed how well the discounters were doing whenever we sent out a mailing. By this time the discounters had also started to do their own marketing. And, even though their mailings were not very effective, they were nevertheless doing more business than us. The discounting revolution was turning out to be a big threat. The facts and figures were staring us in the face, but the problem was that we didn't dare to believe them. Whereas a few years before it had not been unusual for us to take as much as 20% of the money flowing into a new launch, that figure had now dwindled to just 5%.

As we couldn't see a huge increase in the marketing efforts of our competitors, we therefore had to assume that people were getting our literature, taking our suggestions on board but placing their business elsewhere, merely to save a few pounds. Our help desk told us that they were constantly being asked to match the deal that the discount brokers were offering. It was impossible to quantify how many of our clients were being "promiscuous" in this way. The problem was that in an ordinary unit trust launch we had no way of finding out which people on our lists were buying from other people. The names of the unit holders are not public information. Then suddenly an opportunity came along to establish what was really happening. This came with the launch of an investment trust where we knew we were the only firm that had mailed details to our clients. For the first time we knew for certain that the marketing was 100% ours. It was easy for other brokers to execute deals in the investment trust because our "clients" could simply forward their application forms to them. All the broker had to do was Tippex out our name and put his or her own stamp on it. That was the only work they did, other than post the form to the investment trust group. Once the trust had floated, it was easy for us to obtain the list of shareholders and compare the names with those on our list. When we did that, it quickly confirmed the figures we suspected. 20% of the people to whom we had sent the forms showed up on the shareholder register, but only 5% had processed their application forms through us. The other 15% had gone through discount brokers. The discounters had collected the commissions and shared them with the clients.

Armed with this clear evidence of what was happening, it was obvious what we had to do. The Hargreaves Lansdown board decided to go the whole hog and throw out our existing business model in favour of a deep discount policy. This turned out to be one of the best business decisions we have made, although it cost us heavily in the short-term. At the time we were doing £45 to £50 million of PEPs business a year, which was worth £1.5 million in commission at the traditional rate of 3%. By discounting the entire 3% to clients, it meant we were reducing our profit by £1.5 million. We also knew that it would take 12 months for the full impact of renewal commission to come through. While some providers paid renewal commission on a monthly basis, many paid renewal commission only twice a year. We were fortunate that we had always been frugal, kept plenty of cash in reserve and had no silly overheads such as equipment leasing obligations. (Our policy has always been to buy rather than lease things we need.) While the new discount regime affected our profits that first year, the phenomenal response to the change brought home to us how much business we had been missing out on. Within 18 months, we had moved from doing £45 to £50 million a year in PEPs to a phenomenal £450 million a year, or ten times as much business.

However, the battle for leadership in the PEPs business was still not over. Willis Owen, another innovative firm in the Midlands, had plagiarised a guide produced by another broker. This was a guide to PEPs which they paid to be enclosed in the national newspapers. When the guide fell out of the paper, people had naturally thought it was something produced by the newspaper and endorsed by them (the vast majority of people trust newspapers). I cannot remember now who produced the original guide, though I do recall that it had traffic lights on the front. It wasn't the greatest of marketing documents but it gave John Owen of Willis Owen an idea, which he was to exploit to the full. He visited all the leading investment companies and sold them the idea that they should contribute to the cost of his newspaper PEP guide. His version was much more professional than the previous attempt and the companies were more than happy to support him.

The guides were a clever idea and produced more business than anything that had gone before. Although John was paying for his guides to be inserted in the newspaper, he had also agreed with the newspapers that he could use the newspapers' names in the title of the publications – *The World on Sunday PEP Guide, The Daily Gleaner PEP Guide* and so on. His own identity was to be found in the small print of the application form. From memory I think that one guide went to the extreme of asking for cheques to be made out to an entity that included the newspaper's name. Faced with an invitation to subscribe to say *The Sunday Post Offer*, investors naturally thought that they were investing through the newspapers. The following year, from a standing start John Owen managed to do more unit trust PEP business in 12 months than we did, even with our many years of experience. It was as plain as a pikestaff that we had a real fight on our hands.

As discounting spread across the industry, the original discounters suddenly found that they were not doing the business they had done in the past. We had meanwhile been working hard to persuade the investment companies that those of us who did the most work in generating new business should also get the best discounts. As a result we were able to start offering even better discounts on initial commission. If 3% sounded good, why not 4%? As the pure discounters were doing nothing to create new business, they were no longer getting the best deals so they took it on themselves to discount future renewal commission as well. At first they discounted a full year's renewal commission and subsequently they went up to 1%, equivalent to two years commission. It was a dangerous tactic because, if the market had gone down, it would have taken them at least three years to recoup the money they had invested to compete in the market.

Even this however was not the final act in the drama. That came when a firm called CommShare started advertising that they would surrender some of their annual renewal commission as well. Again the "me too" firms came in and offered to do the same deal. We were dismayed. We went to the investment companies and said, "You cannot offer a commission that is being used for nothing else than marketing." They all agreed with us but did absolutely nothing about it. It was dispiriting because, although we had supported their funds for 16 years, it seemed that they were quite happy for us to die right there and then. While we all knew in our hearts that joining the discounters was the only long-term solution, the complexity that making the change would involve was daunting. It was at this low point in our fortunes that Theresa Barry came up with an answer that changed the whole way we did business. Although we didn't know it at the time, it was to give us a business model that in one leap would put us ten years ahead of all our competitors.

Theresa argued that we had no choice but to compete with the surrender of renewal commission. Clients were already asking us whether they could have it and, while we had so many clients and so much money invested in PEPs that in theory we could have matched it, in practice it was impossible. The problem was that unless we held the investment ourselves, we had no idea whether or not a client had sold it. We would have had to check every single investment that every client had with every group to make sure they still held them. We would have no way of knowing at the point we paid out renewal commission whether or not we had actually been paid it. The whole idea was a logistical nightmare. I do not know how CommShare did that and we still don't know how they do it today. We were dubious that they could. Theresa argued that the only way we could compete with them was if we became a plan manager ourselves and held the assets for all the ISAs that our clients had contracted to own. This was how our Vantage service, the jewel that lies at the heart of our business, was born.

The PEP wars timeline

1995 Chelsea Financial Services offer the first discounts over and above those negotiated with the groups. Around 1% extra is offered.

1996 Many other small brokerages enter the fray offering increasing amounts of discounts and peppering the national press with tiny advertisements.

1997 PEP Shop go the whole hog and offer all their initial commission leading to discounts of up to 4%.

1998 Most other discount brokers offer to rebate their entire initial commission.

1999 A few brokers start to add the first year's renewal commission to their initial commission discount, giving a total discount of up to 4.5%.

2000 Discounting reaches fever pitch when a few firms offer up to two years' future renewal commission on selected funds, adding a further 1% to the initial discount.

2001 CommShare enters the market offering a share of the annual renewal commission going forward for any contract which lasts for five years.

2002 HL launches Vantage with a 5% discount and up to 0.5% renewal paid to clients as a loyalty bonus.

Chapter 7

The Tesco of the Retail Investment World

Developing Vantage

Vantage wasn't just something we plucked out of the air. It took time and a great deal of effort to create. The people who should take most credit for it are the competitors who had tried to muscle in on our space with a concept that amounted to nothing more than "we will sell it to you cheaper". The fund industry had cooked its own goose. For years, I had tried to tell the industry that they would never succeed if they rewarded all their agents equally. The example I used was that of Heinz and Tesco. How would Tesco react if Heinz informed them that they were moving to a new regime in which all retailers could buy Heinz beans at exactly the same price? The only sensible answer from anyone in the industry came from Anne McMeehan, who was at Framlington at the time. When I used the Tesco example on her, she said, "But, Peter, Tesco have over a third of the UK market. What is your market share?" It was a fair point but not entirely valid. If you give the same remuneration to people who do nothing as those who are offering shelf space and promoting the product, you are rewarding mediocrity. I pointed out that we were spending several million pounds per annum on promoting the fund industry's products. Even Tesco didn't do that for Heinz. They merely provided shelf space. The discounters were doing nothing but advertise cheaper prices. None of them was doing anything to grow the market.

That started to change with the advent of Willis Owen's newspaper guide, which could at least claim to be promoting products to newspaper readers who had never thought of owning a fund before. The fund groups recognised the value of doing that by offering to subsidise these publications (something that the press eventually pilloried, even though their advertising departments had gleefully taken the money). In our case, we had responded to Chase de Vere's original PEP Guide with our own version. We called ours *The PEP Handbook*, eventually superseded by *The PEP Discount Directory*. It was at that time that we invented what has now become our main advertising strapline: "the best information, the best service and the best prices". This perfectly captures our business philosophy and ambitions. When we first joined the discounting game, we mistakenly believed that investors would be happy to accept a lower level of service and less information in return for having their initial charges discounted away. In practice, we found that the people who want the biggest discounts are also the quickest to complain at any reduction in service. Anyone who goes down the discounting route quickly realises that cutting the level of service is not an option.

We also have to thank Fidelity for providing the stimulus for us to create Vantage. Their contribution to the story starts way back in 1987 when PEPs were first introduced. At the time, I was not sure that we wanted to get involved in providing PEPs. They were difficult to administer and had to be invested in individual stocks and shares, an area in which we had never claimed expertise. However, Fidelity offered an administration service and Stephen, who had always been keen for us to manage money and become more involved in fund management, pursued the early PEPs using their service. Fidelity has always been decisive about cutting services that were not earning their keep. When the company first arrived in the UK, they offered a discount stockbroking service but promptly axed it without warning. Then they also cut their PEP administration service because they weren't making a profit out of it and, at the time, PEPs looked as though they would be a damp squib. As we had enough technical people to take the job on ourselves, we ended up using our computer programmers to produce our own PEP administration system. It showed we were not afraid of accepting the challenge of running new services.

It helped that Broker Focus, the new stockbroking system, had a PEP administration service which was built into the software and completely integrated with the system. That meant that whenever we allocated a stockbroking deal to a PEP, it automatically updated the client's PEP account. Whilst this prototype was not a full forerunner of what Vantage has since become, it was a considerable step along the way. In the late 1990s, Fidelity again forced our hand. They had developed what initially was called a fund supermarket but is also known as "a wrap" or a "platform". It employed open architecture, meaning that visitors could buy a unit trust from any UK provider, not just Fidelity's own funds. Fidelity called their supermarket "Funds Network". We felt strongly that this was the way forward for the industry. The attraction was that clients could hold all their investments in a single account, could see the valuation of their entire portfolio on one visit and could deal as and when they wanted. We were one of the first firms to sign up for Funds Network. Fidelity made much of the fact that we were one of their first users in their initial publicity.

However, this was also the time when the deep discounters were starting to eat into our business. I made my standard argument that providers like Fidelity should be rewarding brokers on the basis of how much effort they were putting in to building the market. Fidelity sympathised and told us they would be spearheading a drive to reduce the level of commission for those who did nothing but discount. After months of waiting to see Fidelity move, however, it became clear that it was simply not going to happen. Whether we were strung along or not, I do not know. However we were incensed. It was at this point that Theresa came up with her brilliant idea that we should hold our clients' PEPs in our own PEP administration system. If we did that, we could afford to give clients what we now call a loyalty bonus, to be taken from our share of the annual 0.5% renewal commission. Although the accounting implications were horrific and the amount of programming required daunting, we set about developing this concept with a vengeance and eventually launched Vantage in 2001. It helped that, while we were developing Vantage, a number of unit trust groups were becoming unhappy about Fidelity having a monopoly with their fund supermarket. At that time Fidelity was the UK's biggest unit trust group, the risk of allowing it to become even more powerful was clear.

Refining The Concept

As a result of this dissatisfaction, four rival unit trust groups clubbed together to produce a rival to FundsNetwork. It was called Cofunds. We launched Vantage pretty much at the same time as Cofunds. This meant that there were now three firms promoting fund supermarkets at the same time which, if nothing else, helped to capture the public's imagination. Although our relationship with Fidelity had soured somewhat, we were still keen to do business together and our two marketing departments frequently exchanged information. I remember saying to someone at Fidelity that I knew how much it had cost us to develop our Vantage system and that I would be surprised if Cofunds would make a profit until it had achieved at least £7 billion of business. This was because the pure fund supermarkets operated on a wholesale margin of just 0.2% whereas our margin as a retailer was 0.5%. My contact at Fidelity smiled when I made this suggestion and said, "Our figure is £9 billion!" In the event, we both underestimated Cofunds' breakeven point and it may not be profitable even now.

Before we came up with our new business model, no one operating on the retail side of the investment funds business had made a lot of money. The fund management side of the unit trust industry was extremely successful and created many profitable businesses and multimillionaires but the bonanza had never fed through to those at the sharp end of the business. It was the fund providers who made the big money. The reason was that fund management, unlike the broking business, produced quality earnings in the shape of a reliable income every single year. As long as the retail investment business remained tied to sales commission, it had no hope of emulating those quality earnings: as a broker, you got paid when you made a sale, but there was nothing afterwards. Every year you had to go out and win the same business all over again. The introduction of a business model based on renewal commission was to change all that. For the first time, a firm like ours could look forward to a regular and sustainable flow of income from year to year. The only reason it had not happened before was that nobody else before us was prepared to forego high levels of sales commission today in the hope of achieving a smaller but more reliable annual income tomorrow.

Our main reason, therefore, for launching Vantage was commercial pressure. It was only after we had made the switch that we realised we had stumbled across the only enduring business model in the industry. What made it more rewarding still was that the new model also turned out to be the one that best served the interests of investors as well. They were able to buy their funds more cheaply, with big discounts on initial commissions and a share in the ongoing renewal. They were getting one all-embracing valuation for all their investments, while we were also still fulfilling our other two main goals of offering the best information and the best service to our clients. Having taken the initial pain, this business model has proved to be both scaleable and enduring. Over the following years, we set out to move all our businesses onto the same model. It took us around seven years to complete this. None of our major competitors will be able to match what we have done unless the fund providers do for others what they never did for us, which is to provide financial support.

When Theresa suggested that the only way we could compete against the discounters was by building our own investment platform, it sounded a tall order. Fortunately we found out that the broking system to which we had by now committed ourselves could be modified to do exactly what we wanted. Don't get me wrong. This was not a 20-minute workover but an entire systems upgrade that probably cost us many millions of pounds – though that's probably £30 million less than it would cost to build a similar platform today. We also had a big advantage over anyone else in the market in that we already had almost 20 years of experience in dealing with the investing public. We knew what they wanted and what they didn't need. The problem with most new computer systems is that they are over-specified. The design teams that big companies put together are paid to think of every possible eventuality, 95% of which will turn out to be completely unnecessary.

The problem with engineering all possible eventualities into a new system is that it makes the system unwieldy and difficult to use. Every time you create an option that only one client in a million will need, it means you have to include or exclude that option whenever you come to enter a new investment or client on the system. As there are so many more things to go wrong, you have to make an exponential increase in the number of your administrative staff. There is also the very real danger that the system will overload and you will no longer be able to give your clients any service whatsoever. The best example I can think of is the National Health Service computer, where I daresay the system can cope with a tropical disease which only two people have ever had (and that is halfway up a mountain in Borneo, when one of them had one leg and the other was blind in one eye and both were allergic to various different medicines). You can be sure that the committee which put the National Health Service computer together decided that they would have to allow for this one in a hundred billion chance. It's this kind of thinking that has made the National Health Service computer so user-unfriendly and so unworkable that you can guarantee, even if the cost escalates to £100 billion, it will still never work effectively.

Even with a sensible specification, we still had a lot of work to do. Many of the valuations provided by other wrap platforms were not easy to interpret. This is not surprising, since the accounting and background information that sits behind the valuation pages is exceedingly complicated and difficult to collate. Our model produces information that most other statements don't such as, for instance, a tax statement which you can clip to your income tax return showing all your taxable income and other relevant details. The most important benefit of having our own platform is that, alongside keen prices and the popular loyalty bonus, we can also offer clients something that the rival business-to-business platforms cannot. Because the other platforms are used by a wide range of different investment brokers, they cannot make comments or give information on the various underlying investments. Any comment that is less than laudatory would upset the people who ultimately pay for the cost of the platforms – i.e. the fund providers.

It is difficult therefore for the other platforms to provide objective opinions. Even if they could, they also have the problem of deciding which opinion to give. You have to remember that every broker has a different view of almost every investment. Some will like a fund that others hate. Investment is, after all, a matter of opinion and the variety of opinions is what makes the market. In our case, as we only have our own clients on our platform, we can give objective comments about any investment which our clients hold. We don't need to worry about upsetting any fund providers. If we don't like one of their funds, we simply don't suggest it to our clients. For example, we have never heavily marketed property funds despite huge pressure from their promoters, a decision that has proved to be very right.

In addition to all the programming, administration and systems design work, there were other problems we had to solve. One was that the draconian regulation of the time required us to attach a full "key features document" to any client proposal. These documents provide the same detailed information about every investment including charges, performance and a thousand other things. We set out to design a single document that could be used for all types of investment so that clients could write in any product which they wanted and we provided. We would then buy it for them. As if designing such an all-purpose form was not bad enough in itself, negotiating with all the various parties involved was a nightmare. It took us many months to perfect our document but only a matter of weeks for it to be copied by all our competitors. I don't think one of them acknowledged how much easier the piece of paper that we designed, invented and produced had made their lives, but I suppose we should be flattered that they copied us.

Simplifying application forms has been a constant theme of ours throughout our history. To this day, I look with dismay at most of the application forms which are produced by businesses (not just investment firms) and the public sector. They seem to have been designed by incompetent chimpanzees with no thought for the client whatsoever. It is particularly dangerous to allow salesmen to design application forms. A salesman will always design the most complicated form he can. Perhaps this is because he thinks he has to have a prop of some sort to sound convincing. Or perhaps it's because a complicated form which no client can understand makes him indispensable. My experience of salesmen is that they can rarely fill in the forms that they have designed. I would like to think that our forms are the easiest to complete of any forms used in the investment world. The application forms that life companies produce for a pension plan can stretch to 27 pages. In fact, all the life company needs is the client's name, age, how much they are going to invest, at what frequency and into which funds. That is six pieces of information at most. Is it any surprise that the life assurance industry is so widely hated by clients and that their share of investors' funds is shrinking?

There is very little doubt that business needs competition. We have lamented for many years the demise of other brokers' newsletters, as it means we now have nothing with which to compete. We make do with competing against a previous edition of our own newsletter. We enjoyed our battles with Chase de Vere when their PEP Guide gave them an early lead in the PEP Wars. More recently, the other investment platforms have proved to be our most direct competitors. Fidelity Funds Network, although widely regarded as the first UK fund supermarket, was in fact the second. Skandia had been doing something similar since the beginning of the 1990s, albeit in a different way, in that most of the funds that brokers could buy through the Skandia platform were life or pension funds. It was only later that a number of investment groups, concerned at being beholden to the investment platform of their competitor (Fidelity), grouped together to set up the Cofunds platform.

One further advantage of having our own platform was that it gave us a much more accurate insight into how well we were doing in the market. Just as politicians are always optimistic even on the point of defeat, figures for sales and repurchases of unit trusts have always been somewhat exaggerated by fund providers. As we launched our platform right at the start of an investment recession, it took us some time to realise how valuable its sales tracking capability would turn out to be. We never had any doubts that the list of investors (and potential investors) that we had built up over 20 years was our single biggest asset. Its value stemmed in particular from two significant features. First, the list had rarely, if ever, been augmented by "bought lists". The only way you can get onto the Hargreaves Lansdown investment list is if you either request it yourself or someone else requests it on your behalf. The only exceptions have been the list of investors in Equitable Life which we managed to acquire when it ran into financial trouble and a list of Venture Capital Trust investors that we compiled ourselves from shareholder registers.

Our Goal: To Be "The Tesco Of The Retail Investment World"

Originally, the race to develop an investment platform was a three horse race, with Fidelity as the initial favourite with a couple of laps start, ourselves and late out of the stalls Cofunds. We never for one moment thought that we would grow our platform faster than these two extremely powerful competitors. We were just one brokerage competing against all the other brokerages in the land. To win the race we would have had to obtain a market share of more than 35%, which would make us the Tesco of the retail investment world. However, we did have some important advantages. First of all, we were the only brokerage in the land that was totally dedicated to gathering assets on a platform. All the other brokers still used some of the groups' own ISA administration systems and only slowly converted to the idea of the investment platform. Some brokerages had started with one platform and then changed to the other, meaning their clients were fragmented across the two. Some even had to include two lots of application forms, key features and everything else associated with each platform.

Initially, Fidelity refused to allow their own funds to appear on the rival platform offered by Cofunds and the four owners of Cofunds took the same attitude to the Fidelity platform. We were able to make significant mileage out of the fact that you could buy anyone's fund on our platform and it was the only platform where you could do that. Skandia, the other potential rival, only had a limited range of fund management groups initially so we were able to make a good showing. In the early days, we managed to grow our platform faster in the first quarter of the year than the others but had to settle for last place during the last nine months of the year. Nothing could alter the fact, however, that the years immediately following our launch (2000-2003) were not good for retail investment in general, coming as they did in the wake of the 2000 stock market technology bubble.

Remembering our experience in 1988, when we used our computer records to send out valuations to clients, Theresa came up with the idea that we should talk to our investors in a similar way. We knew that a single valuation for all clients' investments was something that the broker market had never offered before. Historically, what tended to happen to IFA clients, even those who had invested every penny they had in a range of different products from different companies, was that the IFA would never be seen again. The only way you could get a valuation of clients' assets was to write to all the product providers and ask for the value of each investment. With our new platform, as our computers were able to link up with real-time pricing services on a daily basis, we could produce this kind of comprehensive valuation overnight. Now, any Hargreaves Lansdown client can go online at any time of night or day and find a valuation of their investments. The prices will be 24 hours old at worst. Theresa came up with something which she called a "portfolio healthcheck", to take advantage of the huge administrative team that we had built up to handle the volume of business at the end of 1990s. We didn't want to lose them as it takes time to train people and there simply are not enough people with that expertise in Bristol. Her idea was to ask the clients to send us details of their current investments and allow us to value them all without charge. It was extremely labour-intensive but immensely popular. We found that it created massive goodwill and a stream of new business. Clearly, there were many advantages to being on the platform and that is why we gave it the name Vantage. Reinvestment could be done by letter, phone or online.

To change an ISA or a PEP, was a tortuous operation because you had to first of all ask your present PEP provider to sell the investment but keep it in the PEP wrapper. Then you had to ask your new PEP provider to pick up the funds from the original PEP provider. And then, when the funds arrived, the new PEP provider had to reinvest them in the right place. On occasions, this process could take six weeks. In Vantage, the ball starts rolling after a 30-second telephone conversation and transactions are completed within five days. Initially, many clients only transferred some of their assets. But once they started seeing valuations and how convenient it was to have everything in one place, clients started to bring together all their investment portfolios under the Vantage umbrella. During the period from the end of 1999 to the end of 2003, the stock market fell 23% but we were able to increase our revenues by 64%, mainly as a result of investors transferring into Vantage in droves. Since then, we have made the transfer process even simpler. The general lesson is that it is when markets are declining that clients need most comfort and hand holding.

The Vantage service proved its worth in another way during the bear market. At such times clients desperately want to do something to counter their losses, even though they'd be best to do nothing. With our portfolio healthcheck and asset transfer campaign, clients could at least feel that by checking their portfolios on a regular basis they were doing something that was worthwhile. The other benefit that comes from being prepared to talk to your clients during the bad times is that they are grateful. Brokers who can't be seen for dust when markets turn ugly deservedly lose their clients. Keeping in touch also provides us with superb market intelligence. When markets emerge from the doldrums, there comes a moment when investors once again become prepared to invest. With our huge client base, we are often the first to spot the change in sentiment. It gives us a chance to hunt through the bargain basement for investments that have gone down further than they should. The return of investor interest also tells us when we should increase our marketing spend, allowing us to steal market share while our competitors are asleep and still floundering to get their act together. The bad times have always been our golden hours. In bull markets, the amount of business you do is immense but every Tom, Dick and Harry is in there trying to market investment and it is more difficult to steal market share.

Changing our business model had been a painful process, with a lot of belt tightening along the way. But the new model did not take long to prove itself. By the late 1990s, we had established something which had never been achieved before in the investment industry. We had a profitable, highly sustainable business with quality earnings. Most other investment retailers, or investment advisers as they sometimes call themselves, have to create their income from scratch each year. When they wake up on 1st January they have no idea how much income they will receive that year. Everything depends on their ability to make sales. Hargreaves Lansdown no longer earns its living from sales commissions. We still sell some investments on initial commission when no alternative method is available; when the products are good, we are not shy about promoting them to clients. Since we created Vantage however, our objective has been to change our business model wherever possible to one where we can supply clients their investments with little or no initial charge. By its nature an initial charge reduces the amount of money that is available for a client to invest. If you write a cheque for £100 and £5 is immediately lopped off by way of an initial charge, only £95 of your money is left to invest. By eliminating the salesman's upfront take, our new approach gives our clients a clear head start over any other business model. From day one they know that 100% of their money is working for them. I am proud to say that no other broker has done more to negotiate away the initial sales charge. It saves our clients millions of pounds a year.

Chapter 8

Fearlessly to Market

The Golden Years

In the spring of 1998, I received a phone call from one of my co-directors who had in turn received a phone call from the director in charge of what we now call our financial practitioners. They had an applicant for a job that neither of the two directors quite knew what to do with. They didn't think he fitted into either of their parts of the business but his enthusiasm and apparent desire to succeed made a strong impression on them. He was in one of our interview rooms so I dropped in to see him. This turned out to be one of those moments when someone seems so suitable, ambitious and able that you wonder whether they are too good to be true. Although only 26, Adam Norris had never lacked ambition, having initially tried to become a Tour de France cyclist after attending Millfield School. After taking his degree, he decided to enter the financial services industry and was already earning a significant income through his hard work and ability. He had set his heart on joining Hargreaves Lansdown, however, and said he was prepared to work for next to nothing if need be.

Sometimes that can be a sign of foolhardiness but, in this case, it struck a chord with me. I also had a sense of déjà vu with Adam. He was in a very similar situation to the one in which Stephen had been when we first set up the business many years before. He had a young wife who was pregnant and expecting their first child. What Adam wanted to do was to set up a venture under our banner and persuade us to finance it. We had no idea what he could do but he had some ideas of his own. Negotiations were quite tortuous because I don't think he had dealt with such a straightforward firm as ours before – something we have found more than once with new employees. Eventually, we put together an agreement for a joint venture company. The venture we agreed on, selling pensions through the post, was a daring one for anyone with knowledge of our industry. To explain why, you have to appreciate that Hargreaves Lansdown's main business had always been direct marketing. We conducted most of our business through the post and did this by sending out investment suggestions through our newsletters. Sending out an investment proposition through the post is an expensive process. Some of our mailings have cost as much as half a million pounds. With mailings of that size, you have to be absolutely certain that everyone who receives it is a potential respondent. When I give lectures on marketing financial products, I usually ask everyone in the audience whether they have ever tried mailing a financial product to their clients. When I ask for a show of hands, invariably every person in the audience raises their hand. I then say, "If it was unsuccessful, keep your hands up." In general most of the hands remain up. I would then say, "Put your hand down if what you mailed was a pension product." Every single hand usually drops.

As the pensions market has long been one of the most lucrative markets in the investment industry, it would seem obvious to try to sell pensions through the post. Life companies frequently try to persuade brokers who deal with them to mail pensions. The reason pension mailings have traditionally been unsuccessful is a simple question of mathematics. Most brokers' investment clients are already retired and any broker worth his salt will have already sold a pension to anyone who is eligible, while most of the clients who are still working will already be in pensionable employment. With a typical investment mailing, a product of universal interest might produce a 2% to 3% response. But as pensions will only be of interest to at most 10% of recipients, you don't need to be a brilliant mathematician to work out that 2% of 10% is bound to be a damp squib. "What do we never try to sell through the post?" I ask the audience at regular intervals throughout my lectures. They reply by shouting "Pensions!"

The joint venture with my new young tiger was therefore a bold attempt to take on the apparent lessons of experience. I didn't let

Adam go into the matter entirely blindfolded. Having explained why pensions were difficult to sell through the post, I was able to say that we did have a significant advantage in the form of our existing mailing list, which by then was approaching a million names. The plan we agreed on was to ask all the clients we mailed regularly whether pensions were of interest to them. What we were able to create was a sub list of all our clients who weren't retired, who weren't in occupational pension schemes and who had pensionable earnings. To give Adam some comfort, bearing in mind his family status, I told him that we would finance the business for two years at a loss. What I didn't tell him was that I would only run it for two years at a loss if I thought it would eventually become profitable. If it hadn't shown potential, I would have suggested something else to him. This is one area where I think many large companies go wrong. They start a new venture and say, "We shall give it two years." They then do give it two years even though it becomes quite apparent after the first six months that it will never make a profit.

Just as I expected, Adam went after his new venture with a vengeance. He was given every assistance by our marketing department because everyone wanted him to succeed. Within six months, Hargreaves Lansdown Pensions Direct, the name we gave his division, had become profitable. We were also helped by a lucky break from a most unlikely source when the Government introduced a new type of pension arrangement known as a stakeholder pension. It allowed any citizen of the United Kingdom under the age of 75 to place at least £2808 into a pension and add back basic rate tax resulting in a £3600 investment. People could claim back the tax even if they didn't pay tax. What this meant was that suddenly everyone on our mailing list, except those over the age of 75, could buy a pension and claim the tax relief. It was an absolute bonanza and one that no other broker in the country was either in a position to capitalise on or seemed to understand. The stakeholder pension was fantastic for our clients.

Those over the age of 55 had another option. If they wanted they could take out the stakeholder pension for £2808, have it grossed up to £3600 by the Government and start taking a benefit the very next

next day. In other words, they would get a tax free sum equivalent to 25% of their fund (a cheque for £900) through the post and, in addition, could immediately obtain a pension for life. The net cost was £1908, equivalent to their £2808 contribution less the £900 cheque they immediately received back. The income on this sum would then be in excess of 10% per annum. Yet no other broker in the land seemed interested in promoting this amazing deal. I suspect as a firm that we must have written the vast majority of all stakeholder pensions at that time. We had the market to ourselves for approximately three years. What is more, this all happened in a period when, because of the technology stock bubble debacle and the subsequent depressed stock market in the early part of the decade, our other businesses were not performing as well as they had.

One of Adam's strengths was that he knows how to recruit well. Indeed, I am ashamed to admit that he has always taken greater care in his recruitment than anyone else in the firm. He is quite prepared to recruit people who he thought might be better than himself. This is a difficult thing for most people to do because they fear that the person they have recruited might steal their job. Alex Davies, one of the young men that Adam recruited during this period, has since effectively taken over Adam's old job and is now running Pensions Direct. Adam himself had no shortage of good ideas. And it was not long before he came to us with an idea for another new venture which, just like my idea years before of moving to a deep discount model, was not universally well received. He felt sure that we could compete in the group pensions market, even though it was not a business where we had any experience. I certainly didn't understand the business very well and I doubt any of my co-directors did but Adam was so enthusiastic and so excited about it that we reluctantly said, "As you have got Alex running your Pensions Direct business, I suppose it wouldn't do any harm to let you have another chance at starting a new business in corporate pensions."

Group pensions turned out to be a whole new ballgame. The lead time between finding someone who was interested in a corporate pension arrangement and their agreeing to do business was very long. We recruited someone who showed us the way. For the first large case that he "pitched for", he turned up at the offices of the company half an hour early, as he always does, to make sure that he couldn't possibly be late. When he presented the potential client with our proposed pension arrangements, he produced a complete pack of tailor-made documentation enclosed in a folder printed in the company's livery. It included application forms, details of the scheme and a fact-sheet, all of them printed with the company logo on top. The company was amazed to see so much documentation laid it out in front of them. "We are only checking to see whether we might use you," the finance director said. "You seem to assume that we have already given you the job."

Our consultant had his answer ready, "I know exactly what the situation is, but I thought you would like to see what you will get from us if you were to proceed. There is absolutely no obligation. I know you have not even decided whether or not you are going to change your pension arrangements. But don't you think that anyone who is going to be in charge of such an important part of your company and your employees' future should be able to demonstrate to you that that they will do everything you want in a highly professional manner?" This was game, set and match to Hargreaves Lansdown. And it taught the rest of us how important it was to be utterly professional in the important sphere of advice.

At the same time as we were putting together our corporate pensions division, Adam was taking an increasing interest in our private client advice division which I eventually suggested we rename Financial Practitioners. This division had in the past been purely a service for clients who wanted advice. We had already developed a multi-manager proposition and the new idea was that there would be separate advisers who would promote our Portfolio Management Service. This was a crazy situation because it meant we had two divisions competing with each other. Adam was able to pull everything together and eventually created an advice model that fitted perfectly with our business plan. As with our funds service, it was based on investors having to pay no initial commission. Instead, the clients pay a fee. Initially the adviser could choose to rebate some of this fee, but we have since set the fee in stone.

More important than the initial fee was the fact that we built in an annual management charge to be funded partly by the investment groups and partly by the fee that we earned for running the portfolios. We could then share a small portion of this annual management charge with our advisers. What it meant was that for the first time our advisers had a vested interest in looking after their clients. If clients complained, and we discovered after investigation that the adviser had not done what he was paid for, which was "to service the client to death", he would lose his servicing fee. Our regulator loved this new arrangement, which introduced a badly needed element of accountability into what until then had been an all too one-sided relationship between client and broker!

The Equitable Life Shock

It was during this period that Equitable Life, one of the most respected life companies in the UK and a big name in the with profits business, went bust. The great and the good of the land had been putting their pensions and life assurance business with this historic life company for decades. In part, this was because of its much-repeated promise that "we don't pay commission". Many of those who put money with Equitable believed this proposition. Sadly, the promise was deceptive. It was true that the Equitable didn't pay commission directly to brokers. But that did not stop them paying huge amounts in commission to their own sales force. The commission was simply hidden from public view. As a firm we were alarmed by Equitable's demise as it reflected badly on the whole industry. I think many people would agree that the management of Equitable was culpable in allowing the business to continue to trade when it appeared that the firm's liabilities, including its pension guarantees, far exceeded its assets.

We were also surprised when a rival broker, who had served on a committee of Equitable's disgruntled policyholders, managed to obtain a list of its policyholders. He got into serious trouble for using this list to further his own business. Naturally, we wondered whether we would be able to obtain the same list. We made a speculative request for it and, to our surprise, the Equitable agreed. I think it had to be made available because it was a public document. We were duly informed that a box of listing paper weighing 25 kilos was waiting in Brighton for us to collect. Although we had cheekily asked for the list in electronic form, all we got was a printed list. We frantically researched how best to get the list in a format that we could use. Of all unlikely places, the Philippines turned out to have the best combination of quality and price. When I rang one of the freight companies to discuss getting the list out to the Philippines, they suggested picking up the box from Brighton, taking it to an airport and flying it out to Manila where it could be delivered to the firm which would key the names into an electronic format. I had no idea how much all that would cost. Had he suggested £1000, I wouldn't have blinked. When I asked the question "How much?", the surprising answer was £60. It made me realise how badly I did not want to be in the airfreight business! Although the cost of keying in the data was another invoice, for a tiny outlay we gained access to the Equitable list and as thousands of people were desperate for independent advice on what they should do with their Equitable policies, we happily provided it to anyone who requested it.

Continuous Development And Improvement

Many years before we launched our Vantage service, we had recruited a young law graduate straight out of university. As most graduates did in those days, he started out on the help desk. He then moved to our stockbroking division where he eventually assumed command. As stockbroking and the Vantage platform were so interlocked, he had also by default assumed command of the whole of our back office client accounting administration. One day he came in and made the point that by concentrating solely on the tax wrappers known as PEPs and ISAs, we were missing out on a huge amount of business. The vast majority of unit trusts are not held within tax wrappers but owned directly by investors in the ordinary way. His suggestion was that we should offer these investors a Vantage Fund Account which would sit alongside the Vantage PEP and ISA service. In practice it worked like a dream. The Vantage Fund Account created a symbiotic relationship with our clients. By transferring their funds into Vantage, our clients benefited from having a single valuation for all their investments as well as the loyalty bonus we happily provided to those who stayed with us from one year to the next.

On our part, we suddenly received for the first time an income from investments that in some cases we had sold up to 20 years before and on which we had earned nothing since that initial sale. Another advantage was that we could also earn, for the first time, an income on investments that clients had bought through another intermediary. We received a share of the annual management charge paid by the fund provider – the beauty of it being that, while we gained additional profit, the clients were no worse off than they had been before. Indeed, the clients were actually better off because they also benefited from loyalty bonuses on funds they had bought many years before.

Taking all these new initiatives together, it meant that while most of the industry was floundering at the beginning of the 21st century because the stock market was performing so badly, we were firing on all cylinders. Our transfer business was bringing in more funds than the new business we had obtained even in our best years in the past. Our stakeholder pensions captured the public's imagination. Investors in Equitable came over to us in droves. We established a new business in funds management and our stockbroking division was established as the number one distributor of new issues aimed at private investors. We also had a successful corporate pensions business which brought in new investment clients as they retired and sought advice. We were providing investments with reduced charges, giving clients a service that they could only have dreamed of before that time and at the same time producing the best research. Not surprisingly, this happy combination of advantages helped make us the most profitable company in the sector.

It wasn't enough. Adam and his young recruit Alex Davies wanted us to go down the tortuous road of being able to offer pension solutions to clients directly from our Vantage platform. Legislation had been changing and the product we fixed on was something that Stephen had previously suggested we look at. This was the SIPP, or Self Invested Personal Pension. Until that time, SIPPs had always been expensive products with high charges. They were something that Chartered Accountants set up for their wealthiest clients. The reason for the SIPP's success was that, while it was merely a tax shelter, the client could invest within his SIPP exactly as he wanted. He was no longer confined to the range of funds, many of them poor performers, that was typically on offer in pension plans run by life companies.

People who placed their money in a SIPP could choose all the investments that we were now offering directly through ISAs and PEPs. We didn't need to make any initial charge and we could earn our living exactly the same way as we did from selling our other investments which was through renewal commission. Of course, SIPPs were very new to us but we did have the experience of our Pensions Direct business to fall back on. We also knew that many of our own investors would prefer a SIPP to their existing pension arrangement. New legislation made it much more difficult than before for life companies to prevent the transfer of accumulated pension funds elsewhere. Our clients transferred their pension arrangements in droves. Most were disillusioned with the poor performance and the lack of information offered by conventional pension providers. Our SIPP business has continued to grow. At the time of writing we have around 10% of the SIPPs in existence. And although our funds business remains the biggest part of our operation, I suspect it won't be long before SIPPs have overtaken at least our ISA operation in size.

One thing SIPPs have given us that we have never had in the past is a proposition for clients in their 40s and younger. Our typical client previously was over 50. What with school fees, property prices and all the other claims on their finances, we rarely got to talk to potential investors until their children had left home. However one financial commitment that many people do make before that time is contribute to a pension. This means that we are talking to our potential clients much sooner than we have in the past.

It soon became apparent to us that there was another business opportunity in the pensions business, which was in the sale of annuities to those who have reached retirement age. The unusually low interest rates that prevailed during the early part of the 21st century had a profound impact on the annuity rates that could be paid by pension providers. In fact, annuity rates were becoming so meagre as to be derisory. Clients were naturally extremely annoyed at how little income their accumulated pension funds were capable of producing. The situation highlighted a real problem with compulsory purchase annuities. These are one of the few financial products I can think of where the more money you put in, the worse rate you stand to get. Someone who places £50,000 in an annuity will get a better rate per pound of annuity income than someone who places £500,000. The reason is a simple matter of longevity. Life companies many years ago noticed that people who had the most money in their pension funds were also the ones who were most likely to live the longest. Since an annuity is an income for the rest of your life, it therefore makes sense for the life companies to be more cautious about paying good rates to people with large sums in their pension funds, given their greater life expectancy. This should be a salutary lesson to all citizens: the more financially comfortable you can make your retirement, the better and longer will be your final years.

All this led to clients taking an increasing interest in what is known as a drawdown pension arrangement. With a conventional pension arrangement, when you retire you can take up to 25% of your accumulated pension fund as a tax free cash payment and buy an annuity with the balance. The annuity provides you with a fixed income for the rest of your life, based on the value of your fund at your retirement date. Under a drawdown scheme, you still take out 25% in cash but the rest of your money remains invested inside the pension wrapper and can continue to grow in value even though you are now taking an income from it. Of course a drawdown scheme is not without danger as, if you take too large an income from your fund and the stock market performs badly, you could end up seeing your pension fund fall in value, even perhaps to zero. However, for many people the advantages of drawdown schemes are significant. As a result, huge numbers of our clients began to transfer the amount they had accumulated in their pensions into our SIPP and start a drawdown pension.

When the stock market started to recover after the bear market of 2000-2003, we found that we had the best business model of all our competitors. We had the best proposition for the investing public and the volume of investment that we were attracting also made us the most profitable business in the industry. We were finally categorically giving clients the best prices, the best service and the best information, as we had always wanted to do. Twenty-five years of toil and a quest for constant improvement had turned our formula into gold. However I would always emphasise that everything we have done has been based on a simple three point rule, one that all our staff know and understand. It is: Put the client first. Put the business second. Put yourself third.

Deciding on flotation

With any successful business, the time comes when you have to start thinking seriously about the long-term future. For Stephen and I that moment arrived in the early years of the new century when Vantage, and the new business model it represented, had become well established. As the business bears our name, Stephen and I were keen to put in place a structure that would give the company every chance to survive in perpetuity. This objective naturally counted out a trade sale to a large institution. This was not a difficult decision in any event, because any large institution would almost certainly have ruined the business. (God knows, we have seen it happen enough times in our industry.) At a stroke it would introduce bureaucracy, a meetings culture, grading of staff, and status symbols such as secretaries and car parking spaces; all the dreadful things which large companies instigate – and which detract from the long-term success of a business.

Ruling out a trade buyer still left us with options. One was to remain a private company. The families of the major shareholders could have continued to hold the shares and with a sensible dividend policy, this could have made for a good long-term investment. However with an entrepreneurial business, it is always difficult to find and retain the best people if ownership of the business remains closely held in private hands. Another option at some stage was a management buyout led by the senior staff. This, however, would only have delayed for a short period of time the next step, which would be either a trade sale or, more likely, seeking a quotation for the shares on the London Stock Exchange, something that today is called an IPO (Initial Public Offering), or flotation.

We decided that if that was the most likely long-term outcome, we would rather be in control of the process ourselves. Why not go straight for the flotation option while the two of us were still in charge? It had been in the back of our minds for many years that the most sensible future for Hargreaves Lansdown would be as a public company. Despite the fact that many public companies moan about the short-termism of the City, in the end we ignored the doubters and opted for that outcome. My view is that companies that fare badly with the City usually do so for a good reason. The management may be dishonest, or incompetent, or overpaid, or simply incapable of explaining the business to professional investors. It is true that becoming a public company introduces a lot of tiresome red tape that is of dubious benefit to anyone, but the disadvantages are overemphasised. It is only really onerous for people who have run their businesses as fiefdoms rather than with an eye to the long term. We have always tried to run the business as if it was already a public company. Perhaps unlike some public companies, when times were hard we made sure that the highest paid people at the top suffered first, and we tried to protect our clients and staff from periods of poor trading.

Despite all these positives, I nevertheless found the decision to go for a flotation surprisingly difficult. I suppose that I was the main dissenting voice. Being a vocal opponent of bureaucracy in any form, I didn't know how I would take to all the procedures, process, regulation and reporting. I also felt it might be more difficult to make good long-term decisions at the cost of short-term profitability, as any successful business has to do. Stephen was the most confident that we could be a success as a public company, partly because he had always handled the regulatory and legal side of the business and knew better what to expect. He also pointed out that neither of us was getting any younger and while I was older than him, he had more outside interests. His two children were already in gainful employment elsewhere. When you have given over a quarter of a century to a business, it is only right that you should have an opportunity to reap the benefits and put in place a structure that enables you at some stage to "take it easier". Another factor was that in both our cases 98% of our assets were tied up in one single investment. As investment advisers, we would never have advised our clients to be in such a situation.

Theresa had a more interesting take on the possibility of a float. She felt that as a private company we didn't always make hard decisions. Arguably, she felt, we had gone a little soft. When you run a highly successful private company, it is easy to become complacent. She felt that competing with other public companies would force us to improve our systems, our marketing, our financial reporting, our research and our administration. In other words, it would keep us on our toes and make us a fitter, stronger business. There is no doubt that as a quoted company we are a much stronger and fitter business than we were, and some of this improvement was down to the positive effect of preparing for flotation. I would like to think that we are still delivering the same "knock your socks off service" to our clients.

I suppose I had another more philosophical reason for agreeing to the flotation. I felt quite strongly that it would have been more difficult to recruit and train the right people if we had continued indefinitely as a private company. I was mindful of the experience of a marvellous hotel in South Wales that I know well. The hotel building is one of the best in the UK. While the building from the outside is not the prettiest in the world, inside it is a wonderful conference centre and resort. That's where the positivity ends. The owner is not an hotelier and although he recruits people to run the hotel, the truth is that there is no career path for any of the people who work at the hotel. They have to wait for someone else to leave before they can move up. There is no incentive to do well at senior management level because there is little chance of an internal promotion. The best people leave to join top hotel chains. The result is constant staff turnover. They consistently lose the best. I felt that spreading our wings to give people the chance to become a director of a public company would help to retain and motivate our key people. We could also of course grant share options to keep the right people and with a real share price rather than an artificial one (like the shadow price that many private companies adopt) they could feel confident that there was always a market for any shares granted to them.

However, more than anything, my age came into play. Whilst I have always said that I never want to retire, the City will doubtless have something to say about that the older I become. They might well believe that at 60 I have the drive and energy to carry on until 65, but they may become sceptical of someone aged 65 saying that they wished to work until the age of 70. While I am in excellent health, there is always a concern that your health could deteriorate. (Warren Buffett, the great American investor, is still going strong in his late 70s and his sidekick Charlie Munger is in his 80s; but even they have had to start planning the succession when age finally catches up with them). Therefore, if a flotation was the preferred option and it was going to happen, it seemed right to do it sooner rather than later.

Making The Flotation Happen

Once we had slowly become used to the idea that we would float the company, it was time to confront the potential problems and start talking to potential advisers. We knew from the outset that a float would involve an immense amount of work. We also knew that everyone would expect the flotation of one of the UK's leading investment brokers to be perfectly planned and executed. Our clients and competitors would certainly be watching. We were also acutely aware that there is no other business quite like Hargreaves Lansdown in our industry, and it was therefore going to be difficult to value.

There are many ways you can approach a flotation. Most people, I imagine, go initially to their accountants, a process which I would not necessarily recommend. When one of our earlier firm of auditors had taken us through the process some years before, I left their presentation after ten minutes as I realised that they knew, if anything, less than we did about it. I suspect that some City accountancy firms would acquit themselves somewhat better. Another route is to go directly to the corporate finance department of a leading investment bank. You can find them easily enough by looking at which banks other companies have used for their flotations. The problem for a medium-sized company like ours is that if you go to someone with too high a profile, there is a chance you may get their B team. Alternatively you can end up with an investment bank that wants you as a client and is ready to put a lot of work in, but may lack the right team to perform the duties properly. We certainly had no idea who would be interested in handling our float, who could do the job superbly and who would give us the best team available.

We therefore took what we believe for us was the best route and a route that we would probably recommend to other companies who are contemplating seeking what is now widely known as an IPO (initial public offering of their shares). We interviewed four firms who all suggested they were experts in guiding firms through an IPO. Of the four firms we ended up deciding to talk to we rejected a couple immediately. That left two in the frame. To save the blushes of the two firms we rejected out of hand, and the one who failed at the final hurdle, I will not divulge their names. To be honest, all these three firms would probably have done a good job for us, but there was one with whom we immediately felt most comfortable. They weren't the biggest or the best-known of the four firms, but they impressed us with their knowledge and commitment. We all got on well with the team that they fielded and we were assured that this would also be the team that would stick with us throughout the process. Having heard all the presentations, my board was unanimous that Lexicon Partners were the firm for us, and we decided to retain them.

The first thing Lexicon had to give us was a feel for how much the business might be worth and on which basis it was best to value it. To do that, they had to understand the business, they had to understand our competitors and they had to establish the viability of our business model, the sustainability of profits and in general the quality of our management and our ability to grow profits and survive in all trading conditions. This was a relatively painless process, though it did involve their having access to all our key people.

Having done that, they suggested that we hold another beauty parade similar to the one that we had conducted to find them. They told us that we would need two firms, not just one. This came as a surprise to us. They felt that we should appoint a leading investment bank to be the main sponsor and also a co-lead manager, who would take a smaller role but whose analysts would cover our stock once we had become a public company. I will again spare the blushes of the firms that failed to win the business. Over the course of two days, most of the top City firms came and presented their views on what they thought of our business, what they thought it was worth and how they would bring it to the market. I was astounded by the difference in how much preparatory work each bank had done. One firm had done their homework very badly. Another big firm whom we felt should have been at the top of the list seemed not to have realised one important fact about Hargreaves Lansdown. (According to Lexicon, the guy who was making the presentation appeared only to have read it for the first time in the taxi on the way to Lexicon's offices!).

It was only about halfway through his presentation that he realised what a potentially valuable float Hargreaves Lansdown would be, given our strong and close relationship with all the unit trust groups. As all the big banks have equity departments which court the unit trust groups to try and win their stock exchange dealing business, doing a good job for us in the flotation could be worth a lot of money to them. Quite simply we were the customers of their best clients. Having missed that one fundamental point, it left us wondering what other points the firm might miss as well. (This particular individual, to give him credit, did subsequently pester me to death with numerous phone calls in an attempt to recover the situation, but it was by then too late).

After the initial round, we were fairly sure who our first choice in the process would be, but decided to call in the top two again so as to talk to the analysts who would be covering our stock after the flotation. Unfortunately the bank we initially preferred had an overworked analyst in our sector who didn't acquit themselves terribly well. Although the bank later tried to recover by offering us another analyst, the job was already slipping away from them. The firm we eventually retained was Citibank, the world's largest financial organisation. We were frankly amazed, and somewhat flattered, that they had fought so hard to get our float. Nevertheless we were clear that they had been chosen on merit, not because of their size. It helped that they also were able to offer us the top analyst in our sector, which was an important factor in our decision to retain them.

I am not easily pleased, but I have to say that we could not fault Citi for the work they did for us. From the moment of making the decision, we not once regretted their appointment. Their team was every bit as good as the Lexicon team and we felt that we now had almost every part of the equation in place. We then dropped a small bombshell by saying that we weren't going to do what most companies do, which is use a firm of City lawyers for the legal work that accompanies a flotation. Instead we insisted that we were happy using our local firm, Burges Salmon, whom we knew well. We had a particular high regard for the partner who we would be dealing with on the flotation, and we knew that as an important client we would get that partner, whereas if we went to one of the leading City firms we suspected we would end up with someone several levels down from partner. Citi and Lexicon were slightly nervous about this, as they had never worked with a local firm on a flotation of this nature before. Once we invited them to meet our lawyers, they realised that we had also made a good decision in that area.

Then the real work began. Recognising that the worst thing you can do in a flotation is to take your eye off the ball, I made a pact with the directors who were going to be involved with the flotation that I would concentrate on running the business. The bulk of the work involved in the flotation fell to Stephen, Martin Mulligan, the finance director, Nigel Bence, the compliance director, and Theresa Barry, who was adamant that the tone of the prospectus should not be any different from the way we deal with our clients. There is a fine line to be drawn between selling a company and giving the right message to both clients and potential investors. The fifth person in the team was Tracey Taylor, our group accountant and company secretary, who burnt much midnight oil again during the period of the float.

True to form, we had the satisfaction of dropping two more bombshells on our advisers before we were finished. One was to say that we wanted to act in the sale of our own shares, something that to our knowledge had never been done before. We were informed that we simply couldn't do this, to which we replied that our advisers should show us which part of the legislation explicitly precluded us from doing this, otherwise we said we would go ahead. We had absolutely no doubt that we would promote our own shares to our own clients more fairly, more efficiently and with superior administration to anyone else. The City has always been assiduous at protecting its monopolies, but we were not going to take no for an answer. The only problem was that everyone agreed we could only sell the shares ourselves on the basis of a full prospectus. For IPOs, these are lengthy documents that earn a fortune for the lawyers and bankers who spend weeks drafting them and filling them with small print that nobody reads. Since there are a million people on our primary circulation list (that is how many people have dealt with us over our 20-odd years in business), we clearly could not send out a full prospectus to everyone. The cost would have been astronomic.

As it was, we did discover what a gravy train flotations can be for those who are part of the conventional process. It would appear that firms of security printers spend hundreds of thousands of pounds lavishly entertaining the investment banks. They can do this because when it comes to documents printed by security printers, nobody seems to check how much they charge. As the investment banks can simply charge the cost of a "prospectus" straight on to the client, they are indifferent to how much it costs. This goes for all the documents relating to a corporate event. There are lots of unnecessary add-ons. For instance, the printers often say they have a full team of "typesetters" working overnight to make last minute changes to the prospectus, even though today, with modern technology you can do it in your own office with an ISDN line. Copy for printing can be changed seconds before it goes to press without any typesetter touching it. My guess is that many companies pay 10 times more than is necessary for their prospectuses and other corporate documents. We discovered this thanks to a tip-off from someone we have been involved with floats for many years. Since we buy huge amounts of print ourselves, it was easy for us to get a quote for the job from our own printers. Of course "security printers" make a lot out of the fact that confidential documents are safe in their hands. All I can say is that in the two major insider dealing incidents we have ever come across, one of them was perpetrated by someone who worked for a security printer.

In part because of the cost, we decided at an early stage that we would have another first and make the Hargreaves Lansdown private client offer an internet-only offer. To our knowledge this was the first time that an IPO in the UK has only been available on the internet. All previous internet offerings had required people to print out an application form and send the application form with a cheque. Ours was the first offering that enabled people to subscribe directly for shares online. The only stipulation was that the money had to be in place already in our nominee account. The reason we had to do this was that if the issue price of the shares was to change at a late stage, as does happen, we would have been required to inform all our clients of the change in final strike price. It would have been physically impossible to contact them any other way than via email. This was difficult to explain to those clients of ours who did not have internet access, and were therefore effectively debarred from the issue.

Looking back, the flotation process was every bit as time consuming and involved every bit as much work as we had been warned it would. The most stimulating part of the process was the final roadshow. While the thought of it filled me initially with trepidation, it was very enjoyable explaining our business – the business that we love – to potential investors. We were asked both pertinent and impertinent questions and welcomed them both. In the event, as history records, the flotation was an overwhelming success and was many times oversubscribed. Although we set a strike price of 160 pence, the shares immediately started trading above £2.00 and during the summer of 2007 reached the dizzy heights of £2.40. I have some good memories of the process. After one particularly tiring day in London during the roadshow, Martin, Stephen and I decided to watch a European Championship football match in a hostelry that was screening the matches. Liverpool were playing Chelsea and since our finance director is from Liverpool, of course we had to support them. The only seats we could find were three barstools at the back. It seems that at one stage Stephen had to hold me up because I nearly feel asleep and fell off the stool. By the way Liverpool won. Another amusing incident came one afternoon when I had sneaked off from the roadshow to go racing. I had a horse running at Ascot in the afternoon and a horse I shared with another guy was running in the evening at Kempton Park. In my absence Stephen and Martin did the afternoon's roadshow without me. At a meeting with one of the investment groups that know me well, one of the fund managers asked the question: "Who challenges Peter when he is wrong?" Stephen, very quick-witted, looked at them and said "Is that a hypothetical question?"

The flotation, looking back, was clearly the most time consuming and important thing we had ever dealt with in such a short space of time. I was particularly pleased that we managed not to take our eye off the ball during the flotation period. The business did not suffer. Indeed the higher profile it gave us enhanced our business. Having always strived to make everything we do the best in the business, we certainly felt that we had surpassed our own high standards with the float. There were two firsts – the first time a broker had marketed its own shares and the first genuine internet-only offer for sale. At the "Awards for Excellence in Investment Banking" later that year, our IPO was awarded a prize for the "European Mid/Small Cap Deal of the Year".

I have one other personal memory of the flotation process. The first week of our schedule was arranged so that most of our presentations were in London, apart from a brief foray north of the border to Edinburgh and Glasgow. The last meeting of the first week on the Friday afternoon however was with our old friends Perpetual in Henley. It was funny sitting at the other side of the table from these guys who for years and years and years had been selling us their wares. It was of course friendly fire and made for a lovely end to our first week of intense marketing. We had arranged for a car to pick us up at Henley. Stephen and I normally make sure we never travel together, for obvious reasons, but we made an exception on that Friday afternoon. As we were driving back along the M4, I brought up the subject of the important match that Bristol City were playing the following day. Stephen is chairman of Bristol City and the match turned out to be the one that clinched their promotion to the Championship from the First Division. You need to know that Stephen had recently treated himself to a small executive jet. As I was talking, he suddenly mentioned that Amy, his daughter, was coming down for the match. She is a doctor and at that time was working in a hospital on the North Cumbrian coast. "Are you sending the plane up for her?" I asked. "Yes" he said. Then he turned to me with a big grin on his face: "We really haven't changed much since we started out in your spare bedroom, have we, Peter?"

PART TWO

What I Have Learned (so far)

A Brief Introduction To Part Two

It should be clear by now that luck, coincidence and fate can play a great part in the rise of any organisation. I have already referred to the happy set of coincidences that led me to work alongside Stephen in the first place. Had it not been for a number of seemingly random decisions, Hargreaves Lansdown would never have come into existence. I would like to think however that we have made the most of our "luck". Even now I have never really known where Stephen's role starts and mine ends. Outsiders may think that I have the ideas and Stephen is the one who makes them work. It is certainly true that he makes the peace while I tend to make waves. He is happy doing the things that I hate, like legal stuff and paperwork, and vice versa. But no lasting business relationship is ever that simple. There are always different roads to take in business and there is often time to try them all, if you wish.

One of the secrets of success, I have found, is to be able to identify dead ends early on and concentrate on the ones that can make the most difference to your main business. I think I have always been good at running with the great ideas at full tilt. Stephen on the other hand has been more inclined to do things which were likely to produce slower results. The newsletters, for example, were his idea. I wasn't keen at first because I felt they were likely to become a rod for our own backs, a chore that we would still need to do at times when we were too busy to be bothered. A newsletter requires a lot of discipline. The newsletters however have set us apart and on a different level to all our competitors, and there is no doubt that he was right to insist on doing them.

In this section of the book, I am going to look at the lessons I've learned in both business and investing. The views expressed here are personal, deeply felt and sometimes contentious. You don't have to take my word for what follows; but I hope that you will recognise the years of experience and reflection on which they are based. I don't read many business books, because I don't believe you can teach being an entrepreneur or a good manager. One book about business I do rate very highly however. In fact you could say it has more or less become my bible. It was written in 1970 by an

American businessman, now dead, called Robert Townsend. *Up The Organisation* is, in my opinion, the most humorous, readable and sanest thing ever written about how – and how not – to run a business. His views may be controversial and politically incorrect, but they are none the worse for that. I loaned my original copy to someone, but as anyone will tell you, you never get back any book that you lend, do you? *Up The Organisation* draws on the story of how Townsend revolutionised the Avis rent-a-car business, turning it from an unprofitable mess into America's most successful car rental business. If you get the chance to read it, and have any kind of business mind, I guarantee that you will be shouting out loud "that's so true!", "fantastic!", "yes!" all the way through.

Chapter 9

Finding Your Customers

Marketing

Hargreaves Lansdown stands more or less alone in the retailing of investment because we are a marketing-driven business in an industry that is almost entirely sales-driven. In reality, unless you buy your investments on the basis of your own research, anybody you go to see for financial advice will turn out to be some form of salesman, whatever euphemism might be used to describe their job. They will earn their living from placing you in whichever type of investment they regard as their bread and butter and taking a fee or more likely a commission for advising you. Once you have paid for that initial advice, they will not earn anything again from you unless you either choose to change your investments at a later date or you have some new money to invest. At that point, they will again be paid commission on any home for your money they can direct you towards. A sales-driven approach to investment advice may not be elegant, and in the wrong hands can certainly produce painful consequences for the clients, but it does at least have the merit of simplicity. Note Hargreaves Lansdown's service is different (see section The Golden Years).

Marketing on the other hand is a more difficult route to take. Your aim is to provide potential investors with excellent information and first class investment opportunities and allow them to make their own minds up in their own time. We take the matter one stage further by offering clients ongoing information, not just at the point of sale. All the investments that are bought through our Vantage platform are kept under constant review. We add a current comment on every one of the investments that appear on clients' valuation reports. More importantly, whenever we think there may be a reason for the investor to look again at one of their investments, we give clients relevant information. If, on the basis of that information, they decide they wish to change that investment, we also give them information on alternatives which we feel have greater potential. We make no charge to effect any changes they decide to make.

Marketing is a strict discipline. It costs money – significant amounts of money. When you market a range of products to the investing public, it is simple to calculate the cost of your campaign and assess the results. You cannot hide from the numbers. Being a successful marketing company therefore forces you to innovate. Our view is that whether you want to buy shares or unit trusts, or whether you want to place them in a tax wrapper, you should be able to buy those products at a one stop shop. With our Vantage online platform, everything is made as clear and simple as possible and there is no pressure on investors from a salesman. They are free to make their choices in their own time and in the comfort of their own home. I am proud that our innovations have changed the way that investing happens in the UK. Investors can now buy an ISA on the telephone in just a few minutes and can do the same online or by post. I am particularly proud of our success in simplifying the application process.

In our first ISA guide of the 21st century, we suggested seven investments that would be suitable for inclusion in an ISA. At that time, because of the need to include key features documents and all the other regulatory requirements, the application booklet for these seven ISAs alone ran to 40 pages. By relentlessly chipping away at the problem, we have now reached a stage where we can produce a single unified application form that allows people to invest in 2000 different investments either directly or though one of four different tax wrappers, a total of 8000 different investment combinations. This one form, which once would have consumed an entire forest's-worth of paper, runs to just 30 pages. I like to think that it is one of the best improvements the funds industry has benefited from in the last 25 years.

Innovation; the value of great ideas

Some of our greatest innovations have taken place out of necessity, when market conditions were at their toughest. Communicating with our ever-increasing client base in a cost-effective way has also been a constant spur to innovation. Postage is one of our biggest costs. Unfortunately that means one of our largest suppliers is the Royal Mail, which is one of the most intransigent, incompetent, inefficient, bureaucratic organisations in the country. At one point, it stopped us from picking up our own post even though it was failing to deliver it to us on time and it would have saved them the cost of delivery. This was on the basis that we were already getting our post sooner than anyone else. The Royal Mail has since gone further and now charges us extra for the privilege of delivering our mail, even though every single item has already had the postage paid and in some cases we have used business reply-paid envelopes. This is supposed to be what is known as a timed delivery. It is not what we want but it's the only way the Royal Mail will do it. Amazingly, the compensation we receive when the post arrives late is less than the amount that they charge us. If all monopolies are bad, State-run monopolies are the worst.

Faced with this nightmare of a supplier, we are constantly on the lookout for ways to contact huge numbers of our clients simply, cheaply and economically. The incompetence and inefficiency of the post office is sounding its own death knoll. One good idea we had was to switch to simple postcards for mailings. Because a postcard has the address of the recipient on it, if he or she simply puts the card back in the post by way of reply, we found that it often went straight back to the client. This was true even if the postcard had our business reply-paid licence mark on it. How to get round this problem was something we thought about for days. In the end, we came up with the idea of perforating the card and giving the clients specific instructions to write our abbreviated postal address on the front and rip off the section where their own address appeared. This simple solution has worked marvellously for ten years and must have saved us many millions of pounds as a result of our no longer having to put the item in an envelope.

Another example of innovation was our realisation that there was significant money to be made for investors when the building societies and later the mutually-owned life companies started to demutualise. Whilst we did not benefit directly ourselves, we were able to help by writing guides to how our clients could profit from the demutualisation trend. We still racked our brains to work out how we might turn this to our benefit as well. In the end we invented something called the demutualisation PEP. The simple idea behind it was that investors could place their demutualisation shares in a PEP and so shelter any gains they made from future capital gains tax. When the Halifax demutualised, we took this idea another step forward by creating what we cheekily called the eXtra PEP, using part of the Halifax's logo. We applied for Halifax shares in the placing and after buying them placed them directly into clients' PEPs. That proved to be a resounding success. When we received a call from someone at the Halifax, far from complaining about our use of their eXtra logo, his main comment seemed to be how much better our application form was than theirs, despite their having spent many times the hours on their version. It showed that we had a better idea of what the general investing public wanted.

The Government privatisation programme provided us with another chance to demonstrate how innovation could help clients. I don't think any other broker had read the small print of the prospectuses as closely as we had. We noticed that in the prospectuses it said that any application for shares made by a PEP would have preferred status when it came to shares being issued. Having sought clarification from the Treasury, we took that to mean that any bid from a PEP, because it involved a finite sum of money, would probably be filled in full, rather than scaled back as often happened with the most popular share issues. To my certain knowledge, in one privatisation the PEP bid we submitted for our clients accounted for the lion's share of all the PEP bids from around the country. The clients were delighted with the result, although we wondered why no one ever came and checked our PEP bid to ensure that it was bona fide, given that our PEP bid amounted to such a huge percentage of the total bid by PEPs.

The privatisations were a gravy train not just for the private investor, but also for brokers who were given the privilege of being headline "share shops". Our marketing plan was streets ahead of most of our rivals, but we did have to give credit to one small stockbroking firm in Blackpool which offered investors who applied through them for shares a chance to win a ride on a brand new attraction at Blackpool Pleasure Beach called The Jumbo Jet. Apparently this cost all of £10. It proved a fantastic marketing coup, as I don't think there was a single national newspaper that didn't write up the offer.

Investors can often be their own worst enemies, and we have always been on the lookout for new ways to nudge them out of the bad investment habits that they seem to pick up and never lose. Chasing past winners is a good example: too many investors are guilty of buying shares or funds solely on the strength of how well they have done in the past, when what really matters is how they are likely to do in the future. I therefore noticed with interest an article in *The Economist* which showed how over the course of the 20th century, had you placed $1 at the start of the century in the asset that proved to be the best-performing investment that year and each subsequent year again chose the best at the beginning of the year then rolled up your profits, your capital would have grown by the end of the century to become a sum that would have made you richer than Bill Gates. However, had you placed that $1 in exactly the same investment, but one year later, when it had become the previous year's best-performing asset, you would have had just $219 by the end of the century. It sounds amazing, but I would not dispute *The Economist's* figures. The whole article revolved around a smart family they called the Foresights. The other family, the one that followed the losing strategy, were called the Hindsights and were paupers. We asked *The Economist* whether we could use their characters and invented Felicity Foresight and Henry Hindsight. Our clients loved the idea and although we haven't brought the Foresights into our newsletter for some time, we still get asked might we resurrect them. One day we shall.

Free guides have always been a big part of our direct marketing. In the late 1970s and early 1980s a firm called Julian Gibbs had run a clever advertising campaign in which you had to send off £1 to obtain a guide to investing. It was a good campaign because you could see the value of the advertising straightaway by counting how many people responded. The fact that investors had to send in £1 meant that you could eliminate all the timewasters who reply to advertising without ever intending to do anything. The publication that produces most potential clients isn't necessarily the best place to advertise as it can also produce the greatest percentage of timewasters. They can cost you a lot of money before you establish that they are never going to invest with you. While a lead of this kind might only cost you £20 and so look cheap, you would also have to waste a further £50 on sending out information to these people. When we ran our first advertisement, you may recall that we didn't know why it cost more to advertise in the *Daily Telegraph* than the *Sunday Telegraph*. Even though it produced fewer potential clients, the reason was that it produced better potential.

We developed our own "send £1 for a guide" concept and also hit upon the idea of sending copies of the guides to journalists. Normally we always put a price on everything we send out. This is on the basis that whether people pay for it or not, they always perceive value in something that has a price written on it. However we found that offering a number of free copies of our guides to newspaper readers was a powerful draw. It helped the journalist as the guide helped them to write their columns and it helped us because the journalist would offer readers the chance to have the guide for free if their readers contacted us. It was a great way to produce cheap leads and we were able to turn the opportunity to good account for almost ten years. Needless to say, when you have a good idea, you get flattered by your competitors copying it. I remember one issue of the *Daily Telegraph* in which almost every article written offered a guide of one kind or another, from an investment group, a broker, a bank or some financial organisation. It was probably the last straw for the advertising departments of the newspapers. Why would anyone bother to advertise in future if journalists were willing to publicise guides and generate leads for nothing – especially as the endorsement by the journalist would often produce three times as many leads as an advertisement?

Eventually, the newspapers decided to start producing guides themselves "in conjunction with a broker". There were all sorts of deals. Sometimes you had to pay through the nose for the guide to appear with your name attached. On other occasions they produced what is known as an "advertorial", in which the journalist wrote a piece to advertise the guide, but the article is clearly labelled as an advertisement rather than an ordinary piece of editorial. At the same time I suspect that journalists were finally told to stop giving free plugs in their columns to brokers' guides. When Willis Owen started producing its guide to PEPs, which dropped out of the national newspapers, it showed that the newspapers were ready to get in on the act. Soon they started to ask for a share of the earnings too. Willis Owen refused to do that, so another brokerage picked up the mantle, but I don't think they got a payback because their timing was so poor.

The other idea we developed during a quiet time was what we called The Investor's Guide to the High Street. As many clients wanted to know how to choose shares, the idea was to explain how they could become their own best analysts. We suggested if they walked past a shop which had queues at the door, it would be probably a better indication of success than waiting for an analyst to notice that the profits were going up in that particular retail chain. We listed all the various High Street shops so that when people saw a store doing well they could look to see whether they could buy shares in it. The idea was based on my own experience. Back in the 1960s, as a keen motorist I joined a motoring club and noticed how many of the members were using Duckham's 20-50 oil, a multi-grade oil that was effective over a wide range of temperatures. I bought some shares in the company that made the oil and was able to bank a handsome profit when it was later bought out.

I also made a considerable sum of money after joining a David Lloyd sports centre. When I went there with my wife I couldn't believe how expensive it was to join. I confidently told her, "We must join because we will have the tennis courts to ourselves" only to find that the first time I turned up, the courts were booked solid for a week! I couldn't believe people were paying so much money just to become a member of a sports centre. Again, I bought the shares and within two months the company had been bought by Whitbread. I reckon that the profit on the transaction will pay my membership fees for the next 20 years! It reminded me of something I had read in a book by Peter Lynch, the famous Fidelity fund manager in America, where he mentioned a company called Dunkin' Donuts. This was a fast-food chain that I had visited when it was in its infancy back in 1976. While I couldn't believe anyone could call a place Dunkin' Donuts, I do remember how good the coffee was. Apparently Peter Lynch had also gone into a Dunkin' Donuts outlet at the same time. Having decided that it was the best cup of coffee he had ever tasted, he bought a huge slug of the shares and they then went up tenfold. The Investors' Guide to the High Street proved to be a fantastic source of leads to people who liked the idea of being their own analyst.

My Golden Rules Of Advertising

The rest of our industry wonders why we have always done our own advertising. The perceived wisdom is that, essentially, advertising agencies come for free. The agencies come up with the creative ideas and produce the advertisements and in return they are paid by the commission they earn from the various media that they use. It all sounds very reasonable and I have no doubt that using an advertising agency is good value. What I am not so sure about is whether advertising agencies actually provide what you want. Many advertisements I see on television and in the newspapers leave me wondering how the marketing team could sign off such inappropriate, puerile and pathetic work. I think that advertising agencies are often so obsessed with creating fancy artwork that they forget to tell you who is advertising and what they are advertising. The advertisements make someone feel good but the problem is that it doesn't produce any business.

If you are not interested in producing advertisements yourself, then I am sure an advertising agency will give you a lot of guidance and prevent you going too far wrong. However if you like advertising, then my best advice is: do it yourself. In 25 years we have courted a couple of advertising agencies and used them in a minor way and while we couldn't complain about the results we still missed doing the work ourselves. Much of the world's greatest advertising is, I believe, produced by companies in-house. I am sure that Ryanair don't use an advertising agency and when I look through the newspapers, I find many examples where companies would have done better to do the job themselves. We have always gone by gut instinct. We have been told many times that some of the things we do "aren't what you do in advertising". Having looked at some of the things that it appears you should do in advertising, I don't think I have had any cause to worry. These are some of the golden rules of advertising, as I have come to learn them.

There Is no point, in my view, in doing any advertising other than coupon response (or its modern day successor which is 0800 Freephone advertising).

Why let somebody see your advertisement without giving them an easy way to respond? Response advertising is a powerful discipline. It produces hard results by which your business lives or dies. You cannot hide behind pretty pictures. In the early days, our advertisements were literally not much more than a coupon, the space in the advertisement where potential customers could write their name and address. I have seen huge advertisements from well known firms with a coupon at the bottom that only gave the respondents one line for their whole address yet elsewhere in the advertisement there were huge amounts of white space. What is the point of that? The first thing you do with a coupon is make sure that you can easily write a name and address. Today, however, there is very little traditional coupon advertising, partly because most people are too lazy to fill in a coupon, then put it in an envelope and spend money on a stamp. Most advertising now uses Freephone 0800 numbers. You publish a telephone number on your advert and use a 24 hour seven days a week agency to take people's names and addresses. The calls are free to the potential client. But things never stand still. The internet is the newest advertising medium, and growing in popularity by the day. It involves new skills and a different way of doing things. We are trying to bring the same common sense approach to the internet that we have used in the national press.

The most important thing in advertising is obviously to offer potential customers something that they want.

There is no point in telling potential clients all about yourself. Our original advertising offered information and suggestions about buying unit trusts. Later on we developed a technique whereby we produced a guide to some investment topic and then offered it to clients. Sometimes we asked them to pay a small amount of money (this made sure that you only received a reply from people who were genuinely interested). On other occasions we offered them something for free. We have also advertised information about a specific event. When Fidelity chose to split its flagship Special Situations Fund into two component funds, for example, it gave us a golden opportunity to discover the names of people who owned that unit trust but who had bought it from someone else. We offered information on what was happening and then to update them as events unfurled. Other guides we have produced over the years include a PEP Handbook, Investing in your 40s, Investing in your 50s, and Investing in Retirement. We have also offered numerous guides to pensions, PEPs, with profit bonds and so on. Although occasionally we have used professional journalists to write guides when we did not have the time to do it ourselves, we generally produce both guides and advertisements ourselves.

I hate seeing adverts with lots of white space.

If you have paid for six square inches in the newspaper, my view is that you should make full use of it. Your headline should go right across the top of the advertisement. If you can't fit what you want to say in one line, then use two, as the message is the key. Your bullet points should be in maximum type size and leave the minimum of white space. When no one knows who you are, there is absolutely no point in trying to build a brand. For the first ten advertisements, preferring to highlight the reasons why anyone should respond. Once you become reasonably well known, it makes more sense to ensure that people can see your company name. Whether you are advertising a product or a service, you no longer need to hide your light under a bushel. The scope for branding only really comes however after many years of successfully trading.

Negotiate, negotiate, negotiate!

This is another of the reasons why we have always done our advertising ourselves. Most magazines, newspapers and other media have what is known as a rate card. This is the same as the rack room rental for a hotel room. It shows the maximum price that they are going to charge you. In practice almost all advertising is negotiable. We have always felt that we were likely to fight harder to get the price down than an advertising agency. As agencies get a percentage of the value of the advertisement, it is obvious that the higher the cost the higher the value of their percentage will be. The other thing is that as we were dealing directly with the advertising managers of the various publications, we were able to form relationships with them. They also knew that we were capable of quick decisions. There have been numerous occasions when for one reason or another, they haven't been able to fill an important space with only an hour to go before they had to "put the newspaper to bed". Instead of having to go to an advertising agency and ask them if they had a client who might take the space at 5 o'clock on a Friday afternoon, they found they could always ring us. While they knew we would screw them to the boards on price, we would at least make the decision to run an advertisement. (I am sure I would embarrass one or two newspapers about how much we have paid for prime position at 5 o'clock on a Friday if I was to publish the prices here.)

Use Distress Space

Sometimes we have been offered what is known as distress space. This occurs when newspapers have space in the newspaper of an unusual size that they haven't got an advertiser or editorial to fill.

We have an in-house graphic designer who is happy to play around with the text of an advertisement in order to fit a funny shape in the paper. We would get the space for nearly nothing and quite often an unusual shaped advert will catch the eye. We have had adverts only two or three centimetres high across six columns and other weird and wonderful sizes, but invariably they seem to work. It was more difficult when we had to fit a coupon into funny size adverts, but now with 0800 numbers it is considerably easier. If you deal with advertising agencies, you never get to know about things like that. Nor do you have the fun of sitting down with a graphic designer with just 20 minutes to produce an advertisement that will both fit the space and, just as importantly in our industry, comply with the advertising rules of the Financial Services and Markets Act.

Advertising is a discipline.

It makes you think about your business and tells you what your investors and potential investors want. Too much advertising is what I call ego trip advertising. That includes advertising in prestige publications which have excellent editorial but low circulations and never produce any business. It amazes me why companies advertise in magazines that comment on economics or the political spectrum. Perhaps they just like to see their company name in the "right places". Looking through the upmarket magazines will show you which companies are wasting shareholders' money on this kind of unproductive and wasteful advertising. My advice is: don't get involved in it with your own business.

Avoid image-building advertising, where a company advertises nothing but its name.

All that this kind of advertisement says is "We are big and international" and we have a nice logo. When any company starts image building, you know that they have gone soft. I think it's a signal to sell the shares and certainly not a signal to buy them. An image advertisement doesn't tell you what the company does, it doesn't tell you where it is and it doesn't offer you any reason to go to the company to find out further information. No doubt it makes the chief executive happy that while he is driving to work he can see the name of his company on a huge billboard, but of course he already knows what his company does. Next time that the CEO is held up, I suggest he jumps out of the car, points out the advert to the person in the car behind and asks the guy what he thinks. He might learn something interesting. Companies certainly make some amazing claims. A big oil company claiming to be green – what a nerve! Aircraft manufacturers which carry out research and technology in an area where there is unemployment – who cares? Is it going to make you fly in one of their aircraft? As it is airlines which choose which aircraft you get to fly in, it would make more sense if the aircraft industry advertised to the airlines, rather than to the world at large.

Something has happened over the last 25 years which has made advertising less effective. This is the fragmentation of newspaper sections particularly Sunday newspapers. In the 1970s the *Sunday Times* started splitting up the newspaper into various sections and many newspapers followed suit, a trait that eventually Saturday newspapers emulated. It strikes me that if advertising agencies had any nous at all they would have objected long and loud at this practice. When all the various sections of newspapers were in what is known as the main run of the paper it did mean that even people who didn't normally read certain sections sometimes skimmed through them as something caught their eye. Now that it's all sectionalised it makes editing extremely easy for the readers. Indeed, I have seen people take out the three or four sections they don't want and dump them at the point of purchase to save them carrying home unwanted sections.

We noticed, for example, how advertising response rates went down when they split the financial section of the papers into City and personal finance pages. Without going into the detailed costing of individual newspapers, I am sure that few could survive for long on their cover price revenue alone. Most of that goes in distribution costs and the retailers' profit margin. If the biggest source of revenue is advertising, with print advertising coming under pressure from the internet and other new media, it is obvious to me that newspapers ought to be making their advertising more, not less, effective. To date however, our lone voice on this subject has cut little ice with the newspapers and advertising agencies. What we have seen with our own eyes however is the effect that fragmentation of newspapers has had in reducing response rates. Isn't it time that the industry itself took notice?

Reflections on Sales and Competition

There is little doubt that in some industries salesmen are the most important cog in the wheel. They can be the highest paid, sometimes earning more than the chief executive. When they are worth it, they are worth it and they should be paid accordingly. However salesmen do have limitations. They are only good at three things – sales, sales and sales. You should never let a salesman do anything other than sell. You should never let them price a deal; you should never let them design a product; and you should certainly never let them design an application form. Left to his own devices, a salesman will always give your product away. A poor salesman will always try to redesign the product as well, even though poor salesmen will never sell it however many features you allow them to add to it. And in my experience they probably won't clinch the deal even if you let them sell it at a loss.

The other big mistake that many salesmen make is chasing "the one big deal". Instead of putting all their eggs in one basket, the most successful salesmen have lots of different deals on the table at any time. Among other advantages, that means they don't have to hassle the people who are considering their proposition. However I will reiterate – never let the salesman run the business, have access to pricing or the cash. A salesman will make a sale at all costs. It's the famous story about the firm that sold widgets for £100 a widget. The widgets cost £90 to make. Left to his own devices a salesman would sell them for £95 a piece (on the basis that they would sell twice as many!) or would suggest we could sell ten times as many at £90 – no profit at all. Leave salesmen to selling.

Something that we could never convince the Government to do in its privatisations was abandon the registration process. Insisting that people register to apply for shares in a privatisation was an utter waste of money. The reasons advanced for registration, such as "it creates tension in the market", were entirely spurious. The reason is that investors are only in the mood once. They may be in the mood when they register, but nothing says they will be in the mood again when they get the prospectus some time later. Those who might have been in the mood when the prospectuses eventually appeared would never receive them, as they weren't in the mood at the time they should have registered. We were always very much against a two step operation of this kind. Why not send the whole pack out first time and then let the client decide there and then if they wish to participate?

This is related to what I call the shirt and tie syndrome in sales. I am not sure why it happens, but when someone buys one of something from a supplier, they invariably tend to buy something else as well. From my own experience, I know if I go out to buy a suit, and find one I like, I usually end up buying three or four other items of clothing as well – not just a shirt and tie to go with the suit, but maybe also another pair of trousers, a pullover and so on. When people place a deal with a firm for the first time, a second purchase in some way seems to ratify their decision to do business with that firm. It provides a measure of comfort that they have made the right decision. You see this happening in all walks of life and well run businesses will make sure they are ready to take advantage of it by pushing you immediately towards repeat or additional purchases.

I can understood why people feel that having something exclusively, or being the only outlet in a particular area, is good, but in my view the whole exclusivity thing is a fallacy. 30 years ago you could find 20 car accessory shops at the end of Deansgate in Manchester, by which I don't mean 20 similar shops in one area, but literally 20 similar shops side by side in a row. On the face of it that seemed crazy. However in those days you could still park easily outside and you knew that if you went there you were bound to find what you wanted. That worked in the interests of all the car accessory shops. Sure, you would go into the shop that was nearest where you parked, but if they didn't have what you wanted, they were smart enough to direct you to another shop that did stock it. They realised it was good business if you were successful in finding what you wanted. It meant that the next time you wanted something for your car, you would come back to the same place. Everyone prospered as a result. We have seen something similar happen time and time again in our own industry. If a product captures the imagination of all the brokers, and they all promote it at the same time, the chances are it will grow the size of the market. Everyone does better than they would have done by trying to negotiate an exclusive arrangement. While we were initially surprised to see a number of our competitors in London move near us in the West Country, we have since come to the conclusion that we should be flattered rather than worried. Whatever their reasons for moving, at the end of the day it means that more people will be happy using firms in Bristol and Bath to do business, whereas previously they might have only used firms in London.

PR – Is It Useful?

The one thing you learn in PR is that the easiest way you can get your name in the paper is to "slag something off". In fact two of our competitors are regularly quoted in the newspaper because one of them publishes a black list of unit trusts and the other one produces "a list of dogs". It is easy publicity, but I don't know why they feel so proud about it. I don't think they realise that although they get their name in the paper, their name is associated with something that is bad. You can always find bad products in all industries. The problem is that by publishing a list of the worst performers, people come to believe that the whole industry is bad. I cannot argue against the suggestion that there are huge numbers of investments that are bad. That is why it is very easy to quote statistics such as that the average unit trust hasn't beaten the index. Whilst this is true, we don't think we have ever recommended "the average unit trust". The averages are pulled down dramatically by some of the horrible funds that are managed (or should I say not managed?) by banks, building societies and life companies.

The thing that everyone should remember is that if you court publicity, you also have to take the brickbats. Whether PR does as much good as is often cited is a moot point. It is always difficult to gauge whether being constantly in the newspapers produces new clients, but it does give existing clients comfort that the firm they deal with is being sought for expert advice. However if you ever do anything wrong or make a mistake, then you can also guarantee that that is the day when you will hit most of the newspapers. It constantly surprises me that people in the public eye who court publicity get angry when newspapers turn against them. If they have courted journalists to further their careers, they should also accept that when they transgress those same journalists will be the first to criticise, and rightly so.

Is PR useful? I suspect PR is much like advertising. Lord Lever of Lever Brothers fame (which later became Unilever) allegedly said that only half his advertising worked. The trouble was he didn't know which half. It is the same with PR. You don't know for certain how much benefit you gain, but I am pretty sure that in our industry some firms who use PR in place of advertising to get noticed would certainly not be in the position they are without it. By the same token I am not sure how many new clients PR brings in, but it does without any doubt give our existing clients a warm glow when they see the firm that they deal with frequently consulted by the national press. The drawback of a high profile, we have sometimes found, is that sometimes we have people approach us meekly suggesting that perhaps we are too big and too important to be interested in their small investment matters.

What I say to them is that Hargreaves Lansdown was built on servicing the needs of small investors, and that is never going to change. We have always found small investors to be the bread and butter of our business. They appreciate what we do and the fact that we treat them the same way as all our other clients. Our view is that small clients can easily one day turn into big clients. We are happy to welcome clients from all walks of life. They all have different amounts of money to invest and different requirements. The one thing I am absolutely sure about is that the best PR is the PR you do yourself. You have to be interested in it however, you have to want to do it and you have to be prepared to comment. Journalists will only ring you a couple of times and if you dither, or worry about what you are going to say, or tell them you are going to ring them back, the phone call doesn't come again.

Chapter 10

Making Your Organisation Work

Avoid Meetings Like the Plague

Let's get one thing straight. Meetings are the scourge of industry. Anyone in business should be constantly campaigning to abolish all meetings. If the public sector abolished meetings, it would probably be able to operate with 3% of the people that it currently employs. Meetings stop people from doing their jobs. If you cut out the meetings, you could probably also lose 90% of your middle management. I have never relented in my quest to stop meetings. The truth that a camel is a horse designed by a committee is so true that it's sad. Often when I see a meeting in progress in Hargreaves Lansdown, I open the door and join it. I sit down at the table. The striking thing is that when I sit down, someone will look up and say, "We are just finishing." I remain seated. Someone else will then repeat, "We are just finishing." Then I say "Well, finish then." They all walk out. Had I not gone into the meeting, you can be sure that they would have stayed there another hour. One good way to stop lengthy meetings is to make sure there are no chairs – in fact, nowhere to sit at all. You can always find out which are the worst parts of your business. They will be the ones where the meetings culture is greatest. Meetings are where people go to abdicate their responsibilities.

I once read an article entitled "A day in the life of...", which featured the chief executive of a well-known British airline. Apparently this guy worked so hard it wasn't true. His day started with a breakfast meeting at 7 am. All that a breakfast meeting does is extend your working day. It costs money because somebody has to organise and pay for the breakfast. Breakfast meetings are terrible things because they happen at the best time of the day for getting things done. The telephone doesn't ring early in the morning because everybody else in industry is having a breakfast meeting. After his two hour breakfast meeting, the article reported that the chief executive's chauffeur drove him to his "first meeting of the day" (which actually was his second). That lasted an hour and a half. Then the chauffeur drove him on to the next meeting of the day, which lasted for two hours. He then had a lunchtime meeting (for lunchtime meeting, read a breakfast meeting that costs more and lasts longer). After lunch he had a board meeting which went on all afternoon. He got home at 8 o'clock at night.

While he could claim to have spent long hours on his job, in my book he hasn't done any work at all. What he should have done that day was buy a ticket and fly incognito on one of his planes. That way he would have found out what was really going on in his airline. He would have found that the seat he had booked had been cancelled because the plane had been changed. He would find that even though there was a huge number of staff, there was still a queue at the check-in desk when there didn't need to be one. The reason being most of the staff were pretending to be busy elsewhere. When the plane was late leaving, he would have discovered that there was no communication from anyone about why and the information about when it actually really would leave. He would have learnt more from that one trip travelling incognito then he would have learnt had he been in six months of meetings which probably was the agenda for the next six months. It was many years ago and he is no longer the boss but even without him his airline hasn't got any better, so I assume they still have the same meetings culture. In other words the chief executive probably thinks he is working hard because he is in meetings all day long. I shall continually fight the meeting culture as long as I am chief executive of Hargreaves Lansdown.

Meetings should take place in the following way. If you want to meet someone, walk over to their desk. (They might even be there if you have abolished meetings at your firm). Your arrival will almost certainly cut short a phone call and in the time you have saved, you can say what's on your mind, get a response and be back at your desk, all within five minutes. In my firm, you won't be able to sit down because there won't be a chair near the desk. If you really want to stay any length of time, you will have to get down on your knees to talk. Believe me, there is nothing that makes a meeting shorter than having the chief executive on his knees next to somebody's desk.

The way the average large company now operates is very different. In between board meetings, the directors tend to spend the rest of their time talking to the next tier of management below them. That takes up about half that tier of management's time, and they in turn spend the other half talking to the next level down from them. And so it goes on, all the way down the line of command. What that means is that the company is actually being run by managers who are a long way down the management chain. Many of the people who have been promoted to do the job of running the company are in fact merely passing on messages up and down the line – a completely fatuous and pointless exercise. In my view one of two things should happen if (by ill-chance) you happen to find yourself in charge of a company that is run this way. One way is simply to sack all the upper echelons of management, including the board, and while you are at it, get rid of their secretaries and assistants as well, so as to free up the space that they are occupying. The cost of employing them will drop straight into the bottom line, increasing profits. The alternative is to pick the eight people who are really capable of running the business and let them get on with it. That way, while you wouldn't save quite as much in the way of meetings rooms, secretaries, assistants and middle managers, at least it would be clear who was running the company and could therefore be held to account for how well it was doing.

If you get no other message from this book you should get the message that meetings are bad for business. Even when they are essential, you should always decide in advance how long the meeting should be. If it's going to be half an hour, start it half an hour before the end of the working day, or half an hour before lunch. There is no better stimulus to finish a meeting than the start of the lunch hour, or the closing bell. Sometimes meetings are not just a waste of time, but positively detrimental. When we started advertising in the press, for example, we talked regularly to one particular gentleman on a national newspaper. In our minds we had a clear and positive picture of this individual. He was efficient, we liked him, he helped us, we gave him business and everything was hunky-dory – but it was never the same after he came to see us. His visit shattered our image of him. He turned out not to be the guy we thought he was. The same went for a journalist that I used to get on with very well. We talked regularly on the phone and she gave us huge amounts of publicity by quoting us in her articles. Although I had suggested meeting a couple of times, she had always declined. I should have left it at that. When eventually I did agree to meet her for lunch in London, she stood me up. What is more, she never contacted me again and never quoted us again. To this day I don't know why. I learnt the wisdom of that old adage "if it ain't broke, don't fix it". If someone is doing good business with you, why risk the chance of ruining the relationship by meeting them?

Getting The Best Out Of Employees

Most businesses seem to accumulate unnecessary staff. Government ministers are the worst offenders. They have a diary secretary, a private secretary, an assistant or two and then another secretary to look after all these hangers on, plus one other person whose title evades me. In the private sector, where you have to make a profit, this is a hopeless way to operate. I can't think of anyone in the business world who has enough work to keep a secretary busy all day. We have a team of two whom I suppose you could broadly describe as being in the secretary/assistant category. Stephen and I could not possibly find enough to keep them occupied the whole day long. Both of them in effect have other jobs. For example between them they handle much of the correspondence from clients who have queries about our procedures and the reports produced from our investment team. They also do secretarial work for Mark Dampier and a few others on the research team. Even then we struggle to keep them busy.

Neither is allowed to waste their time in "make work" jobs such as making appointments. Making appointments through your secretary is four times as tortuous as making them yourself. If she makes an appointment, she has to come and ask you if it's alright. Then she has to go back and tell the other people whether it is alright or not. If it isn't alright then they come back with another date which she then asks you about and then she goes back and confirms it then she comes back to you and tells you which one she has booked. If you had made the appointment yourself, it would all be done and dusted in ten seconds, without the need for being interrupted 16 times to discuss whether the appointment was appropriate or at the right time or on the right day or not.

The other thing that secretaries do is intercept phone calls. That means she takes a call, which wastes her time, then tells you who is on the line and what it's about, which wastes your time, and then you have to decide whether you are going to take it or not. If you had taken the call in the first place, you would have got rid of it in four seconds if you didn't want it and there would have been no time wasted. Even worse is the secretary who decides for you which calls you should take. She rejects the one you wanted, which means they phone six times more, and puts through the ones you don't, which you could have got rid of in four seconds anyway. If someone is persistent and finds that everybody is fending them off, in my experience it won't stop them phoning and wasting everyone's time. If you take the call, their mission to speak to you is over straightaway. You can normally tell within five seconds whether you want to speak to someone or not. At that point you thank them politely and tell them you are not interested, or if you are not sure how interested you are, my preferred method is to stop them in full flight and then give them just 30 seconds to interest you. If you count down the last five seconds, ("five, four, three, two, one") and hang up, you can be sure that they will never phone again!

Some firms have departments that handle office services. They will do you a photocopy if you want, but in my experience they always give you three, just to be on the safe side. That costs you money over and above the wage of the person who has just given you three times as many photocopies as you wanted. Since you or your secretary had to go there to get the photocopy, you might as well just have walked over to a photocopier and done the job yourself. Some people have assistants too. An assistant is a secretary with a fancy name who costs you more, does less and takes three times as long to do something as you would have done had you done it yourself. It takes you twice as long to vet what they have been doing and to find out they didn't do it right the first time. You therefore have to make them do it again, so despite spending twice as much time again as you could have spent just doing it in the first place, you have still not got it right. The other people you should never have are section leaders. As soon as somebody becomes a section leader, they stop working and then stop everybody else in their section working as well. What then happens is that the section gets too big, so you have to split the section in two and now you have two section leaders who both need two more because they are causing so much grief within their own sections.

If you can avoid it, nobody should be given the job of manager either. In one of our most successful businesses, the young man who runs it is clearly the boss and everybody knows it. But his secret is that he has great people running different parts of his business. There is somebody in charge of his help desk, somebody in charge of administration and somebody in charge of marketing. All he did to find those people however was put a group of people together and then tell them to get on with the job. In each case somebody just naturally took charge. The person who everyone went to, the person who communicated what was happening, was the person who took responsibility. They weren't asked to take charge. They just did it. Of course that person was the perfect person for the job, even though the chances are that you wouldn't have picked him or her yourself. We have seen that situation in our office time and time again. When we have given someone responsibility, they haven't always been the right person to do the job. When someone left another of our businesses to have a baby, the guy in charge at the time appointed someone in the section as the new person in charge. He was just the wrong person with the wrong ideas of what a manager should do. Eventually we just moved him and the person who should have been given the job stepped forward.

It is important not to give people grand sounding titles. If we simply called everybody an employee, they would muck in for the general good and that's the best way for businesses to run. You have to give everyone a chance to come up with ideas. Our experience has certainly been that the best decisions we have made originated from a range of different sources. No one can remember now, for example, who decided that we should move into stockbroking. At the time we had tried a couple of "collaborations", one that worked well and one that did not. One of our employees knew a big firm of stockbrokers in Bristol and organised a meeting. I shall not easily forget it. An arrogant and conceited senior partner walked into our offices, clearly without any knowledge of our operation. His demeanour, tone of voice and the comments he made were denigratory. He described us as *"investment bond pushers"* – which was ironic, given my well-known views on the subject. I pointed out to him that the real investment pushers were his half commission salesmen, while ours was a marketing driven business. Had he done five minutes work, he would have discovered that it was his operation that was commission hungry and unsustainable. The meeting didn't last very long. Many years later he effectively gave away his business for nothing, selling it for shares rather than cash to a company that went spectacularly bust. Despite this false step, it was Stephen who put the wheels in motion and put our stockbroking business together. It was to become a significant part of our business.

How we came to develop our stockbroking systems was another story again. It had its roots elsewhere in the organisation. Having recruited a bright, intelligent, young chartered accountant to work on our systems, we sent him out to find a system that had not, unlike those of many of our competitors, been made obsolete by the revolutionary changes in settlement procedures that had followed the Big Bang. Readers may not appreciate that the "back office" of any stockbroking firm is arguably the most important part of its operation. No stockbroker has ever gone bust because of its failure to persuade clients to trade stocks. It is almost invariably the inability to handle back office work that forces failed stockbrokers out of business. The business of settlement, issuing certificates, making reconciliations and handling corporate events such as rights issues, stock splits, new issues and so on is the bread and butter work on which the financial health of any stockbroker depends. Unglamorous though it is, get that aspect of the business wrong and you are finished.

While we were deciding what to do, I remember going to Leeds with the young tiger in question to visit one of our biggest competitors and look at their system. He immediately dismissed it as not right for us. When he did eventually come up with his favoured solution, its credentials were dubious. The system was being built for a major clearing bank, had never been used and was produced by Broker Focus, a tiny software house in Dublin that nobody had heard of. My team was adamant, however, that it was right for us. What they saw clearly in the new system was that it obeyed good accounting principles. A lot of software looks clever and produces pretty reports, but is not robust from an accounting perspective. A second key attraction was that £20m-£30m had already been spent on the project by the bank, and no doubt there had been a contribution from the EU, with the aim of creating a state of the art stockbroking system. It helped that we got on well with the team in Dublin. They were all on the same wavelength as far as accounting procedures were concerned. Given the importance of the back office function, it was a big decision to defer to the judgment of such a relatively young and inexperienced newcomer in the office, but in the end we decided to make the brave decision to step into the breach (later we also bought the software house in order to help secure its future).

The Importance Of Company Culture

Many things have contributed to the success of Hargreaves Lansdown. Our marketing has been good. We have an outstanding systems team. We were fortunate to start out in business at the start of one of the greatest bull markets of all time. And so on. However I believe there is something more important than any of these which has been key to the firm's success. The only words I can find to describe it are "a special culture".

The culture of the firm can only be set from the top and it starts with simple things. For example, from the beginning of the firm, if I saw a leaf had been blown in by the wind in reception, rather than ignore it, or send for someone else to do something about it, I felt it was important to stop to pick it up myself. The first time I went to one of our new offices, it was difficult to find the entrance and even more of a nightmare to gain someone's attention when you did. Remember that I was the boss. God knows how difficult it would have been for any clients who turned up: if I had been a potential client, I would have left immediately.

My solution was to get the office to buy signs that pointed to the door and make sure that when clients did arrive, they were greeted appropriately. When we have leased offices where they throw in reception staff as part of the deal, I have often been appalled at how poor the central services can be. Offices like this are invariably overmanned. Of course building managers don't care about costs, as they can always charge it to the tenants and put on a percentage. The more they spend the bigger their percentage. It is amazing how unfriendly and unwelcoming some businesses can be. It is usually because the boss hasn't tried dealing with his own business as a customer. It is always said that the best phone call a boss can make is a call to his own firm to see what happens. I am sure that this is true and it is advice worth heeding.

A strong culture in a firm goes much deeper than making sure that clients are received well and that when they telephone they are efficiently transferred to the appropriate department. You have to remember that clients do not understand your business. They only see one firm. The worst response anyone can get is, "Oh, that's another department." When I hear that kind of remark, it makes my blood boil. Our staff are trained to give the impression that Hargreaves Lansdown really is just one business and that visitors can expect to be helped on any aspect of the firm' activities. Our culture is one of equality throughout the business. That is why we have dispensed with company cars. The trouble with company cars is not only that they cost three times as much as any individual would pay if it were their own car, but they also seem to bring out the worst in people.

It seems to be quite in order for example for an employee to spend four days off work test driving a range of different models. Then people seem to need a hire car when their company car goes in for servicing, added to which there is always a huge amount of management time wasted on deciding which model of car an employee is entitled to. If employees want to add a bit of their own money in order to obtain a slightly better model, when it comes to changing the car later the extra they have spent seems to be automatically added onto the value of their new model. Depreciation rarely comes into the reckoning with company cars. For some reason they always seem to do fewer miles to the gallon than the road report indicates. I can't think of any reason why that should be the case unless of course the fuel is fuelling two cars! Fortunately after the changes to the tax regime for company cars, it no longer makes sense to have a company car. The worst thing is that for many employees company cars become a status thing. The car becomes their consuming passion. Nothing could be worse for creating a healthy working environment.

In a well run organisation everyone should be treated equally. The only differentiation between employees should be salary and a bonus that is completely dependent on how much of a difference they make to the firm. In our offices today everyone sits in an open plan area. Nobody has their own private office, and everyone has similar size desks and similar toys on their desks. We found that when we started acquiring the latest flat computer screens, they soon became a status symbol. It quickly became known that if your old screen broke, you could get a flat screen as a replacement. It was amazing how many computers broke that week. When we changed tack and started to replace old VDUs with even older models from someone else's desk, it was equally amazing how quickly they stopped breaking. Since then we have changed the policy so that flat screens go to whichever department is most crowded and has the least amount of cooling equipment. It may have cost our IT department a lot to move so many screens around, but it has probably saved us thousands more in replacement cost. It is a much fairer system than either allowing senior people to have them first, or replacing "broken" ones.

Expenses are another potential horror story. They can quickly run up into huge amounts of money. No boss should ever charge anything through expenses which is not wholly incurred in the course of business. If the boss is cheating on his expenses, you can be assured that everyone else in the firm will hear about it and it will become part of the firm's culture. Stephen and I prefer to go to the other extreme. There have been many times when I have spent all day moving round by taxi in London and never claimed the fares. I wouldn't expect employees to act the same way, but I have never treated the company's money as my own and never felt the company's money was less valuable than my own. Many people seem to think that company pounds are far less valuable than their own and that therefore you can spend them twice as fast.

Corporate entertaining is grossly unfair. I suspect that only 2-3% of any firm ever gets invited to lavish entertaining events. Employees who are key contacts for our suppliers on the other hand could probably spend half the year at major sporting occasions if they accepted all the invitations that came their way. We have a strict rule with corporate days. Unless the occasion is solely designed to enhance the knowledge of people in the firm (for instance an investment seminar), all corporate days have to be taken as a day's holiday. When we have an invitation for more than one member of staff, we always ask if people from departments who never get invited to such wonderful events can go. It's not usually what the donors want, but it's what we want to reward people who aren't at the glamour end of the business, but whose jobs are just as important in the growth of the business as any other.

A good rule in business is that if large companies or the public sector do it you can guarantee it's wrong. One good example is in grading of staff. At one of my early employers, the grading system became an all consuming preoccupation. Those who reached a certain grade automatically qualified for a company car. It was remarkable how the HR department, because they knew how to manipulate the rules, managed to get most of their people up to that grade! There was also a better car for a better grade. I suspect that in many companies today grades dictate length of holidays, size of desk, who has a secretary and a whole lot more. It's all bunkum. The reason it's bunkum is that when the grading takes place, it is always the person who is graded and never the job. A job may be incredibly important to the firm, but if at that particular point in time it is occupied by a complete drongo, the job will get a very low grade and nobody will ever want to take the job in the future. Conversely you will sometimes have a superb employee doing a brilliant job in a menial task, thus giving that job a high grade. The way a grading system works there is never any sensible progression in the firm. People aim to jump from grade to grade rather than from job to job.

That is why the only thing better employees should get is a better salary and bonus. The only person who knows how much they should be on is their boss. It is not the job of an HR department. At Hargreaves Lansdown we look at every single person's salary and bonus individually. We do not have across the board pay rises and we do not have standard bonuses. Stephen and I personally go through every single department's salaries and proposed bonuses. It's a huge task, but no task is more important to get right. We always say to our managers that we know they aren't doing their job if we find them suggesting a flat salary structure, and similar pay rises and bonuses for all members of their departments. That cannot ever be right. Some of your employees will have worked far harder than others and some will be far more able. That ability and effort should be rewarded disproportionately.

The other thing that all bosses of organisations should do is read complaints that are personally addressed to them. It is very rare that a client feels so incensed that they feel they have to write to the boss. They often have a good case, and it is vital that the boss knows when something is going wrong. If it is about a one-off mistake by one of the employees, that is unfortunate but rarely serious for the business. However if it is a regular complaint, it may mean that there is something systemically wrong which needs to be fixed. The other good reason to take complaints is that it allows you to deal directly with the occasional professional complainers. These are normally people who have retired from a bureaucratic job with nothing better to do than sit at home and make mischief. If their complaints are unreasonable, we usually end up by suggesting that Hargreaves Lansdown is not the right firm for them and suggest they go somewhere else. It's surprising how many people beg to stay. However, with the really awkward ones, we don't give them the opportunity. We just get rid of them. You cannot afford to go on dealing with people who think it is their mission in life to try to disrupt your business with spurious complaints. It is easier for the boss to tell them the company doesn't want their business any more.

When I said that individual mistakes were rarely serious, I meant it. I have never yet come across a case where the person who made the mistake was not also the one who was most upset. As our business involves dealing with other people's money, it is imperative that anyone who handles people's money is as meticulous as possible. Employees who have made a mistake are often astounded when I go and see them personally to console them and show them the letter that I have written to the client. This says that while we are sorry for the mistake, the person who is most upset is the person who made the mistake. If there has been any cost incurred by the client, the client will be compensated.

The reason we behave in that way is because we do not want employees covering up their mistakes. Employees are encouraged to own up to mistakes and we have a policy throughout the firm of no recriminations. Even though some of our mistakes are costly, we have never needed to discipline the employees involved. We know that they have probably had sleepless nights and been punished enough already. Of course if someone repeatedly makes careless mistakes, and shows no sign that they will ever improve, then clearly they are in the wrong job. Similarly if the same mistake is made persistently by different people, it gives us a clear indication that the way we are carrying out the process is what is wrong and needs to be changed.

Most large companies allow senior management and directors to pamper themselves. They buy art to adorn the corridors of the "directors' suite" and sit in ostentatious boardrooms. They have secretaries, assistants and chauffeurs who are all available for their private use. They have ever larger offices with ever more expensive furniture and designated parking spaces which are never used because the chauffeur picks them up and takes them home every night – that is if they are not flying first class round the world on the very generous leave they award themselves. While they are junketing, it means that someone who could have gainfully used their parking space is missing out. The ideal parking arrangement, in my view, is one where there are no allocated spaces and the first in get the best space and the last ones in are unlucky. This system also happens to be good for office timekeeping. (I have to admit that unfortunately we have too few spaces to use this system, but I can assure you that we shall at our next offices).

Timekeeping is an important part of business. Some modern innovations should be avoided at all cost. Flexitime, for example, is a licence for lazy employees to pretend to pack an entire week's work into two days, during which the last few hours are completely unproductive because they have already been in the office for so long. The other three days their phone is unmanned and some other sucker has to deal with their calls. My advice is: never allow flexitime – and bear in mind that the most important timekeeping is the boss's timekeeping. If the boss gets in at 10 o'clock, has three hours for lunch and leaves at 2.30 to play golf in the afternoon, you can guarantee that this is the regime all the staff will aspire to. One of the most famous rags to riches stories in British business is that of Jack Walker. It is said that Jack Walker's family couldn't afford dining chairs when he was a child and they sat on wooden boxes for their meals. Jack and his brother built up the UK's largest steel stockholder. They even had their own industrial estate and their own road leading up to it, Walker Industrial Estate on Walker Road, Blackburn. Despite having sold the business for approximately half a billion pounds, he carried on making money right up until the day he died. (The Flybe airline is something that he started).

When I worked in Blackburn in the early 1970s, I had cause to go over to a factory that the firm I worked for had in Darwen. My route passed Walker Industrial Estate and no matter how early I went to work, there was always a Rolls Royce parked either side of the front door. The offices were fully lit and you could see from the road that everyone was in. When I left and went home in the evening and drove back past the Walker head office, everyone would still be in and the Rolls Royces of the two Walker brothers would still be parked there. It is a story I often tell my managers. The moral is that if you want everyone in first thing and working a full day, you can only lead by example. One of the reasons why the Vietcong beat the Americans in the Vietnam War, it is often said, is that the Vietcong generals "enjoyed" (or perhaps more accurately endured) exactly the same conditions as their troops. They never sent their troops anywhere where they wouldn't go themselves. Whilst I am not going to moralise on the Vietnam War, it is a salutary lesson. If the boss won't get his hands dirty, you can guarantee that the foot soldiers won't either.

Making the best use of your time

A famous entrepreneur once told me the secret of a good day's work in business. First ask yourself, he said, two questions: "Which task do I least want to do today?" and "Who do I least want to speak to today?" Then first thing in the morning get the guy you don't want to speak to on the phone and deal with everything you have to talk to him about, however unpleasant it may be. Immediately afterwards do the task you least want to do. Once these unpleasant chores are out of the way, your mind will be unclogged and you can get on with your day without having to worry about them any longer. This simple piece of advice will save you a huge amount of heartache and greatly improve the effectiveness of your day's work.

Other little things can also help the smooth running of your organisation. One is to make sure that your staff are always ready to ask the question "why?" Just like the two ladies I visited as an auditor (the full story is related in the section on management consultants a few pages on), who had been doing their jobs for 20 years without one person ever looking at the information they were producing, there will be hundreds of things that are done in any firm for which there was a reason when they were first instigated, but where that reason no longer exists (see later section). Good employees will ask the question "why?" and unless someone can give them a good answer, the chances are they are right and it shouldn't be done.

Another practice that you want to try and stamp out is what I call pending file syndrome. Employees who constantly pick up and put down a file without getting to grips with it are a terrible drain on any organisation. Every time you pick up a pending file, you have to refresh your mind with what's already in there. If you had dealt with it the first time, it would have saved you days. In the same vein I have never understood why people send holding letters. You know the kind I mean. It is the one that says, "We acknowledge receipt of your letter," (normally dated at least two weeks earlier), "which is being considered and we shall be issuing you a response in due course." Nothing is designed to irritate people more. I have never understood why you can't answer the whole letter promptly the first time round. It's quicker, the client will be happier and the job is solved immediately.

A consultant I met once had been on a management course and was adamant that you should never take a call if you are already busy with something else. His argument was that you should choose when you want to speak to someone, and not be dictated by when they want to speak to you. He could not have been more wrong. If somebody takes the trouble to call you, decide whether you want to speak to the caller or not and then take the call. If you don't want to speak to them, tell them so politely and then say goodbye. Why is that the better course of action than not taking the call? Because if you don't take the call, you can be sure that the caller will phone another ten times – which means another ten interruptions. Another tip on phone calls that I have found useful is to have an excuse ready for getting callers who you know will talk forever off the line as quickly as possible. I often say "I'm just about to do something." They immediately say "Should I phone you back?" You say "No, lets do it now – but please can we be brief?" You are then ready to end the call as soon as they have finished talking, rather than having to waste time on the line discussing the weather and the cricket, or moaning about the government.

One thing we educate all our people to do is never to make things up. On our help desk, if someone doesn't know the answer to something, they are instructed to go and ask someone who does. Better still is to hand the phone to whoever knows that answer and listen in yourself. There is nothing more irritating than hearing someone say "Wait a minute. I'll go and find out." You hear a conversation in the background and eventually the person you were talking to comes back to you with an answer. What then happens of course is that you immediately ask a follow on question to which they also don't know the answer. You are then subjected to a further blank pause while they find out the answer to that one, and so on ad infinitum. Had the person who did know the answers taken the call, the conversation would be over much quicker, and the client would be happier.

How To Recruit Good Staff

When we moved to Kendal House, we had 70 people in a space which we knew would take 200. As it had taken us 15 years to grow to 70 people, we assumed that we would be OK for at least another 15 years. Unfortunately, despite being careful with how many people we employ, we grew to 650 and occupied five separate buildings by the spring of 2008. What we found as we progressed was that we were constantly competing for people against the overpaid and inefficient public sector. Recruitment became more and more difficult. Bristol may be the administrative centre for the whole of the South West, but unfortunately ours is a unique business that isn't listed in the careers manual at universities. Although a few people who were interested in investment management sought us out, we had very few investment management jobs to offer. Accounting staff were easier to recruit because lots of people go into accountancy, but the rest of the business was not so lucky.

We also had a logistical problem in that 60% of our business is normally done in the first four months of the year. Fortunately we discovered that many graduates who had taken obscure degrees were finding it difficult to find jobs in the areas in which they had studied. So we put an advertisement in the local paper seeking unemployed graduates for temporary assignments that could lead to fulltime employment. We would take on significant numbers in the first three months of the year, some to answer the telephones on our help desk, others to process applications in our administration department and some to fulfil client requests for brochures, leaflets etc. None of them seemed to mind doing this fairly menial work, because it was a temporary job and they were earning a few quid whilst looking for the job that they really wanted. A good number of the graduates who came on a temporary assignment, not thinking they ever wanted to work in our industry, found they loved our business and remain with us today. Many of them have progressed to senior positions in our business and some indeed are directors on our executive board.

One year things became so busy that we didn't even have time to interview anyone. We would simply offer ten graduates a temporary job and ask them to turn up for work. We told them the rate we would pay and paid them all their first day's wage. When we had worked out which ones were going to be useful, and which weren't, we told the ones we didn't want not to come back the following day. I have not yet thought of any better way of recruiting. What I am keen on is cutting out employment agencies. I still do not know the purpose of employment agencies. From what I see of them, they do little more than act as a post box. They advertise that they can find jobs for people and then pass on their names and addresses to employers without doing anything in the way of vetting. It means you are paying a fee to someone who has done no more than give you a few people to interview. I believe that most firms should advertise directly and that potential employees should choose the firms that only advertise directly. Why? It's a symbiotic arrangement. Employers know that people who are prepared to look through situation vacant columns in the newspapers are likely to be more hardworking and conscientious than those who simply wait for agencies to send them potential employers. Employees should also be able to work out that employers who take the trouble to do the job of recruiting themselves are likely to be better employers.

I suspect there are a few recruitment specialists who do the job properly. Any one of them reading this section will do so with great indignation. However they would appear to be so few and far between that up to now I have only met one. I came across three young chaps who really did work hard both for the employer and the potential employees. They specialise in jobs in the City of London for graduates and go to the trouble of telling the graduates all the various jobs that are available and even do psychometric testing to establish which jobs suit which graduates. This means that the graduate gets the right job and the employer gets the right graduate. I was so impressed not only with the enthusiasm of their team but with their professionalism and attention to detail that I was delighted to invest in the business. They are called Benedix and specialise in jobs in the City of London for graduates. They go to great lengths to identify the ideal role for their candidates, while providing further intensive training and consultancy to ensure that their candidates are of the highest standard and ready to go from day one.

The best advice I would give to people about recruitment is "always pick the best". I recently went through all the people who had originally come to us as temporary employees. One now runs my help desk, one is in charge of training, one is in charge of Vantage administration, one is a director, one is the senior marketing manager, one is in charge of administration on corporate pensions, two work in our investment management team, two are very senior in compliance – I could go on. Many have moved to completely different parts of the firm. Some work in systems, some work on the internet, and so on.

We would not have the brilliant head of compliance we do if we had not learnt this lesson many times. The Financial Services and Markets Act, the legislation that lays down the way that financial services in the UK are regulated, is one of the most draconian pieces of regulation in the country. Whereas originally our chief accountant of many years ago had been in charge of compliance, eventually it all became too much for him and he went out to advertise for help. He came to me after his recruitment process and said: "Peter, one of the applicants is absolutely perfect for us. She is a young lady who I think will be fine and do the job. The other applicant is really too good for us. I think at this stage of our development we don't want anyone quite as good as him." Fortunately I insisted on only seeing the young man who was meant to be too good for us. It was astonishing how much he knew about the industry, even though he was fresh out of university. We employed him and he later learned that he had gained a first class honours degree. I will still back him today as the best compliance officer in the entire country (and for any competitor or major financial institution who is reading this book, I would add: beware, he loves our culture too).

Dealing with customers

My experience is that many firms are terrible at dealing with correspondence. Whenever I have needed to complain, there is usually more than one thing with which I am not satisfied. More often than not an answer comes back, but the most important complaint remains unanswered. We try to educate everyone in the firm to make a point of finding out what a client's main complaint is. Quite often people don't put the main point first. They may put their grievances in chronological order, or start with something minor before hitting you with their real grievance. Our policy is to try and answer the main complaint first, and if we have made a mistake, to admit it straightaway. There is nothing better then telling a client that you have made a mistake. It immediately puts them on your side. However if no mistake has been made, you should never apologise.

Many businesses run away from trouble. When financial markets are volatile (the industry's euphemism for falling), many firms simply disappear from view. Their clients call, but the principals are nowhere to be found. Our policy, in contrast, is to remain visible at all times. We are always prepared to take calls and, when necessary, give forthright answers, however unpalatable they may seem at the time. Clients never forget that you were there to hold their hand in hours of need. The important thing to remember is that where there is trouble, there is always business to be done. When markets are bad, our experience is that clients who had previously been happy to paddle their own canoes greet our Financial Practitioners with open arms. Having someone to share their worries, and if necessary tell them what to do, even if the advice is simply "do nothing" is a great source of comfort. I remember sadly the case of one lady who telephoned us one day and insisted on selling all her investments, on the strength of having read in a couple of Sunday newspapers that the end of the world was nigh. It was a shame because no sooner had she sold than the market bounced up again. It was nothing more than panic. Investors should remember that all the bad news they are reading in their newspapers, or hearing about on the television, is already in the price of their investments. Investments always discount all the bad news in the market place. When the news is widely known, it is always too late to sell.

The adage that where there is trouble, there is business is truer than most people realise. A good example occurred when I worked for Burroughs Machines (now Unisys) in sales. Although I had qualified as a chartered accountant, I wasn't too proud to have a go at sales. My range included Visi-Record machines, which were mundane bits of kit that carried out a range of basic accounting functions. As it happened, we had an excellent builders merchant package and while making a call to a potential customer, I noticed that there was a builders merchants next door. I had about 20 minutes to spare between the end of my first appointment and the next. Opportunistically I knocked on the door and made what is known in the sales business as a "cold call". I went to reception and presented my card. The receptionist said "Oh, Mr Brocklehurst handles your sort of people." I thought it sounded ominous, but she was already calling Mr Brocklehurst on the internal phone. I was immediately summoned to his office. As I went through the door, a Burroughs adding machine nearly hit me as it came flying across the room. I won't repeat Mr Brocklehurst's language exactly, but the gist of it was that he wasn't terribly happy with his adding machine, which it seemed had never worked particularly well.

The following day I went back with a new device that we were marketing at the time, a product called an electronic calculator. In those days they cost about £250 and did slightly less than the equivalent machine you can buy for a fiver today. When I saw the receptionist, I told her that I had a small present for Mr Brocklehurst. When I got into his office, I placed the calculator on his desk, apologising for the fact that his complaints had clearly not been handled well before. I rang him about a week later to ask him what he thought of the calculator. It turned out that he was delighted. Being an accountant, and careful with the pennies, he had always been too mean to buy one before. Three months later I sold them £42,000-worth of computer equipment. All you need to do to pick up the business that goes with trouble is handle it correctly.

The only other rule I have about handling complaints is one that I learnt from a maître d' of a restaurant. He said to me once that no matter how good your chef or your waiters are, something will always go wrong from time to time. People will get the wrong meal, things will be undercooked, things will be overcooked, the meal will be cold, etc etc. The worst thing you can do in these cases is make an offer to the person who is complaining. "Never, ever tell the customer what you are going to do" was the maître d's advice. Why? Because whatever you come up with will inevitably be deemed insufficient. The best thing to do is ask the person who is complaining what they would like to see the establishment do to make them happy. The customer will almost invariably ask for something less than you were prepared to suggest yourself. What is more, the way they respond will tell you immediately whether they are reasonable or unreasonable. If they are reasonable, and you treat them well, the odds are that they will come back again later. On the rare occasions that you are facing someone who is completely unreasonable, the best advice is simply to ask them to take their business elsewhere. They will be nothing but trouble. Encourage them to be a trouble to your competitors.

Keeping Costs Down

When you have been in business for 25 years and pushed out the boundaries in what was previously nothing more than a cottage industry, you are going to ruffle a few feathers. The retail part of the investment business does not create many sustainable businesses, and I think I know the reason for it. The problem is that the rewards for selling products for commissions can be so lucrative that it becomes a drug: there is little incentive to build a long-term business. With so much upfront income to live off, few firms pay enough attention to controlling costs. The owners or directors take money out of their businesses to support champagne lifestyles which their businesses are frankly unable to support. There is little doubt that, had we employed such a philosophy, we would be a far smaller business than we are today, and we might well not even exist at all.

It took something like £50 million to create the back office systems and platform that we call Vantage, an investment that virtually no other broker in the UK could contemplate. We would not have been able to spend that amount of money ourselves had we not kept such tight control over our spending. Even today the monthly invoice run is checked through by both Stephen and myself. Some people might call that petty, but it means that every manager who makes purchases on behalf of the firm knows that they may get a query about anything that looks unnecessary or expensive. Containing costs has been heat-sealed into the culture of Hargreaves Lansdown from the beginning. In our early days when we saw an envelope come in with stamps that had not been franked, we would, if we were quiet, steam the stamps off and reuse them. Any paper that is spoiled on one side we still encourage people to reuse as scrap paper, provided that there is nothing confidential on the front.

Our frugality is nothing however compared to a businessman that I once met who had a crane hire business in Reading. He operated out of a very old battered caravan on a plot of land that he had acquired very cheaply from British Rail in the 1970s. British Rail had offered to fence it off for him, but he'd preferred to do the job himself. I suspect he may have been rather generous with where he placed his posts! I got along with him well from the start. It was remarkable how many of the business ideas he used were no different from ours. When I asked him whether he had steamed stamps off envelopes when he started out, as we did, he replied "Don't be stupid, we still do it!" He told me a hilarious story of how he would go out in his suit in the morning to survey a job and then turn up in his overalls with his crane in the afternoon to do the actual work. In crane hire, it seems, however big or small the job, everyone always charges for a full day's work. My friend would often invent an excuse ("the traffic" etc) to turn up at the crack of dawn on jobs. Some days he could use his crane three times and get three full days pay for it.

My crane hire friend had an instinctive feel for PR opportunities. One day he'd read somewhere that a famous escapologist was going to escape from a sack suspended from a chain. When he rang up the promoters and asked how they were going to organise the stunt, they said they were going to hire a crane. He told them he was in crane hire and offered to do the job for free. What he didn't tell them was that he had placed the name of his firm and his telephone number in letters two foot high on the boom of his crane. In effect his business had a free 20-minute advertisement on television. I have no idea what that was worth, but it must have paid for his time many times over. It just shows that some people will always make money no matter what business they are in.

We have been lucky that, apart from a couple of brief interludes, Hargreaves Lansdown has always grown consistently on every measure – turnover, profit, space and personnel. But we have never stopped trying to work out how we can do things better. Indeed we often say that we turn the business on its head at least once every two years. I remember my father-in-law walking into the office in the late 1980s and saying, "Too many staff." He was absolutely right. We were throwing people at jobs, rather than perfecting our systems and sitting down to work out how to do things more efficiently. We have always been big spenders on technology, but our systems people work on the same basis as our marketing people. My instruction to the marketing director is always the same,

"Get me £10 million-worth of advertising for half a million pounds." In the case of systems, we want £40 million of systems for £2 million. Sometimes, as when we bought cheap PCs, we find that we have made a false economy, but in general we have found that there is good value to be had by those who go out and look for it. Even with suppliers that we have used for ten years, we always get an alternative quote. Although we are faithful to those that have served us well, and they would have to do something really bad before we ditched them, we do constantly check that they are still providing the same value that they offered us when they won our account.

The costs of something as mundane as our newsletter are also kept under constant review. In the early days we used to print out the text and paste it up ourselves. Later we used a firm in Bristol, which typeset it for us. Their trained designers made it look much more professional. Although it was their business, they sadly didn't move with the times. I remember telling the managing director for months how unhappy we were with the turnaround time of the newsletter. Sometimes it took as long as two weeks, which on occasions meant that the information looked very dated by the time our clients read it. He never offered any suggestions for improving the turnaround time. One day one of his competitors, who had been courting us for some time, turned up in my office and said we could halve the turnaround time by switching to his firm. The clincher was that it would also be substantially cheaper. When I rang the firm we had used for years to ask them one last time whether they could turn it round more quickly and improve the price, I was told it was impossible – so we moved. Within a week the old firm had come back to us with a better turnaround and price. By then it was too late. Why couldn't they do it before?

The same thing happened with another huge task that we wrestled with every time that we sent out a newsletter, which was stuffing the envelopes. In the early days everybody in the office stopped to stuff the envelopes by hand. No one was spared. Stephen, Theresa and I all mucked in with everyone else. We even had competitions to determine who could stuff the most. Eventually we brought in some temporary staff to do the job, but they became complacent and lazy. When I went into the room that they used one day, I don't think that more than 10% of them were working. Those that were working were working at snail's pace. Having got rid of them, we later used an agency that was based, surprisingly, in deepest Devon. Theirs was a cottage industry that involved delivering the packs to ladies all over Dartmoor. We pictured them happily stuffing our envelopes with our newsletter whilst watching Coronation Street. Of course we don't really know what happened, but that's what we assumed.

In time they too became complacent and didn't move into the machine age. When the circulation of the newsletter topped 100,000, the only way to get them out quickly and efficiently was with machines. This presented huge logistical problems, as until that time all our pieces of literature came from different sources. For example the unit trust groups provided the leaflets while the envelopes came from somewhere else, and so on. Although our instructions on size, and how they had to be packed and folded, were always very specific, we never got them exactly as we wanted them. Time and again our contract packer had to charge us surcharges. Deliveries were late, purely because we were not in control of the pack.

Eventually we decided we had to take the radical step of producing all our own literature, sourcing our own envelopes, using agencies to laser print our letters, and controlling the printing and fulfilment of the job ourselves. Today everything that we produce we produce ourselves. We design our own application forms to ensure that they are easy to complete and process. Everything is under our control and the only people we can blame when anything goes wrong are ourselves. We like to claim that *The Investment Times*, our current publication, has the largest readership of any investment publication in Europe. We have the capacity to send out two million copies at a time, as well as the addresses of two million households where we could send it (and these are not bought names – you only get on our list if you ask to be added to it).

Over the years as our staff have increased in numbers, we have had to increase the space where they work. For ten years we were in Embassy House. Having started with 6000 square feet, we fortunately managed to acquire 2000 more, thanks to the Indian gentleman. When the business below us went through a lean time, we managed to hive off a small piece of their offices and used this, initially, for stuffing envelopes. Later we moved our insurance broking subsidiary into that space. When eventually we grew out of Embassy House, I had been looking for some time to acquire a building plot and construct our own offices. It was my first encounter with property developers. I am told that developers are generally impossible to deal with, exceedingly greedy and not particularly nice people to boot. Certainly the ones that I have encountered filled that bill. We acquired about five eighths of a building plot, with a developer unfortunately having the other portion. Getting them out was the nearest thing I have come to homicide in my life.

There was an interesting series on television 20 years ago featuring the former chief executive of ICI, John Harvey-Jones. He was famous for his exceedingly bad taste in ties. His garish neckwear was his trademark. The idea of the programme was that he would go into various companies that needed "a company doctor" and offer advice. One of the companies was Morgan Cars, which at the time had a seven-year waiting list for its individually hand-built sports cars, but still couldn't make a profit. The advice that Harvey-Jones gave was hardly rocket science. With an order book of seven years, he suggested that perhaps Morgan could put their prices up. It was a mystery to me why Morgan hadn't come up with the solution themselves. It wasn't as if everybody on the waiting list intended to take possession of their cars. What happened was that when people learnt that their car was about to be built, they would simply sell their place on the list to someone else for a couple of thousand pounds and make an instant profit. Morgan could easily have made that profit themselves. However there was one thing that John Harvey-Jones did say which I disagreed with. He said it was never worth saving the odd penny on buying cheaper pencils or cheaper pens for the staff because all it did, to use his words, was "irritate the hell out of everyone".

He was wrong. Once you allow people to be lax over price vigilance, you open the floodgates. It goes like this:

- Week one: "It's only an extra pound";
- Week two: "It's only an extra fiver";
- Week three: "It's only an extra 50 quid";
- Week four: "It's only an extra hundred quid";
- Week five: "It's only an extra thousand pounds".

And so on and so forth. Before you know where you are, everything is out of control.

One of the few good decisions made by the managing director of the brewery I castigate elsewhere in this book concerned costs. In the 1970s many industries went through tough times. The brewery I worked for was no exception in having to economise. For example they took to driving more modest cars (even though they didn't go so far as to sack their chauffeurs!). One of the cost-saving ideas they came up with was switching off the lights in the lavatories. The chief engineer pointed out the inconvenient fact that as the lights were fluorescent, switching them on and off would actually cost more than leaving them on all day. The laws of physics dictate that it costs more to turn on a fluorescent light than to run it for several hours. After considering the matter the managing director said "We should still turn them off." Why was that a good decision? Because it showed that the commitment to save money ran all the way through the firm. Most people wouldn't know that switching the lights off wouldn't save any money and so the action made clear to everybody in the firm that there was an economy drive going on.

Management Consultants – A Waste Of Time?

One of the most regular unsolicited calls anyone in business is likely to receive is from people who claim they can improve the efficiency and profitability of the business. Many go by the fancy name of management consultants and are to be avoided at all cost. I can give you many reasons. The first is that if you do invite them in, they will frighten everybody in the firm to death. People always assume that the only reason management consultants are coming in is to suggest downsizing. The reality however is the opposite. In the unlikely event that management consultants achieve anything, it is likely to involve you in more, not fewer staff. The reason I say that it is unlikely anything will happen is because most people who use consultants don't know how to deal with them. What management consultants like doing is coming in with a clipboard, talking to everyone in the firm, extracting all your own people's best ideas and putting them into a long report as if the ideas were their own. In a good firm all the good ideas will already have been implemented. In a bad firm, most of the staff will spend their time wondering why they are being asked to do their jobs in a way that is clearly either crazy or unnecessary. I shall never forget visiting a depot of a company I worked for many years ago. This company used lorries to make deliveries. In the delivery manager's office, two ladies religiously recorded the mileage and loads of every single lorry for every single day. As I was an internal auditor at the time, we checked some of the sheets and they were perfect. We couldn't find any mistakes whatsoever. Tick – job done. Well no!

Then I asked the two ladies what happened to the sheets when they had completed them. One of the two duplicated copies, it turned out, was filed in a filing cabinet near where they sat. That was the copy that I had checked. The other one went to the customer delivery manager. I went in and asked him where the customer delivery sheets were kept. He said he didn't know and even when I had showed him an example, he still didn't know. When I showed it to his secretary however, she said "Oh yes. We file them in a filing cabinet in the customer delivery manager's office." And there they were, all neatly filed. When I asked the customer delivery manager what he did with them, he didn't even know they existed. When I asked his secretary what she did with them, she said "I just file them." When I went back to the two ladies who had meticulously prepared the sheets and asked them what they did with them, they said "We just file them." I then asked, "Does anyone ever look at any of them?", to which they replied, "Not our copies." Two years after writing my report, when I went back again, the two ladies were still doing a fantastic job of completing customer delivery records that were completely unnecessary. The local management hadn't "got round to" re-employing them. I doubt that management consultants would find them.

So what do management consultants do? Although they purport to be business experts, very few of them have ever actually run a business. Some are chartered accountants, some are straight out of university, some have been to business school and some have MBAs. An MBA, or Master of Business Administration, is a qualification that is supposed to qualify people to run the biggest corporations in the world. I have only come across a few. In my experience they talk in a form of management speak that no one understands, have no idea how to handle people and invariably if you put one in charge of a department, everyone else immediately wants to leave. Essentially what consultants do is present you with a report which includes all the best ideas that they have gleaned from your staff and charge you a huge amount of money for it. The person who requisitioned the report never reads it and if he does rarely does anything about it. It is no surprise to discover that 60% of all management consultant billing in the UK is to our wonderful public sector. A further 20% of management consultant billing is to companies that were previously State-owned and are now "privatised".

The public sector has a very clever way of using management consultants. When they are criticised by the government or the media or the general public, their answer is always to employ consultants. Management consultants of course take the brief gleefully and produce a report which incorporates all the best ideas of the people working at grass roots levels. These are the people who probably should be running the public sector, rather than the idiots at the top – in any cesspit the biggest lumps always rise to the top. When they get this wonderful report, what do they do with it? Because they have spent so much money on the report, they rarely have any money left to do anything. A couple of years later, they will requisition the same report again, which will once more never be implemented.

If you want a cushy number which massively overpays, perhaps there is something to be said for becoming a management consultant. As a manager, if you genuinely think that you need help in your business, then the thing to do is to ask your staff what is going wrong. They will always give you some great ideas. What you should use management consultants for are things that can be implemented better from outside the firm rather than in-house. However, my experience is that if you ask management consultants to go and sort something out, they will run a mile. Doing work is the last thing that management consultants want to do. All they want to do is talk, report and then skedaddle. We have never employed management consultants in Hargreaves Lansdown, and the first person who suggests we do will probably be asked where they might like to work next.

Making the Most of Your Assets

What follows is a true story, although I have changed the name of the individual concerned. It is an example of how an enterprising businessman makes the most of his assets. This businessman, whom I shall call Jack Thatcher, had an office which overlooked a private car park in (let's say) Exeter. Over the years he came to realise how badly he wanted to own the car park, if only because that way he would have a guaranteed parking space for himself. One day the car park, which had 25 spaces, came up for sale. The price was exorbitant, but unlike the frugal person he was Jack went ahead and bought it anyway. The drivers who used the car park paid an annual rental to use it; and as the new owner, Jack naturally had to honour those deals. However he was not happy about paying over the odds for his parking lot and so he set about making his latest investment produce a much higher return. Two weeks after completing the deal, he informed all the people who were renting a parking space that he was going to close the car park over the weekend, in order to resurface it and make the interior more agreeable. By then he had measured out the car park very thoroughly. Next he announced that he was changing the practice of allocating individual parking spaces. What he could see was that by making the individual spaces slightly narrower, he could increase the capacity of the car park from 25 to 30 cars. He arranged for the car park to be repainted, with nice new white lines marking out the new, tighter spaces. Because nobody had ever counted the spaces before, nobody realised what had happened. They may have found it a little bit more of a squeeze to fit their cars into the spaces, but there were no complaints. Jack's next step was to place an advertisement in the newspaper offering parking spaces in Exeter town centre. When anyone contacted him to show an interest, he always said that the spaces had by now all gone, but that he would get back in touch if anything changed. During the conversation he would make sure he found out what sort of car the caller had and take their telephone number. If they had a large car, he would decline to phone them back. If they had a small car however, he would call back a couple of days later and say that miraculously a place had now become spare.

Having noticed over the years that the car park was never full, Jack was soon able to sell five more slots than there were spaces. After a month he realised that the car park was still never full, so he sold another five spaces (naturally, only to owners of small cars). At the last count, his customer tally had risen to 45. If the car park does ever fill up, leaving drivers without a space, he always has a perfect excuse to hand. Sometimes moonlighters get the blame. He has also invested in a small car of his own, which he parks in a tiny space next to the entrance. If anyone gets really irate at being blocked in, he gives them the car keys and lets them take his car. A brilliant example of how to maximise your assets.

The Ingredients of Business Success

A Good Manager

Effective management of people is a rare and undervalued skill in industry. In the whole of Hargreaves Lansdown, there are probably no more than a dozen who are exceptional in this respect. The key is being able to delegate, to give someone a job and then to let them get on with it. However delegation itself needs to be just that and not what I call abdication of responsibility. That happens when someone gives somebody a job without knowing whether they can do it or not and simply assumes, without ever checking, that they are doing it. If after six months they go back and find that the person wasn't doing the job properly, it may be because they didn't have the talent, but most likely it is because they were never shown properly what to do. The manager then castigates them for getting it wrong. It is not the employee's fault, but the manager's for not checking regularly that they understood what they were doing and were in fact doing it. The manager has abdicated rather than delegated.

At the other end of the spectrum is a manager who can't delegate and is constantly on top of the employee picking fault, taking it back off them and doing it and invariably blowing hot and cold. This type of manager is your friend one day and intolerable and obnoxious the next. As a result the employee doesn't know where he or she stands. Where do I stand in this spectrum? I suspect I am not the best delegator. The one thing I can delegate easily are jobs that I hate doing. Unfortunately I find it very difficult to delegate something which I think I am good at. What I am good at, however, I think, is devoting time to people. No CEO can afford to believe that his time is more important than that of anyone else's. I will normally drop what I am doing, no matter how important, if I get a cry for help from a member of my staff. If someone comes to me and needs something sorting out, or a decision made, I will stop to sort it out for them. Faced with a desk that is covered in paper demanding to be dealt with, it is all too easy to deal with everything in the order in which it appears. I don't think the head of an organisation can afford to work like that. You have to prioritise. If something needs immediate attention, it should never go to the bottom of the pile. It should be done immediately.

If you want a perfect example of what not to look for in a boss, I can recommend the film *The Devil Wears Prada*, in which Merryl Streep played an absolute dragon of a boss, called Miranda Priestly. She is brilliant in the part and epitomises the worst CEO you can imagine. She has the entire firm running around for her, carrying out trivial tasks, most of them unrelated to work. Some are simply impossible. It is a brilliant portrayal of a boss who is convinced that she is more important than the rest of the firm put together. The only way she could get away with behaving so badly is presumably because the fashion industry pays well and is one in which so many people are desperate to work. In the end, of course, even high salaries start to wear thin if the boss is a tyrant and staff decide they can take no more of it. I can think of at least one business in our industry where a bullying leader only hangs on to his people with the lure of money. He thinks he is always right, listens to no other opinion, makes his workforce unhappy and works them ridiculous hours. While he has made an awful lot of money, I doubt he has made many friends.

As a boss you must never forget that your staff are the most important part of your business. You have to give them your time, to praise them when they do well and to refrain from castigating them when they make mistakes, because they will already be more upset than anyone else. In my experience remuneration is less important than creating the right atmosphere in the office, improving work conditions and making sure there is praise for a job well done. The best people rarely leave for more money. They normally leave because they are unhappy.

In the final analysis, there is more to business than marketing, advertising, sales and so on. Most businesses that only have selling skills tend to fail. They have always said of stockbrokers that none ever went bust because of their inability to shift stock. It was never the selling that proved fatal. Stockbrokers invariably get in trouble because of their poor back office procedures, meaning their ability to handle transactions of clients' cash. In any given year we handle between £4 and £5 billion of clients' money. That means we have to have first class systems and first class staff, including 10 fully qualified accountants. We have invested massively over the years to enable us to handle huge numbers of transactions. All those accounts have to be reconciled. We have to prove that the money coming in equals the amount that we have added to our clients' accounts. Similarly we have to be able to reconcile all the accounts to show that the money going out equals the amount that has left all those accounts.

When running a successful business it is all too easy to allow managers just to recruit, recruit, recruit. Throwing people at a problem is only a standby measure. You cannot carry on doing that because eventually your costs will run out of control and you will get to the stage where no matter how many people you employ, they still can't handle it. Without first class systems and strict cost control you are going to be in trouble. If you want to run a great business, I think you have to tend to every facet of it. You have to get the staffing right, you have to get your costs right, you have to get your marketing and advertising right, you have to get your accounting right, but most important of all you must never pay too much for anything. When Jack Cohen started Tesco, he worked out that he could buy tea very cheaply, repackage it and sell it much cheaper than anywhere else. That was how Tesco got going. You can always tell when you are dealing with a great business, as they will try to negotiate you into the ground. We did once try to do a deal with a supermarket (not Tesco) to provide them with a financial service. In the end we had to walk away because we felt they would never rest until we were left with no profit from the transaction. They wanted us to do all the work and for them to take all the profit. It is often said that in business if you can buy it right, you can sell it right. The history of many successful businesses, including Hargreaves Lansdown, bears that out.

Chapter 11

Making Sense of Investment

Investment Success and Wealth

After almost 30 years in the investment industry, and having been interested in money since I was 11-years-old, people naturally assume that I am some kind of expert on the stock market. However, while I have extensive experience in investment planning and know almost every kind of investment product around, I don't regard myself as an expert on individual stocks and shares. What I do know about is the way that the industry works. That knowledge is one reason why I invest the majority of my own money in collective investment products (specifically unit trusts) and use my knowledge of the industry to select the professionals who I believe will make the most of my investments. Most of the senior people in Hargreaves Lansdown also invest nearly all their capital in unit trusts. Although I have one or two major holdings of shares in individual companies for historic reasons, it is my belief that the best way for the majority of the British investing public to invest is through unit trusts. In 30 years in the industry I have never changed my mind about that.

My view is that investors should concentrate on only three areas when choosing investments: deposits, fixed interest and equities. Unless you know what you are doing and have a lot of experience, there is no reason to venture away from these three types of investment. One of the most important things in choosing your own investment portfolio is determining how long it will be invested for. The longer you have as an investment horizon, the greater the amount you should have in equities and the less you should have in fixed interest. The amount you keep on deposit is a matter of taste, but it should certainly be enough to cover your day-to-day needs and any purchases that are on the immediate horizon.

As for property, if you don't own your own home, you might consider a small exposure to a property fund, but investors should not forget that the physical fabric of any property does depreciate from year-to-year, and the only way a property will appreciate in the long term is if the rental income which it produces can be increased. When I started writing this book, there was a glut of commercial property created by the crazy prices that people were willing to pay. A glut of property will always restrict landlords' ability to increase rental incomes, so it was clear to me that the short-term outlook for property was terrible. The problem with property is that it is not easily realisable. If you want to sell a unit trust, a share or a fixed interest instrument, you can pick up the phone and sell it. A property by contrast can take many months and sometimes years to realise. If investors ever become nervous about property, the value of property funds can fall very quickly. The fund managers then struggle to sell their properties into a falling market. In these circumstances their only practical response is to restrict withdrawals by imposing penalties on those who try to cash in. Investors therefore find themselves locked into a fund that is going down in value with no firm idea when they are likely to receive settlement. All this is exactly what started happening in 2007.

I have no argument that property had provided excellent returns for investors over the prior ten years and may one day continue to do so. However property is best regarded as a long-term investment. Don't have it in your portfolio unless you are comfortable with not needing that part of your capital again for many years. Most people have all the exposure to property that they need in the shape of their own home. I would suggest that 10% of an investment portfolio is a maximum sensible exposure to property. We recommended one property fund many years ago. Fortunately few clients invested, but it still proved to be a disaster. That experience has coloured my attitude to the sector ever since. Today we only offer property funds to clients who have already decided they want to buy. We research them and have opinions on them but are loathe to recommend them ourselves. When our financial practitioners discuss property funds with clients, they are informed to advocate caution.

My Investment Philosophy

Over the past 30 years my investment philosophy has changed very little. The initial sensible ideas that Stephen and I absorbed when we started work with Bill Sandham all those years ago, before he went awry, still guide what we do today. It starts with the notion that most investors are better off investing through funds than by buying individual stocks and shares. Although we have successfully managed portfolios of stocks and shares in the past, picking investment funds is what we do best and what we now therefore concentrate on. For 30 years we have remained committed to the view that the best way for the average investor to invest is through unit trusts and OEICs, as many of them are now called. (OEICs, pronounced "oiks", are essentially identical to unit trusts, except for their pricing and legal structure. They were introduced in the 1990s in the belief that they were simpler for investors to understand and easier to administer). There are many good reasons – simplicity, convenience, flexibility – why unit trusts and OEICs remain so popular. For many investment companies, unit trusts are their shop window, being the most visible and transparent example of what their investment teams can do. Having a range of top performing funds is the easiest way for good investment houses to show off their capabilities. While unit trusts are designed for the retail market, many fund management groups use them as credentials when pitching for the chance to manage money for pension funds and other professional clients.

I like to say to investors: "Is it likely that a local stockbroker with virtually no research can manage your money better than a leading investment manager who does nothing else all day and can draw on the most expensive research available?" The answer is obviously no. Equity income unit trusts, in particular, have an unparalleled track record at creating an investment income in retirement. Stephen Lansdown and I have been faithful exponents of their merits from the start, and never had cause to regret the fact. The dividends from income unit trusts can be safely spent in your retirement in the knowledge that next year's dividends are likely to increase often enough to match inflation. Over time the underlying value of the investment should also improve. Once you have secured enough income from your investment portfolio to meet your immediate needs, only then should you start to consider growth funds, where there is a bewilderingly large choice of candidates. The question of how to pick the best of these funds is one that we have – from necessity – spent most of our working lives studying and thinking about.

Why are equity income unit trusts such a favourite of ours? To understand that, you need to look at what equity income unit trusts do, which is invest in the shares of companies which pay dividends. The reason why this is such a good way to invest goes like this. All companies are in business to make profits and to grow those profits year-by-year. This means that a well run company should pay progressively better dividends over time. Obviously there will be periods of poor trading when dividends might not rise. In exceptional cases, when companies get into severe difficulties, dividends are sometimes cut. More often than not this leads to the departure of whoever is running the business at the time. Cutting the dividend is not something that boards of companies do lightly; and they will typically make great efforts never to have to take such a drastic step.

In general, therefore, it is natural to expect that good companies will be able to increase their dividends from year-to-year. It would not be an unreasonable strategy simply to buy shares in all the well-run companies that pay dividends. As companies go through economic cycles and the quality of management varies from period to period, you clearly stand to do better by applying specialist expertise in choosing which companies are most likely to increase their dividends and therefore see their share prices rise. This in effect is what the managers of equity income funds spend their time doing. An equity income unit trust exists to provide investors with a diversified selection of the best dividend-paying shares in the country.

There is an added bonus too that comes from making the dividend the key criterion in selecting which shares to own. This is that over time this approach often produces higher overall returns than picking shares which have what on the face of it look like superior growth prospects. The discipline involved in picking shares with the best dividends often also helps to find the shares that produce higher capital gains in the longer term. All shares go in and out of vogue. A first class income fund manager is constantly on the lookout for companies where the share price is depressed (and the corresponding rate of dividends is therefore high). They need to be patient and may need to hold a share for a long time while they wait for the rest of the market to recognise that the share price is too low. When it does eventually happen, the gains can be substantial. As the shares rise in price, the dividend as a percentage of the share price will start to fall, prompting the equity income fund managers to sell the share in favour of something that is now cheaper. By focusing on the dividend, income fund managers are subject to a built-in discipline that virtually forces them to buy what is cheap and sell what is expensive.

Historical experience and academic research both support the view that a dividend-based investment approach is likely to produce superior returns in the long run. In many periods, as well as offering rising dividend income, income unit trusts also produce better capital performance than funds which are invested purely for capital growth. That in turn means that equity income funds can be valuable investments not just for those, such as people in retirement, who need income, but other investors as well. Those who don't need an income immediately always have the option to "roll up" (that is, reinvest) the income into their funds and thereby increase the capital performance whilst they don't need the income, and revert to taking the dividends when they do. It has always been our belief that no investment portfolio is complete without at least some income unit trusts in it.

It is easier to say what makes an unsuccessful investor than it is to define what makes a successful one. The most unsuccessful investors in my experience are the ones who try to time the markets. In other words they aim to move their money in and out of the market at just the right time – in when markets are cheap, and out when they are expensive. It sounds simple, but there is also a simple reason why it is so difficult to pull off. In practice nobody knows when the market is too low or too high; that is something you only find out with the benefit of hindsight. I have known investors who have been waiting for the market to hit its low point for the best part of 20 years. Whenever the market has gone down substantially, they have always been convinced it would go down further. When it starts to climb again, they have thought it was a false dawn and that the market would sink again. A few months later they realise they have missed it, repeat the process and miss it again. Such behaviour is understandable, but it is not the way to increase your wealth. It is also a great argument for regular savings. Anyone who has saved regularly throughout their lives and puts a proportion of their savings each year into the stock market is likely to enjoy excellent investment results. Sometimes they will buy at the market peaks, but for most of the time they will be investing at more opportune moments, and the results over time will almost invariably be good.

As I have already mentioned, another mistake to which many investors are prone is chasing past performance, forgetting that what matters is the future, not the past. It seems impossible to stop investors every January from buying whatever investment has given the best returns in the previous 12 months. The practice is as old as the hills, and foolhardy in the extreme. I am thankful today that the newspapers make less of a song and dance than they once did about which investment was last year's top performer. It was unhelpful information that merely tempted investors to the wrong thing. While it is a mistake to pick the best performing sector of the past year, it does not follow however that you will automatically do better by picking the year's worst performing sector either. In fact you should never pick a sector purely because it has underperformed the rest of the market. To take one example, commodities were the worst performing sector in world stock markets for more than a decade, starting in the mid 1980s. That changed when India and China led the developing world on a mad dash for economic growth. But if you had decided to bet on commodities solely on the basis of their earlier underperformance, it would have been easy to take the plunge far too soon.

Our many years of experience and involvement with marketing investments helps us to avoid such mistakes, though the temptation to promote the easy sell is one that all investment advisers face. We have seen thousands of investments that seemed to be dream investments from a marketing perspective, by which I mean that we could have sold huge quantities of them, had we wished. If you are running a long-term investment business however, you have to stand back and say "it may be saleable, but is it going to be good for the client?" It would be stupid to deny that we have not had a 100% record in always finding great investments. We trust that our experience, research and due diligence work will help us to avoid poor ones in the future. Nobody will ever have a 100% track record of success in this business. The research team we have developed and trained over the years know, however, that our priority is always to find the investments that are going to perform best in the future, not the ones that we will find easiest to sell. The analytical methods we have developed over the years are invaluable in helping us sort the wheat from the chaff. Knowing that an investment is good on the basis of analysis and experience is not itself enough. We have long since discovered that even the best ideas won't always capture the imagination of investors.

Our problem is that it can be very difficult to persuade clients to take an interest in the things we like. Sometimes they are simply too close to their home market. If they think they know that something is wrong with the UK economy, for example, they will happily rush off to seek opportunities in markets which seem more exciting, regardless of the fact that they know much less about them. We have seen countless occasions when investors have piled into overseas markets, especially in the Far East, only to see their investments plunge later. There have been times when European stock markets have fallen to bargain basement levels, yet because the news is dominated by headlines about unemployment, riots, bureaucratic corruption and industrial action, investors have turned up their noses at these phenomenal opportunities. A little knowledge, or a cursory reading of the newspapers, can be dangerous when it comes to picking stocks or markets in which to invest.

It is often said that a stock market climbs a wall of worry. In other words stock markets seem to defy gravity by continuing to rise even when the news is bad. There is an important reason why this can happen. This is that most of the time stock markets reflect all the best information available at the time. The information they are focusing on is forward-looking. Markets reflect what analysts think the economic situation will be in two or three years time, not what it is today. Everything that is happening at the moment, or is likely to happen in the short term, has already been factored into market prices. Worrying events don't therefore affect the market unless they have not already been foreseen by the combined brainpower of all the professional investors who are trying to work out where markets are going. Most of the UK's best brains now work in the City of London and many of the best brains from abroad also gravitate there. A top engineer can earn more working in the City analysing engineering companies than he can by engineering products. (I have never got my mind round whether it is good or bad). Faced with such intensive competition, the chances that an individual investor can outsmart the market are small. That is one reason why the City of London has never got a general election wrong. If you want to know who has won a general election you only need to go into the wine bars in the City of London on the eve of Election Day before the votes are counted. Champagne will mean a Conservative victory.

The magic of 10%

In most lines of business you won't go wrong by giving your customers what they want. In the investment world, there is an important exception to this rule, which is that giving investors what they think they want (rather than what they really need) can be downright harmful both to them and, in the long run, to your business. That doesn't stop many firms taking the easy option of selling products which investors find tempting but which, in practice, they need like a hole in the head. Taking the easy buck is why there have been so many scandals and examples of mis-selling in the financial world. When we started out, we never realised quite how important saving people from their own worst instincts was going to be. It has turned out to be a key part of our job as brokers and advisers.

The reason for this is that investments are not like packaged goods. Most types of investment have a finite fundamental return. No matter how much you slice and dice them, no matter how glossy the packaging you put on them, they are only capable of producing so much by way of a return. The trouble is that investors don't know what that limit is. And so there are always buyers for the proposition that appears to offer them more – the something for nothing syndrome. High yielding investments are a case in point.

Since we set up shop in 1981 there has been a sea change in the level of interest rates both in the UK and internationally. After the inflationary disasters of the 1970s, when oil prices quadrupled and the world economy sank into a grim recession, interest rates were very high – at one point well into double digits. This was a new experience for almost everyone: you have to go back to the Napoleonic wars to find the last time that had happened. Since then, however, a combination of tough action by the world's central bankers, aided but not always abetted by governments, and the globalisation of the world's financial markets has helped to drive interest rates all the way back down to the levels that were last seen by our parents in the 1950s. For most of the last ten years, inflation in the UK has been running at around 2%-3% per annum whereas in the 1970s it was as high as 25% per annum. Interest rates have inevitably therefore come down a long way too: which in turn means that the income yields on all types of investment have also fallen steadily to record lows.

The problem is that investors' expectations have not come down in line with the dramatic changes in interest rates and investment returns. Most people still hanker after the much higher income returns that they were used to 10 or 20 years ago, not realising that they can only be achieved these days by taking risks with your capital. The 10% yields that were common in the early days of Mrs Thatcher's government are a thing of the past. Investors who had money on deposit became used to these high yields. Yet that has not stopped providers throughout my career dreaming up new ways to offer people high returns with often painful results. What follows are some examples. They all feature products that offered, often with "guarantees" attached, income returns of 10% per annum. All provide education for investors.

One example which rewarded investors ...

Twenty-five years ago, there was an incentive known as life assurance premium relief (LAPR) which was designed to encourage people to save through life companies. Savers in qualifying life company policies were able to gain tax relief and gross up the premiums by 15%. This gave them a significant competitive advantage but life companies 25 years ago were no different than they are today. You always know that one of them will eventually abuse any good deal that is going. The trick with these policies was that, while you had to take out a ten-year policy in order to qualify for the 15% tax bonus, the bonus could not be clawed back once you had owned the policy for more than four years. What the life companies did, therefore, was design guaranteed income bonds which had a life of four years and a day – just long enough to be sure of earning the tax relief. At a time when you could earn a gross return of 10% on a building society account, some of these products offered 13% to 14% net of tax.

This meant that some amazing returns were available: and because they were backed by a Government bond, they were very popular. The clearing banks shovelled in billions of pounds of their clients' money. The life companies made some unbelievable profits and one or two firms were able to make a living purely on the basis of the commission they earned on this one product. Even insurance brokers who knew nothing about investment sold them. The fact that every four years advisers could recycle their clients' money into the next bond in the series made them an ideal product for earning commission. The high-yielding four-year bonds also proved to be good guaranteed products for investors. The only criticism that can be levied at them was that their success was one of the main reasons for the Government deciding to remove life assurance premium relief. Even that turned out not to be a disaster for investors. The yields investors could achieve from guaranteed income bonds were little different to what they had been before the 15% life assurance premium relief had been removed, strongly suggesting that there was plenty of "fat" in the life company returns.

... And Two Poor Ones

Unfortunately, as interest rates declined, even guaranteed income bonds struggled to provide the Holy Grail of double digit returns. One investment that attempted to plug that gap was a split capital investment trust, so-called because its share capital was split into two or more types of share, each with different characteristics. One class of share, a zero dividend preference share, provided no income, just as its name suggested, but was promoted as being "guaranteed" to grow by 10% over its life. (Many split capital investment trusts have a finite life, of say 10 years, after which the shareholders have a chance to vote whether or not it should continue). If you invested in the fund through a PEP, it was all tax-free. I put the word "guaranteed" in inverted commas, however, because the return would only become certain if the trust had made enough money to pay out the zero dividend preference shares on the day the trust was wound up. The remaining capital of the trust was even less secure. Alongside the zero dividend preference shares there were ordinary income shares that received all the income that the trust's equity investments earned.

To many investors it was these shares that looked the tastiest as the initial dividend yield was just above 10%. If you bought these shares, however, your capital was at risk. There was only enough capital in the trust initially to pay out the zero dividend preference shares. To make it possible to give investors the "guaranteed" growth on the zeros, the stock market had first to go up, as the holders of the zero dividend preference shares had first call on the trust's assets. For the holders of the income shares to get their money back as well, the stock market had to go up a lot more. It was only after the holders of the zeros had been repaid that the income shareholders could hope to get any of their capital back. Soon after many of these types of trust were launched, the stock market started to fall and many of those who bought the sexy-looking income shares received their 10% income all right, but ended up losing part of their capital as well.

Another famous deal with a 10% yield was Foreign & Colonial's (F&C) High Income product. The only way you could receive the advertised income yield of 10% was to hold it within the tax-free environment of a PEP. The fund was an extremely clever concept and used some clever derivatives to turn the potential future growth of the stock market into current income. Remembering the little man in Times Square, we took special care to investigate it because we knew it would capture our clients' imagination. F&C had a computer model that purported to show how the fund would have performed had it been launched several years before. Stephen and another member of the firm spent several days at F&C's offices carrying out due diligence. When they examined the back-tested results of the fund, the concept seemed to work well.

The proof of the pudding was sadly very different. While the fund continued to throw off the 10% income it had advertised, the value of the investor's capital soon began to erode. Eventually, F&C was forced to reduce the fund's target yield. The fund still exists today. At the time of writing it produces an income yield of 6.4%. Those who invested at the outset, when the yield was 9%-10%, will have lost about 15% of their capital. Because of the income it has returned, the investment certainly hasn't been a disaster, but had people invested in an ordinary equity income fund instead, they would be considerably happier.

One That Disappointed

While some companies were still producing reasonably attractive guaranteed income bonds in the early 1990s, others were desperate to replace the vast amounts of revenue that the old life assurance premium relief guaranteed income bonds had generated. One company, Sun Life, decided that it would allow single premium investments straight into its with profit fund. The whole purpose of a "with profit" fund is to iron out the peaks and troughs in the stock market. It is a long-term savings vehicle in which part of the returns in the good years are held back to improve returns in the bad years. As such the concept works best with regular premium contracts.

Before Sun Life came along and changed the game, investment into with profit funds had always been reserved for people prepared to pay so much per month, quarter or year. The single premium concept conferred ever more risk to the life companies.

For a while however, the flaws in the concept were not apparent and the single premium investment bond took off. For a period in the late 1990s, the with profit investment bond was the most successful investment product the life companies had ever produced. Billions of pounds poured in. In those days the rules on advertising and projections were more lax than they are today, and the life companies were able to feature fabulous headline rates of "growth" in their literature. The advertised growth rate on the original Sun Life bond, for example, was something like 14%. So well did these bonds catch on that even Standard Life and Scottish Widows, the two giants of the industry, who for many years had been vocal critics of the single premium with profit bond, were eventually forced to swallow their pride and produce their own versions. Their sales and marketing departments were doing no business and so were screaming for something new to sell. Any notes of caution that their actuaries may have sounded seemed to be swept aside.

There is no better illustration of the commercial pressures which drive so much of the investment business and which make it so important for investors to stay on their guard. It was only when you read the small print in the prospectus for the original with profits investment bond that you discovered that the headline growth rates being used to tempt investors into the fund depended entirely on Sun Life being able to maintain their bonus rates. In order to get round the risk that some investors in the with profits fund might profit at the expense of others when markets changed direction, the life companies introduced something known as an MVA. MVA stands for "market value adjuster" and a more innocuous euphemism you could not imagine. Essentially, it means that the life companies reserved the right to levy penalties on anyone who tried to take their money out of the fund at a time when markets had fallen. Naturally, as markets were rising strongly, nobody took much notice at the time.

If so, it proved to be an expensive oversight, for it was not long before nemesis arrived. One reason was that with marketing departments demanding bigger and bigger headline rates of return, the managers of with profit funds had started to invest more and more of their funds in higher risk equities. This was the only way that they had a chance of producing the higher returns they had offered in their promotional literature. It was also a reversal of traditional practice as the whole ethos of with profits until then had been to invest in a balance of cash, property, fixed interest and equities. The diversification meant less exciting returns but greater safety, a combination that had traditionally been the basis of the with profit concept's success. The actuaries had been right to warn that the idea of a single premium contribution to a with profits fund might be storing up trouble for the future.

Shortly after Standard Life had changed its mind and entered the market, the stock market went into freefall, falling 50% over a period of three years. Overnight the billions that had been invested in with profit fund bonds before the market peak became liabilities of the fund. The more the stock market fell, the greater those liabilities became. By the beginning of 2003, with the stock market still heading down, some life funds looked like becoming insolvent. In other words they no longer had sufficient assets in the fund to pay out the policyholders in full. Many were getting so close to that point that they were forced to start moving the funds out of equities and back into safer investments such as bonds. Unfortunately they were changing investment policy at just the wrong time. Early in 2003, the world's stock markets started to recover. Instead of capturing the gains that they had previously lost, the with profit funds were trapped in fixed interest investments that did nothing to help performance. Many companies were forced to wheel out their MVAs: in some cases, investors who tried to cash in their bonds found that the effect was to slice 15-20% off the headline value of their capital. In other words, when investors tried to take their money out of the bonds, they could only do so by taking a significant loss.

Even now therefore, although markets have partially recovered, the returns on profit investment bonds have continued to lag behind those of other investments. In my view it will be many years before with profit funds will once again be able to declare meaningful bonuses. Many investors are still locked in to their with profit bonds. Having been snubbed before, the actuaries who advise the life companies on their investment policies are hell-bent on restoring the reserves that were so badly depleted during the boom times. In my view the failings of the with profit investment bond has been instrumental in discrediting the whole with profits concept. Will it ever recover? I doubt it. If there is a future stock market crash and with profit bonds weather the storm better than other types of investment, maybe that will restore a little of investors' confidence. It will all depend on how much the reserves have been replenished.

The new capital gains taxation rates introduced by the Government in 2008 have, however, made these bonds look even less attractive from a tax perspective. Today investors are far more sophisticated than they were and these days can much more easily achieve their own diversification. They no longer need a life company to ride out the peaks and troughs of the stock market on their behalf.

Precipice bonds

If the F&C fund and with profit bonds deserve criticism, the products that came to be known as "precipice bonds" were in my opinion in a different league. I thank my investment research team on a daily basis for the fact that we have never promoted them. Precipice bonds were based on derivatives. While the income was guaranteed, the repayment of the investor's capital was dependent on the stock market performing in a particular way. If you read the small print in the brochure, you could see that you would only get your capital back if the stock market performed in a specified manner. The sting in the tail was that if the stock market fell by more than a certain amount, the potential loss increased sharply – to the point where in certain extreme cases, the returns literally "fell off a precipice". Since most of these products were launched at the end of 1990s, which was just before the stock market fell by 50% over three years, it meant that many of these bonds produced huge losses for investors.

It is important to emphasise that there is nothing wrong per se with the use of financial derivatives. In the right hands, they are a valuable tool for investment professionals – those that understand them at least. (The onset of the credit crisis in mid-2007 showed that the management of many of the world's biggest banks were not amongst those who did understand how badly derivatives could go wrong. The banks have ended up with hundreds of millions of near worthless derivative securities on their books. Indeed derivatives were the downfall of the world's largest insurance company AIG). Some fund managers have been very successful at using derivatives to protect the value of their funds in difficult or volatile market conditions. The trade off is that these types of funds tend not to perform as well when the market goes up. You can be sure that, for good and ill, we shall see a lot more of these funds appear over the next few years. Hedge funds and absolute return funds are two examples of funds that use derivatives to help them manage their exposures to different kinds of risk. Just as with any other type of investment, they need to be researched thoroughly. Many are geared; in other words in good periods their returns go up faster, but in bad periods they fall in value further. You really have to understand how they work.

The marketing of precipice bonds was extremely deceptive (not that it stopped them being sold in droves by commission hungry or incompetent brokers). In my view the manufacturers were the real culprits. Their literature was so misleading it bordered on deception. If you showed a man in the street a leaflet with a big headline that said "10% guaranteed income", he would naturally expect to get back both the 10% per annum and his original capital. That wasn't, however, what the providers meant. The wording of precipice bond literature was carefully manipulated to give that impression but it wasn't the real position. While it was true that the income was guaranteed, the return of the investor's capital was not.

Similar products are unfortunately still being sold today, and while they no longer advertise such huge headline rates of income, they are still poor products in my view. If you want to be in the stock market, you should be investing in a simple stock market instrument. If you buy a product using derivatives make sure you understand it and whether the derivatives are used to make it more risky or less risky.

As my episode with the "little man in Times Square" makes clear, you should always remember that when a return on any investment looks exceptionally attractive, this is the time to beware. Whatever the regulators may try to do to prevent abuse, there will always be somebody trying to take money from suckers. It is the nature of the world. As I wrote this chapter I was shown an investment with "indicative" yields of between 15% and 17%. It had all the features you would expect in an investment that was designed to sell well in 2007: property; the name gold (although what that had to do with it I have no idea); speculative; geared; lots of lovely photographs in a glossy brochure. Words like "barge pole", "wouldn't", "with" and "touch" spring to mind.

Since writing this book but prior to publication this section has turned out to be exceedingly prophetic. The demise of the Icelandic banks revealed the folly of seeking the highest yield. No investor, nor for that matter the newspapers who showed the Icelandic banks' deposit rates as the best buys ever, questioned the reason for those high rates of interest. At that time the financially strongest institutions were offering the lowest rates of interest on deposit and that is exactly where everyone should have been putting their money. Seeking what offers the highest yield is a dangerous strategy.

Choosing The Right Investments

Our opportunity-led research process gives us what we feel is a great advantage over most other investment businesses, which remain driven by what can most easily be sold – a sales imperative, in other words. Mark Dampier, our head of research, eats, sleeps and dreams about investment. His ideal day involves sitting down with a group of fund managers, investment analysts or economists to absorb and debate what they are thinking. He has as good an insight into where markets are going as anyone I have met. He has been around the block so many times that he can spot areas of potential quicker than most. Because of our leading position in the market, many fund managers are happy to tell Mark not just where they see the best opportunities, but also when is not a good time to buy their funds. They are astute enough to work out that attracting huge amounts of money from clients of the country's leading unit trust broker into a fund which subsequently underperforms is not a smart idea. They only tend to talk up their funds when they are confident about having the right kind of portfolio for current market conditions.

Although Mark's track record is first class, we have always wanted to make sure we have as much evidence as possible before making our recommendations. With that in mind we have developed a powerful screening tool to help us pick the likely winners from the 3000 or so funds that are on offer to investors in the UK. With so many funds to choose from, you cannot hope to have much success without strong analytical methods. But you also need judgment and experience, what I prefer to call qualitative analysis. Any fool can look at which fund or market has performed best in the past, but that kind of research, based on historical information alone, is worse than useless. Originally the Financial Services Authority, the regulator of our industry, insisted that anything we write which relates to historical information has to carry a warning that "past performance may not be a guide to the future". In my view, even that warning was too weak. Our view is that past performance is absolutely NO guide to the future. Fortunately the change has now been made and we now have to say "past performance is not a guide to the future". One of our biggest challenges is trying to help clients not to do the seemingly obvious things that we know from experience are unwise.

Although our investment suggestions normally work out well, there is still the problem that even the best fund managers cannot outperform the market all the time. I have in the past, on occasions, received letters from clients criticising a fund that we have recommended regularly during our almost 30-year history, the Fidelity Special Situations fund, managed by Anthony Bolton. His fund periodically tended to go through poor patches. My advice on such occasions has invariably been to "double up", in other words to buy some more of the fund, in the knowledge that the most exceptional fund managers often come back strongly from periods of underperformance. There are plenty of other cases where fund managers who seem to be top performers for a short period of time start to go through a bad patch and never perform well again. Faced with such examples, we realised that we needed more analytical tools to help us assess individual managers. One thing we quickly discovered was that so-called "style factors" are an important influence on which funds do better than others. Without an understanding of how styles affect fund performance, you have no chance of picking the winners and losers.

What does style in investment mean? The first important style factor is company size, and the second is the kind of stock that a fund manager picks. In any stock market you can rank shares by the size of the company involved – small, medium and large. Within each size category there are also two main types, value and growth stocks. Value stocks are shares which, for whatever reason, are currently priced below their historical average level. Value stocks are typically bought for income funds. These stocks pay excellent dividends. Value stocks come in and out of vogue as investors alternately seek and shun them. Growth stocks, in contrast, are companies which are in sectors or industries that are experiencing above average rates of growth. These companies are often capital intensive and pay little in the way of dividends, the management believing that any profits they create are better ploughed back into the company to finance future growth. As market cycles turn, sometimes growth stocks become too expensive and at other times they look good value. Similarly with value stocks, when the investment herd notices an undervalued stock, they all tend to buy it at the same time and push up its price to a point where it is no longer a value stock.

This has important implications for funds. Any fund manager who happens to own small company growth stocks at a time when the market is being driven by that kind of style will most likely find himself running a top performing fund for as long as those conditions endure. Merely being in the right place at the right time, in other words, is enough to propel his fund to the top of the performance tables. It may have nothing to do with the fund manager's skill. It could just be luck – from which it follows that this is not a fund that you really want to own. What a great fund manager does is add value over and above the style factors that are driving the market at any one time. For example most equity income funds will be predominantly invested in value stocks, as they are the ones that produce the highest dividends. A great income fund manager will consistently outperform other income funds, even though in years when value stocks are out of favour, the fund itself may not be among the best performing funds in the whole market. As a result private investors who just look at raw performance numbers might well not notice the good fund manager.

The powerful analytical search programs we have on our computer system are designed to strip out these style factors in order to distinguish between the good, the bad and the indifferent fund managers. We also take the analysis a step further because, just to make things more complicated, some fund managers invest in more than one style. For instance, some income fund managers use what is known as a barbell approach. They choose high yielding stocks to give them the dividends that they need, but invest the rest of the portfolio in growth stocks so as to produce some additional capital growth. It is very difficult to compare such a fund with a fund that owns nothing but value stocks. To assist us in the complex analysis required, in 2001 we embarked on the creation of a highly sophisticated computer programme built by two Greek mathematicians. (Because of Pythagoras, Euclid and so on, Greek universities throw out more mathematicians than they could possibly ever need in Greece!). The programme is so clever that it can predict how a fund manager is investing purely from the way that the price of the fund moves. It means that sometimes we can even tell fund managers that they are no longer investing in the style they claim to be! Over a period of years we are able to build up a complete picture of the way that a fund manager invests, something we can show graphically using bar charts.

The analytical computer system and program has also proved to be invaluable in the way that we run our multi-manager funds. A multi-manager fund is one that includes a number of individual unit trusts run by different fund managers. We have four – one that includes the best income fund managers, another that includes the best growth funds, a third that combines the best of each type to create a balanced fund and finally one which is managed for the cautious. When we decided that funds were our forte, we also felt that we should give clients the opportunity to let us manage their unit trust portfolios. The way we manage our multi-manager funds is not by trying to second guess which sectors are likely to best, but by trying to find the best manager in each sector. Since inception our multi-manager funds have been managed by Lee Gardhouse, who joined us as a graduate in 1995 and is the man responsible for recruiting the Greek mathematicians. We also enlisted the help of a professor who from time to time comes in to check the sampling and logic of our programme.

The reason we don't try to second guess the market is simply that we don't believe anyone can do that regularly. By picking the best fund manager in each sector, we think we are giving clients their best chance of meeting their investment objectives. Our multi-manager funds have performed well within their peer group without us having to make any big strategic calls about where the markets are going – something that experience suggests is next to impossible. Most other multi-manager funds take small bets in certain sectors. You may find, for example, that they are overweight in Japan and underweight in America. What that means is that if the consensus allocation among such funds is to have, say, 7% of the portfolio in Japan they might have as much as 12%, believing that Japan will perform better than other markets. This type of asset allocation is fantastic when the fund manager gets it right. But when he gets it wrong, it can seriously affect the fund's performance. We believe that sticking to consensus allocations between different markets and spending all our time and effort instead on finding the best fund in each of these sectors is a less risky way to invest. The track record of our multi-manager funds supports that.

The general lesson for investors is that picking funds is a lot more complicated than it appears, just as beating the market is harder than you think. The way we run our multi-manager investment funds stems from the work carried out by Professor William Sharpe of Stanford University, who first pioneered the view that investment style has a huge effect on which funds perform best during particular periods. Style analysis, as we have seen, aims to identify the kind of stocks and shares that do well or badly at different points in time. The secret of picking funds successfully is to be clear about what style the manager of any fund you are thinking of buying is pursuing. If you look only at the way a fund has performed in the recent past, it can present a dangerously misleading picture. If you actually make all your investment decisions on the basis of that past performance, as sadly many investors do, you are virtually guaranteed to have below average results.

We see our job as trying to stop our clients from making that kind of mistake. We can do that in two ways. One is by offering advice that steers them away from funds that have done well in the past but are unlikely to do that well in the future. The second is to give them the chance to sub-contract the choice of funds to our specialist multi-manager team. You would be surprised how deeply ingrained in the human psyche is the idea that funds with above average returns must go on doing the same in future! Many psychologists have pointed out that the human brain is not wired to make good investment decisions; and my experience certainly bears out that this is true. You would be amazed by how much of a struggle it can be to persuade an investor that the funds that have made the most money in the past 12 months are not necessarily the ones they should be buying now. It is even more difficult to persuade an investor to cut his losses and sell a no hope fund with little potential of ever doing well. Private investors hate realising a loss. They prefer to sell their winners.

There can be some mileage in trying to spot changes in market and style leadership. Looking back it seems obvious that most world stock markets have tended to take their lead from the American stock market. Nevertheless there have been times when some individual markets have looked cheap or expensive in comparison. Within individual stock markets, different sectors also move at a different speed to the market as a whole. There are times for example when large companies as a group do better than average, and other times when smaller companies have taken the lead. Specialist sectors such as technology also go from being overvalued to undervalued, and back again. It follows that there will always be opportunities to add some value in a portfolio by spotting these trends and looking to capitalise on them. As with all types of investment, however, patience is an under-rated virtue. You may have to wait a long time for these trends to reverse; and if you are too early your results will suffer.

Glossary

Value stocks – these are shares that, for one reason or another, look undervalued. They normally have quite high dividends. Many income funds hold such stock. The reason they are undervalued is mainly because they are out of favour, but also they are historically in industries that do not offer huge growth prospects and are not glamorous industries. Often the industries are cyclical and typically such industries as textiles, engineering, steel, utilities and banks often feature in this sector.

Growth stocks – these are ones where the management is invariably very aggressive. They also tend to be new high growth industries and typically they pay little or no dividend, the management feeling that they can make more for their shareholders by ploughing back the profits into growing the company more quickly. Typically growth stocks can be in any industry but they are more associated with new industries, new technologies and new business concepts.

Internet Stocks – and Other Sources of Grief

When you are in the investment industry there are in general four types of investments:

Category one
Investments which are likely to do well that clients will buy.

Category two
Investments which are likely to do well that clients won't buy.

Category three
Investments of dubious merit which clients will buy in droves.

Category four
Investments of dubious merit which even clients will reject.

Life would have been simple if all the investments that we were ever offered were in category one. For obvious reasons we have tried to concentrate on the top two categories. The one that you should really avoid is category three. They can make brokers an awful lot of money, but the gains are short-term, since it also risks leaving a huge proportion of their clients disappointed. A good example would be the precipice bonds I mentioned earlier. Barlow Clowes was also in that category, although it failed because the people at the top were crooks. Thankfully we avoided it. However despite our best efforts and considerable due diligence, we have also learnt that things can still go wrong. The most important thing about your business mistakes is to learn from them; and to make sure that whatever you do, your motives are genuine.

The Foreign & Colonial 10% product was one that caused us grief, as already explained. We were the only broker to spend a significant amount of time with F&C carrying out what is known as due diligence. We felt that we had done everything we should have done, but that didn't stop the product not delivering what it offered. Nevertheless, as a broker that had promoted the fund, we received a lot more flak than the manufacturer, something which is all too common in our industry. Product providers often look to duck their responsibility by saying: "We only produce the product. It is up to the brokers to decide whether it is suitable or not." That argument has never made any sense to me. If you go into a well-known supermarket and buy a branded packet of cornflakes and find a dead rat inside, who would you sue? Would you sue the supermarket for not noticing the rat, or would you sue the cornflake manufacturer? I think you would sue the cornflake manufacturer, but in the investment industry the blame always seems to lie with the retailer.

The internet boom, also know as the dot com bubble, is one that nobody in the industry will ever forget. I have had many letters regarding the technology debacle. I am still getting them even now, more than eight years later. Companies with no business, merely an idea, were suddenly raising capital on the stock market through initial public offerings. The share prices of these companies were quintupling or even more after flotation. We realised there was a huge appetite for technology funds, but we were cautious about their prospects. In our 1st January 2000 yearbook we gave some suggestions for funds that clients should consider buying for the PEP season, and included one technology fund amongst 20 other selected funds. By the end of January it had become quite clear that the only thing that clients wanted to know about was technology funds. Our switchboards were jammed with phone calls. We couldn't answer all their questions, which is why we eventually decided to produce A Guide to Technology full of words of caution.

We have regularly been accused of not conveying the risks. I reply by pointing to the introduction to the technology guide, where we listed a huge number of cautionary messages. For example, we said that technology companies would have to improve their profits radically in order to warrant their high share prices. My standard response is to send anyone who complains the lead article in the guide with every word of caution highlighted. I then challenge them to send the article back with all the words that might have suggested they should buy it. Of course, at the time all our words of caution were completely disregarded and investors piled in to technology like there was no tomorrow. Most of the internet companies and funds went into a horrible decline. In 2008, seven years later, none of them were back in profit.

On this occasion, at least, the product providers were also castigated. Was it opportunism or were they negligent? The question has never been tested in the courts. It never will be in all probability. The question we have asked ourselves since the debacle unfolded was whether we were right to produce our technology guide in the first place. Should we have said nothing, it is unlikely that the result would have been any different. Were we better to put out a guide with a massive voice of caution? At the time I think we were one of the few voices urging caution. On a personal note I did buy one technology stock. Years before when we chose our computer system, the fileserver we bought was made by an American firm called 3com. The server was so good that in true Victor Kiam style I bought the shares. At the beginning of the technology boom I sold them at a massive profit, or so I thought. Having paid £15,000 for the shares, I sold them for £45,000. Had I still owned them at the top of the technology boom, they would have been worth more than £1 million! It was an indication of how extreme valuations had become.

Another event that caused us grief was the aftermath of 9/11, the violent terrorist attacks on Manhattan Island on 11th September 2001. I had just been to see the school where I was to send my daughter. On the way back my wife dragged me into an antique shop where the staff were watching a portable television. There was a news report showing the damage done by the first plane to hit the World Trade Center. At first until the second plane hit the other tower, everyone thought it was an accident. I sensed immediately the second plane hit that it would be a disaster for world stock markets. The American people would shun public places, which meant that the retailing boom would grind to a halt. Because of the terrorists' connection with the Middle East, it seemed likely that the oil price would rise. I guessed there would be a flight to quality investments, including government bonds, and that some people would be so terrified there would be a flight to gold. (Perhaps I should have told Gordon Brown my thoughts, as he had just sold the UK's gold reserves in order to balance the budget at a quarter of the price he could have got seven years later). We sat in the office and agonised over what to do. We knew it was a dangerous thing to put out an investment note so soon after such a tragedy. The newspapers the next day showed horrific pictures of people hurling themselves out of the World Trade Center to avoid the heat. Having decided to put together a brief mailing to send to all our clients on the afternoon of the terrorist act, we made the decision to print the following morning and sent them out the following day.

It proved to have unwelcome consequences. On the basis of just 12 complaints, the Advertising Standards Authority saw fit to castigate us. One journalist whose own newspaper had been full of gruesome pictures suggested we were "coffin chasing". Had he read the note that we sent out, he would have realised that what we said was not designed to make us money, which was the implication of his comments. What we did was advise people to reduce the amount they had invested in equities – we make no money when people sell unit trusts, only when they buy them do we increase our income. The columnist cited another broker who had sent him an extremely long email suggesting caution. Perhaps he felt that every broker in the land should have been sending him emails rather than talking to their clients! I remain convinced that we did the right thing in alerting our clients to the investment implications of the 9/11 attack. Many clients took our advice to reduce their equity holdings and congratulated us for the advice. Nevertheless, we were still pilloried by the media. My view is that while you are never going to make the right decisions all the time, as long as you can hold your head up high and say you acted with your clients' best interests in mind, and for no other reason, it is easy to take the brickbats that will inevitably come your way.

The craze to invest in property in 2006-07 has some echoes with what happened during the internet bubble. Low interest rates had driven property to values that would have been considered unbelievable a decade before. We have been cautious about property funds, except for a small proportion of clients' portfolios. In the event many funds rose in value and investors, as they always do, clamoured for more of the same. Did that make us wrong? I don't think so. For one thing the stock market performed better than property during that period. If property proves to perform better than equities in the future, I dare say that some investors will complain to us that they have been cheated. Only time will tell whether taking the high ground in this way has been the right decision. The property markets turned down and investors seeking to sell their property funds en masse could spell disaster because property, by its nature, is not an easy asset to sell. In those circumstances property funds could end up going the same way as with profits funds. Investors will find that they cannot get their money out easily. At the time of writing this is pretty much exactly what has happened.

How To Build Your Wealth

Everyone has a different reason for going into business. For some it is just a desire to be one's own boss. Sometimes people come up with a good idea which they think they can exploit commercially – or it may be they work for a firm that has a fantastic idea or product which is only being promoted half-heartedly. There are lots of different cases. Very few of those who are successful, I suspect, went into business simply to become wealthy however. Those who go into business for that purpose are normally doomed. Businesses need capital and they need nurturing. People who see their business merely as a means to support a champagne lifestyle are almost certainly committing their business to failure. That is not to say that successful business people don't enjoy the trappings of success – houses, cars, boats, etc – once they have succeeded. Some spend their wealth spectacularly well. Those who have obtained their wealth through a talent rather than through business often feel they need to spend it on silly things. I suspect many pop stars and footballers fall into that category. It is a shame that no one ever tells them "you don't have to spend it!"

People are so obsessed with wealth and the crazy salaries that some professional sportsmen command that it distorts their judgment. It annoys me that whenever Bill Gates is interviewed in the UK, the first question the interviewers ask is almost always about his wealth. In fact the least interesting thing about Bill Gates is his wealth. Some say he was lucky and in the right place when he was given the job to write the operating program for the original IBM PC. It was certainly a big error on IBM's part to give away what became one of the most valuable commodities the world has ever seen. Although he became very rich in a short period of time Gates didn't do what many people might have done, which was sit on his laurels. Instead he turned his good fortune into one of the world's most successful companies, fighting tooth and nail with the American antitrust laws along the way in his efforts to keep Microsoft at the forefront of world software. He has gone down several blind alleys and made mistakes, not least when he wrote off the internet. Having realised his mistake, he was honest enough to admit it and turned the considerable power of Microsoft on to the project. The toys that are associated with wealth are clearly not what motivates him, and he seems a happy and fulfilled individual as a result.

Ironically his business partner, Paul Allen, of whom we hear much less but who is almost as fabulously wealthy, does have a thing about the toys of success. It seems he owns three of the biggest ten privately owned yachts in the world. I know one very wealthy man who enjoys spending money and does it spectacularly well. He has a fabulous holiday home, his own fishing stretch in Hampshire and many of the other things that you would associate with wealth. Yet I know another very wealthy man who never spends a penny and is just as content. It may be a mystery to some why people who have no desire for the trappings of wealth can nevertheless create successful and profitable businesses. I include myself in that category. Until I went into business, I had never really achieved anything of note. I wasn't artistic or musical, and I certainly wasn't academic. I didn't get into the school teams for football or cricket, I enjoyed my sport when I was younger, including the crazy sport of fell running, but I was never going to win a race. I was a reasonably competent club squash player but I enjoyed it purely for the exercise and the social life that went with it. I must be one of the world's worst golfers not having the concentration span or patience for the game. Therefore to find something at which I excelled was a wonderful experience.

Epilogue:

The Simple Pleasures In Life

The one thing in life that I do seem to have a talent for is business and that is motivation enough for doing well. If you are a striker at football, the number of goals you score in your career is a measure of your success. If you are a runner, winning races and setting world records are important. If you are a pop star, the number of hits you have is how you count success. The real measure of business success is the wealth you create. If someone has single-handedly built a business from scratch, the wealth accrues to that individual. There is no reason to be embarrassed about it. In other cases dynamic leaders can take on an existing business and create huge amounts of wealth that way. I admire Christopher Gent who took a small spinout from the electronics company Racal and turned it into Vodafone, the biggest mobile phone company in the world. I have also been impressed with how Stuart Rose took the top job at Marks & Spencer and revived it when it was open season for people wishing to denigrate it. He has made it once again one of Britain's favourite retailers. Stephen and I are lucky that, with a huge amount of help from our team, we have been able to build a strong and enduring business. We both hope that the business will live on bearing our names long after we have gone. That is an important part of the motivation that keeps us going, even though we could have retired years ago.

Some people find it strange that I have no desire to spend my own wealth. The reason is simply that it was never acquired for that reason. I am not a great one for extravagant cars. I don't have scores of boats, planes or houses. We live in the knowledge that our family will be financially secure for many generations. I have never understood why people who become successful feel they should change their friends – what on earth for? Yes, when you are successful, you do make some new friends, if only because some of your old friends can't do some of the things that you wish to do. In any case whatever your future path you will make new friends. True friends, I have found, never let you pay for them and would be angry if you suggested it. Stephen still plays skittles with the same team he has played with for 30 years. I still go for a run – well I may be exaggerating, it's more of a jog and a fast walk! – with the same guys that I have run with for a quarter of a century. After the run we go to a local pub for a couple of beers. The first time I went to that pub after all the publicity surrounding the flotation of Hargreaves Lansdown, the barmaid was surprised to see I had turned up. People expect you to behave differently. Yet I don't feel the need. I have never been particularly happy with material things.

My father's philosophy in life was that the more things you own, the more problems they create, and I feel the same. As long as I am still fully occupied with my role as chief executive of Hargreaves Lansdown, I couldn't contemplate having an overseas property. The thought of having to arrange maintenance for a property a couple of thousand miles away doesn't bear thinking about. My greatest pleasure in life, other than my family, is nurturing the business. Outside work, the thing that gives me most pleasure is my half-acre vegetable plot. I have been trying to perfect something that the Victorians did, which was produce fresh vegetables 365 days a year. For the last two years we have managed it, although in April the selection is somewhat limited! In the winter there are few pleasures as good as going out on a Sunday morning and gathering leeks, cabbage, Brussels sprouts, celeriac and a few parsnips for Sunday lunch. Sometimes my hands are so cold it hurts but nothing beats washing the vegetables and laying them out on the kitchen work surface ready for Sunday lunch. Are the simple pleasures the best? You bet your life they are.

Acknowledgements

When I wrote this book I was uncertain of whether I wanted to name names, but my publisher felt that they added to the book. The people named are mentioned because their input was relevant to a part of the story. Some have specifically asked for their names not to be included. However it is only fair to say that every single person who has worked for Hargreaves Lansdown also deserves an acknowledgement from me for their contribution to the business. They have worked into the night when necessary and come in during weekends if there weren't enough hours in the normal working week. They have gone the extra mile in explaining things to clients, obtaining whatever information was needed and holding their hands when markets were volatile. Over 27 years we must have employed more than 2000 people. It is unfortunately impossible to mention all their names here.

The clients of Hargreaves Lansdown also deserve mention and a huge vote of gratitude. The ones that came to us at the beginning took a chance in dealing with a firm that was still so embryonic. All the clients who have sung our praises to their friends have acted as an unpaid marketing arm of the business. I thank our clients for their tolerance when we have been frazzled by circumstances and for praising our staff when they have experienced excellent service. I thank also those thousands of clients who, when we floated the company, sought to buy our shares in droves. Finally I must thank all the people in the industry who have helped us over the years. That includes the original unit trust groups who sponsored us to become their agents and the many who regularly bring their fund managers down to Bristol to tell our investment team about their investment philosophy. We must also thank our suppliers; not least our printers who have turned things round at breakneck speed when circumstances dictated it. We have always been loathe to change our suppliers and we thank them for rewarding our loyalty by providing us with excellent products and services over the years. I would also like to thank my family who have understood that I dedicated much of my life to coming in regularly to the business and often had to tolerate me when prepossessed by problems, opportunities, deadlines or just when things weren't going as planned. It has been a fantastic journey. I have loved every minute of it, and I love it today, but it couldn't have been done in isolation and for that I thank everyone who has had a part to play in the Hargreaves Lansdown business adventure. It has been a wonderful journey, but it isn't over yet.